A SOCIAL HISTORY
OF THE
FRENCH REVOLUTION

by

Norman Hampson

Routledge and Kegan Paul

University of Toronto Press

First published in Great Britain 1963
by Routledge and Kegan Paul Ltd
39 Store Street, London WC1E 2DD and
Newtown Road, Henly-on-Thames, Oxon. RG9 1EN

First published in Canada and
the United States of America 1963
by University of Toronto Press

Reprinted three times
First published as a paperback 1966
Reprinted 1970, 1974 and 1976

Printed in Great Britain by
Lowe & Brydone (Printers) Ltd, Thetford, Norfolk

RKP ISBN 0 7100 6525 6 (p)
RKP ISBN 0 7100 4559 X (c)
UTP ISBN 0-8020-6060-9 (p)
UTP ISBN 0-8020-1248-5 (c)

A SOCIAL HISTORY OF THE
FRENCH REVOLUTION

Contents

Preface

From one point of view major social revolutions are like geological faults. The rolling evolution of the historical landscape is suddenly broken and the continuity of its strata interrupted. What follows is conditioned by what went before, but is not a direct continuation of it. Unlike geological faults, however, social revolutions are the product—however unexpected and unwelcome—of human action. Structural changes which have been proceeding at a slow pace, without deliberate central planning and often without any clear awareness of their cumulative significance, suddenly become an object of political attention. The social history of a revolution is therefore essentially different from that of a society in peaceful evolution, since political action becomes more closely involved in the process of accelerated social change. The nature, extent and significance of the revolutionary modifications in the structure of a society are conditioned by the political context in which they are brought about. To quote only one example, the question of whether change is achieved by consent or imposed by force may be a matter of politics, but the solution adopted will influence both the structure and the social cohesion of the community involved.

This fusion of social and political factors is particularly marked in the case of the French Revolution. To an extent that has probably no parallel in modern European history, the Revolution was a maelstrom of social aspirations ranging from the restoration of an aristocratic society to the creation of a welfare state controlled by a monolithic and totalitarian government. In 1789 aristocrats were demanding the appointment of official genealogists to verify noble ancestry. Within five years revolutionary extremists were struggling with the problems of a national health service and wages policy in national industries. Social aspirations, whether 'reactionary' or 'progressive', ranged far beyond the practical limits imposed by the material conditions of late eighteenth-century society. What was achieved was a mere fraction of what was attempted. In consequence, a simple comparison of the social structure of France before and after the Revolution would be both inadequate and misleading, since the final result was conditioned by the false starts and lost illusions that had preceded it.

A social history of the French Revolution must therefore take account of politics, because a substantial part of politics was concerned with changing social structure. I have consequently tried to integrate social analysis with a description of how social interests and aspirations shaped political movements and how political action modified both the structure of society and what people thought about society and their own place within it. This has involved the adoption of a broadly chronological treatment of the subject and the inclusion of a fair amount of detail on some aspects of revolutionary politics, since it is in the detail that social attitudes are often most clearly revealed and it is only by understanding the complexity of the revolutionary situation as a whole that one can appreciate the specific aims of those who wished to effect social changes and the means which they decided to employ.

Anyone who tries to investigate the social history of the Revolution is immediately aware, despite the overwhelming literature on the subject, of important aspects about which very little is yet known. On any number of subjects, such as the way of life of the provincial gentry at the end of the ancien régime, the use made of the capital paid in compensation for offices whose venality was abolished, the extent to which feudal dues continued to be paid between 1789 and 1792, even the consequences of the sale of the property of the Church and of the *émigré* nobility, information is fragmentary if not totally inadequate. This is all the more serious a handicap to the historian since it is becoming increasingly apparent that conditions in France, both before and during the Revolution, varied very widely indeed from one area to another. A detailed survey of one Department—which itself may be a collection of contrasts —offers no safe basis for generalization about others. Anything in the nature of statistical precision is therefore, for the present at least, out of the question, and it is not possible to do more than make a tentative assessment of the extent to which a known situation in one area corresponded to conditions elsewhere.

Within the dimensions of a book of this size it is often impossible to do more than hint at the range of local variations, even when these are known. To some extent, interpretations that would be better qualified have to be given a categorical form and generalizations advanced without the exceptions that would tie them more closely to the evidence. If the result is at times nearer to a caricature than a portrait, I can only hope that the inevitable oversimplification, without unduly distorting the proportions of the whole, has emphasized some of the main issues that might otherwise disappear in a mass of detail.

This study is intended primarily for the general reader. Although I have not hesitated to omit political aspects of the Revolution which had no direct social repercussions, I have tried to include enough of the basic framework of events to make the whole intelligible to those without any previous knowledge of the period. At the same time, I hope to have provided some new evidence in support of familiar arguments and some controversial interpretations that may interest, and perhaps provoke, readers already acquainted with the subject. If I can help to stimulate those who are unable to accept my own views into evolving new syntheses of their own, I shall be gratified to have contributed this link to the endless chain of French revolutionary studies.

I am happy to have this opportunity of acknowledging my debt to those who have assisted me in the preparation of this book, notably to Harold Perkin, the most helpful and tolerant of editors, to Professor A. Goodwin, and to Malcolm Anderson for their great kindness in reading the manuscript and correcting many inaccuracies, and to Richard Cobb for allowing me to read in proof the second volume of a thesis that is one of the major contemporary works on the Revolution. I am indebted also to the staff of the Bibliothèque Nationale, and particularly to the librarian and staff of the John Rylands Library, for their unfailing courtesy and helpfulness. Finally, I would like to thank my students at Manchester University for teaching me while I taught them.

Manchester
January 1963

To the memory of the late

J. M. THOMPSON

Il faut nous réunir . . . Citoyens, communiquons-nous nos lumières, ne nous haïssons pas.

DANTON

I

~~~~~~

France on the Eve of the Revolution

~~~~~~

La Noblesse cause la corruption de la nation, parce qu'elle décourage la vertu et les talents, elle étouffe l'émulation, elle corrompt la justice, elle dispose des places et des grâces et en fait faire ces distributions indignes.

J. A. CREUZET-LATOUCHE, *Journal des Etats Généraux*

FRANCE since the Revolution has been a divided country. At no subsequent period has there been general agreement on the form of constitution, the economic policy to be pursued by the Government or the position of the Church within the State. While other western European countries have experienced similar divisions, France has been unique in the permanence and intensity of these conflicts, which arise mainly from the Revolution. In the eighteenth century France shared the apparent stability of her European neighbours and the period from 1715 to 1787 was one of relative calm in French history when compared either with the religious wars of the sixteenth century and the Frondes of the seventeenth or with the recurrent revolutions of the nineteenth and twentieth centuries. The understandable attempt by some Frenchmen to present the ancien régime in the eighteenth century as a period of idyllic calm is nevertheless seriously misleading. The nominally autocratic monarchy, the increasingly anachronistic 'feudal' society and the temporal power of an established but discredited Church all gave rise to problems and conflicts that tended to increase

1

in intensity towards the end of the century. An analysis of this society and of the tensions that were to destroy it is therefore the necessary prelude to an understanding of the Revolution and its disruptive influence.

The eighteenth century was a period of declining absolutism in France.[1] The centralized administrative machine created by Richelieu, Mazarin and Louis XIV still governed the country from Versailles and the royal will was still the most important factor in determining almost every aspect of foreign, economic and religious policy. But the palace of Versailles was a complex institution that housed Court and Government under one roof. Louis XIV had tried to keep the two apart, respecting the social hierarchy, with its privileges and distinctions, while he excluded the nobility from political power. Even the *roi soleil* had found this separation difficult to maintain. His bourgeois ministers obtained the *survivance* of their office for their sons and founded new aristocratic dynasties: Colbert may have been of humble origin, but his son was both a marquis and a minister and his grandson was a duke. Louis XV and Louis XVI had neither the ability nor the authority of their illustrious predecessor, with the result that the Court was able to infiltrate into the Government and eventually to monopolize ministerial posts. By 1789 all the ministers were noble, with the single exception of Necker, the Swiss banker whose professional skill and contacts alone kept the monarchy from bankruptcy.

This aristocratic infiltration produced unsatisfactory results. Court society was given to intrigue and family politics, and the fluctuating balance of power that resulted was not conducive to the pursuit of vigorous and consistent policies. To some extent this was true of all government in eighteenth-century Europe, but contemporaries appear to have regarded the situation in France as exceptional. One of the most intelligent diplomats in the British Embassy, writing in 1788, expressed his surprise that a government so inefficient should have been able to accomplish so much.[2] The absence of effective royal control meant that the machinery of government tended to embed itself in hereditary ruts. Once the king ceased to intervene

[1] See the chapter by J. S. Bromley, 'The decline of absolute monarchy', in *France, Government and Society* (ed. J. M. Wallace-Hadrill and J. McManners, 1957).
[2] *Despatches from Paris, 1788–1790* (ed. O. Browning, 1910), p. 31.

and to innovate, the institutions that the monarchy had used in order to control the aristocracy became themselves aristocratic. Perhaps the most striking example of this trend was to be found in the parlements. These thirteen appeal courts, which were also entrusted with the registration of laws, were of political as well as legal importance, since they aspired to turn the right of registration into a right of veto. Even in the reign of Louis XIV the main offices in the Paris parlement were becoming restricted to a few old-established legal dynasties such as the Harlays, the Lamoignons and the le Peletiers. In 1644 the Crown had conferred transmissible nobility on all the councillors of the Paris parlement. This tendency developed in the eighteenth century and spread down to the *maîtres des requêtes*, the legal officers of the Crown from whose ranks the majority of the intendants were drawn.[1] In consequence the intendants themselves sometimes took on a new character, not as a result of deliberate choice, but by the application of a traditional method of recruitment to a changing social structure. Whereas they had been created to serve as agents of the monarchy in controlling the provincial aristocracy, they became noble themselves and sometimes served in areas *(généralités)* where they had family ties with the great local magnates.[2] In 1789 the intendant at Aix was also the *premier président* of the local parlement, a confusion of functions that would have horrified Colbert and Louis XIV. In the Toulouse area the aristocracy was able to play on the social ambitions of the intendant's *sub-délégué*.[3] Where the intendant still tried to defend popular interests against privilege he was often crippled by lack of support from Versailles and confined to a rearguard action against the offensive of the parlement and local Estates.[4]

[1] F. L. Ford, *Robe and Sword, the re-grouping of the French Aristocracy after Louis XIV* (Cambridge, Mass., 1953), *passim*, and J. Égret, 'L'Aristocratie Parlementaire Française à la fin de l'Ancien Régime', *Revue Historique*, CCVIII (1952).
[2] Two *intendances* have been the subject of recent studies: H. Fréville, *L'Intendance de Bretagne, 1689–1790* (3 vol., Rennes, 1953), and M. Bordes, *D'Étigny et l'Administration de l'Intendance d'Auch* (2 vol., Auch, 1957).
[3] R. Forster, *The Nobility of Toulouse in the Eighteenth Century: a Social and Economic Study* (Johns Hopkins University Studies in Historical and Political Science, Series LXXVIII, No. 1, 1960), pp. 28–31.
[4] M. Bordes, 'Les Intendants Éclairés à la fin de l'Ancien Régime', *Revue d'Histoire Économique et Sociale*, XXXIX (1961), 57.

In the same way the wealthy bourgeois who governed the main towns also acquired nobility (*noblesse de cloche*) and tended to become a self-perpetuating oligarchy. The monarchy had been the main source of such dynamism as had existed in the ancien régime. When the king himself ceased to govern there was no alternative force of change. Administration tended to become routine and the agents of Government officers who aimed at assimilating themselves to the aristocracy they had been intended to control. Thus the forces of inertia became preponderant, at a time when social and economic changes were subjecting the system to a growing strain.

In spite of their limited victories the nobility were far from satisfied, for the machinery of centralized absolutism remained intact. Those provincial Estates which had lapsed in the seventeenth century were not revived. The intendant himself might be noble and obliging on matters of detail, but this was small consolation to the provincial gentry whose political influence was no greater than it had been in Saint-Simon's day. Government policy might be in the hands of a duc de Choiseul, but Government methods were as arbitrary as ever, the *lettre de cachet* could still send a nobleman to the Bastille and the Court aristocracy itself had no corporate control over State policy. And so the eighteenth century saw a growing attempt by the various sections of the nobility to challenge the royal Government. The great families at Court, casting envious eyes on the Whig nobility across the Channel, denounced 'ministerial despotism'. The parlements, appropriating the theories of Montesquieu's *De l'Esprit des Lois*, claimed to act as custodians of the traditional constitution of the country, with the right to veto 'unconstitutional' laws. The provincial gentry demanded the restoration of their local Estates and hoped to rescue the monarchy from the influence of a Court nobility that they detested. All were nominally devoted to the king, but each saw the monarch in the rôle it had designed for him and had no inhibitions about attacking the Ministers of the king's choice and the policy they enforced in his name.

The main political conflict of eighteenth-century France was therefore the struggle of the aristocracy against the declining power of royal absolutism. Social divisions were a good deal more complicated: nobility, bourgeoisie and peasantry were

4

divided by internal conflicts, while the slow evolution of the economy was gradually altering the balance of forces all the time.[1] A relatively rigid society, still bearing many traces of its feudal origins, led all sides to think primarily in social rather than in economic terms. In the countryside in particular this produced a general coalition against the local seigneur rather than against landlords as such. It was only when the Revolution had swept away this feudal superstructure that the purely economic divisions within the village were clearly revealed.

Before the Revolution the most important social division in France was that between noble and commoner. This was originally assumed to rest on a distinction of blood, rationalized by Boulainvilliers into the theory that the aristocracy were the survivors of Frankish invaders and the commoners the heirs of the conquered Romano-Celtic natives—in other words, that Germanic blood carried the opposite qualities in France to those which the romantic movement was to attribute to it in England.[2] This argument was scarcely likely to commend itself to a sceptical age and Voltaire enjoyed himself describing the Frankish ancestors as 'wild beasts seeking grazing, shelter and a few clothes to protect them from the snow'. His historical sympathies were entirely with the Romanized Gauls, and his classical age was as hard on 'Gothic' ancestry as on Gothic art. In any case, the developing monarchy had played havoc with this conception of a warrior *noblesse d'épée* by insisting on granting titles to its servants (*noblesse de robe*). Worse still, the impoverishment of the Crown had led it to sell nobility to members of the bourgeoisie *vivant noblement*. The impoverished scions of ancient lineage had themselves completed the pollution of the blood *en fumant leurs terres*, to use their elegant expression, by *mésalliances* with bourgeois heiresses. According to Necker, such matches became particularly frequent during the reign of Louis XV. It was therefore impossible to maintain, in the late eighteenth century, that the nobility as a whole was biologically distinct from the rest of the population, but in both

[1] See P. Sagnac, *La Formation de la Société Française Moderne* (2 vol., Paris, 1945–6).
[2] For Saint-Simon's views on the origins of the nobility see *Mémoires* (ed. Pléiade, Paris, 1953–61), IV, chap. xxix.

épée and *robe* families ancient lineage continued to confer status and parvenus were still treated with some contempt.

In addition to this division, the nobility was separated in terms of function, the military families despising ennobled Civil Servants and *parlementaires* and the latter scorning the *noblesse de cloche* and the prosperous bourgeois who had bought themselves sinecures conferring personal or hereditary nobility. In the eighteenth century the highest *épée* and *robe* families were tending to intermingle, although one or two distinctions were still observed at Court—for example, the *robe* was not eligible for full membership of the much-coveted *Ordre du Saint-Esprit*. Distinctions of status were often sharper in the provinces, where the impoverished *hobereau* had only his ancestry to console him for the continuous acquisition of titles by men who surpassed him in wealth and education.

A third distinction, that between the *noblesse de cour* and the provincial nobility, followed directly from the centralizing policy of Louis XIV. Pensions, grants and employment were reserved for those families presented at Court and often resident at Versailles, a minority variously estimated at between 4,000 and 20,000 out of a total of about 400,000 nobles. The *présentés* were drawn from ancient *épée* families, but were far from including all those who were eligible. This Court *noblesse* affected to despise the rude manners of the provincials, while the latter combined a cavalier loyalty to the person of the king with an outspoken contempt for the gilded sycophants with whom he surrounded himself.

Length of lineage, social function and relationship to the Court all constituted a complicated pattern of status. The first characteristic of the nobility to strike the observer is therefore the fact that it was far from constituting a united order—indeed, one near-contemporary went so far as to describe its series of internal divisions as forming a 'cascade of contempt'.[1] Further than this it is dangerous to generalize, for the wealth, sources of income and *mores* of the aristocracy varied enormously from one region to another. Even allowing for Chateaubriand's habitual exaggeration, his picture of the vegetating Breton

[1] J. Droz, in the introduction to his *Histoire du Règne de Louis XVI* (Brussels, 1839). On the nobility see H. Carré, *La Noblesse de France et l'Opinion Publique au Dix-Huitième Siècle* (Paris, 1920).

6

hobereau has very little in common with the thrifty capitalist farmers of the Toulouse plain, the wine-growing nobles of the Bordeaux area, or the industrially-minded aristocracy of Lyons.[1] Much more detailed research is necessary before a clear picture of the complex attitudes and preoccupations of the nobility can emerge. The order as a whole owned about one-fifth of the land of France, but its individual members included extremes of wealth and poverty. The duc d'Orléans was one of the richest men in France, with an annual income in the region of eight million livres (about £400,000), while some of the provincial nobility were to be seen ploughing their few acres themselves. The division between rich and poor tended to be self-perpetuating, since the main source of income open to the nobility was to be found at Court and the purchase of a post at Versailles was beyond the reach of the majority: an ordinary regiment might cost 40,000 livres, while an important command in the household troops would be worth very much more. The acquisition of such means of advancement was, in fact, one of the main reasons for the frequent *mésalliances*. With a few exceptions, such as sea-borne trade and the glass industry, the nobility were debarred from profitable occupations. There were not many like the bishop of Metz, a Montmorency-Laval and founder of the Baccarat glassworks or the marquis d'Angosse, an important ironmaster in the Basses-Pyrénées, who took advantage of these limited opportunities. Some were associated with companies which obtained mining concessions from the king, but the majority had no industrial connections. The 'landed' gentry themselves sometimes drew the greater part of their income from fixed feudal dues rather than from the ownership of large estates whose yield could be increased by scientific cultivation.[2]

The aristocracy, so varied in most respects, were alike in enjoying a privileged position in society based on the anachronistic assumption that they were a feudal landowning class that shared in the royal Government, served the king in war and preserved order in the countryside. They were exempt from

---

[1] Chateaubriand, *Mémoires d'Outre-Tombe*, Part I, Books i–iii; Forster, *op. cit.*, *passim*, and 'The Noble Wine-producers of the Bordelais in the Eighteenth Century', *Economic History Review*, 2nd series, XIV (1961), p. 18; J. Jaurès, *Histoire Socialiste* (Paris, 1901), I. 79–82.

[2] In the Toulouse plain, however, the sale of grain provided four to five times the income from feudal dues. Forster, *op. cit.*, p. 38.

the *taille*, the original form of direct taxation, and from the royal *corvées* for the building and upkeep of roads, which became generalized in the eighteenth century. The social conservatism of Louis XIV had got the better of his absolutism and the half-hearted attempts of the *roi soleil* and his successors to tax the nobility had met with only limited success. The new taxes, the *capitation* and the *vingtièmes*, were theoretically levied on all subjects, but the noble was exempt on a part of his arable, if he cultivated it himself, and on his meadows, parks and vineyards. Since no previous tax assessments for the nobility existed it was generally easy for them to strike a bargain with the intendant and pay a comparatively small amount. The extent of these fiscal privileges should not be exaggerated—the duc de La Rochefoucauld, when introducing the Budget for 1791, estimated that the former privileged classes would provide only thirty-six million livres out of a total income from direct taxation of 347 million—but they were nevertheless a source of constant irrita-tion to the commoners.[1]

Certain occupations, such as commands in the armed forces, ambassadorships and high preferment in the Church, were reserved for the nobility. In all these fields the highest positions were monopolized by the great noble families at Versailles, and the provincial gentry had to make do with posts of secondary importance. Seigneurial privileges, although much more wide-spread, were similarly restricted to those who owned fiefs. Such privileges were basically of two kinds, concerning land and persons. The latter, which applied to all the inhabitants of the manor, consisted primarily of the *banalités* which repre-sented a seigneurial monopoly of corn mill, wine press and oven, the manorial courts which reinforced the power of the seigneur besides providing him with a source of revenue, and the *droit du colombier* which enabled the lord's pigeons to be fed at the peasant's expense. Hunting rights were perhaps more important as a source of loss to the peasant than of income to the seigneur. The second category of rights concerned land which had allegedly once been leased from the lord on perpetual tenure.

[1] On the fiscal system see G. Lizerand, 'Observations sur l'impôt foncier sous l'ancien régime', *Revue d'Histoire Économique et Sociale*, XXXVI (1958), and C. Ambrosi, 'Répartition et Perception de la Taille au dix-huitième siècle', *Revue d'Histoire Moderne et Contemporaine*, VIII (1961).

The confusing multiplicity of *cens*, *champarts*, *lods et ventes*, *quint et requint*, etc., which included many local variants, consisted partly of a kind of ground rent, of fixed amount, paid in cash or kind, partly of exceptional payments such as those due when a holding was sold, and partly of personal services owed by the peasant to the lord of the manor.[1] The combined incidence of these feudal obligations varied greatly from region to region and even from village to village and family to family, but in conjunction with heavy royal taxation they often imposed a crushing burden on the peasant.

Much more detailed research is necessary before it will be possible to speak with confidence of a rise or fall in the standard of living of the aristocracy during the century. Their expenditure was generally high. If one disregards such untypical scandals as the twenty million livres of debt accumulated by the king's brother, the comte d'Artois, by the age of twenty-four, even in the provinces the nobility were often living well and building or enlarging châteaux. They were also tending to spend part of the year in town houses in the provincial capitals. In an age of steadily rising prices such standards would impose a heavy strain on incomes that were often relatively static. Even the prosperous grain farmers of the Garonne valley could only afford to marry one son and one daughter if their estates were to be kept intact, and the size of their families was almost halved in the course of the eighteenth century.[2] Those of the nobility who could undertake large-scale farming, benefit from the steady increase in rents, speculate with large quantities of grain delivered as rents in kind, encourage the development of industry on their estates or exploit their mineral resources, were presumably able to profit from the long period of rising prices. But any such advantages would come to them as landowners rather than as privileged seigneurs. The more conventional country squire, with his limited estates let out to share-croppers and much of his income in the form of fixed feudal dues, probably found his real income falling at a time when his expenditure was increasing and his more prosperous neighbours were setting a stiffer social pace. It may be that some such division within the

[1] See M. Garaud, *Histoire Générale du Droit Privé Français (de 1789 à 1804): la Révolution et la Propriété Foncière* (Paris, 1958), pp. 45–101.
[2] Forster, *op. cit.*, chap. vi.

FRANCE ON THE EVE OF THE REVOLUTION

provincial nobility influenced the attitude of individuals towards the Revolution and helps to explain why the aristocracy was more prepared to co-operate with the middle class in a relatively industrialized province such as Dauphiné than in backward Brittany.

As we have seen, the nobility had on the whole succeeded in its attempt to infiltrate the royal administration, but on its other flank it was fighting a defensive battle against the growing wealth and ambition of the middle class. The financial power implied by the possession of liquid assets was increasingly at variance with the hierarchy of social status. The monarchy, in need of money but attached to the traditional social order, found itself in a dilemma, since the venality of offices and commissions, which it could not afford to abolish, excluded many of the nobility who could not bid against the well-filled purses of the ambitious bourgeois. The power of money was such that even at Versailles the bourgeoisie had to be admitted to the queen's gaming-table to keep up the supply of gamblers. During the reign of Louis XVI in particular, a series of dykes was built against the threatening bourgeois tide. The difficulties were considerable, for indebted aristocrats would use their influence to advance their bourgeois creditors, but the combined efforts of the aristocracy and of the royal Government gradually succeeded in closing most of the breaches. The king increasingly turned to members of the nobility to fill vacant bishoprics. Indeed, Mme Campan credits Louis XVI with having decided that 'all ecclesiastical preferment, from the most modest priory to the richest abbey, was to be the appanage of the nobility'.[1] Certainly, by 1789 all the bishops were noble. But the most sensational victory of the aristocracy was the Ségur ordinance of 1781 which, with minor exceptions, restricted commissioned entry into the army to those who could prove four generations of nobility. This devalued the titles that the Crown had been busily selling to aspiring bourgeois and created a new division within the nobility. The parlements, which needed no royal prompting, were also tending to recruit their members entirely from the aristocracy.

This aristocratic offensive, while primarily intended to

[1] Campan, *Mémoires sur la Vie Privée de Marie Antoinette* (2nd ed., 1823), I. 224.

10

benefit all the old *épée* families, in fact worked mainly to the advantage of the *noblesse de cour*. The poorer provincial nobles were often unable to take advantage of the facilities offered to them and the five military colleges founded for their benefit in 1777 were promptly invaded by the sons of Court families. In 1788, it was decided that the command of regiments should be virtually reserved for the Court nobility, which put an end to the ambitions of the more obscure noble families.[1] The aristo- cratic offensive was, in fact, being conducted at this stage by the Court nobility, who used their influence to strengthen their own position at the expense of the provincial gentry and the recently ennobled, as well as the middle class. They were to pay for their exclusiveness in 1789 when the noble electorate pointedly re- jected many of them as candidates for the Estates General.

More serious was the check to the social ambitions of the middle class. French society had hitherto been much more mobile than is generally recognized. Necker's estimate that nearly half of the nobility in 1789 had acquired their status within the preceding two centuries is supported by recent research.[2] It would also seem that the movement into the nobility had been accelerating during the eighteenth century, as might have been expected from the growing wealth of the middle class and the impoverishment of the Crown. The ex- clusiveness of the aristocracy now deprived the newly ennobled of some of the most important practical advantages that their status had formerly conferred and consequently created a sharp division of interest between the old *noblesse* and the upper middle class and *anoblis* which accentuated the divergence between the social hierarchy and the economic structure of the country.

During the second half of the eighteenth century in particular there were signs of a seigneurial reaction in the countryside, based on the more rigorous exploitation of his feudal rights by the seigneur. As usual in the ancien régime, different forces were pulling in different directions. The lawyers were increas- ingly hostile to the old conception of feudal tenure and inclined to regard the peasant who paid an annual *cens* as a freeholder.[3]

[1] L. Hartmann, 'Les Officiers de l'Armée Royale à la veille de la Révolution' *Revue Historique*, C, CI (1909).

[2] See, for example, G. Girault, *La Noblesse Emigrée et ses pertes foncières dans le Département de la Sarthe* (Laval, 1957).

[3] Garaud, *op. cit.*, chap. i.

But many seigneurs were simultaneously adopting a more businesslike attitude to the management of their estates and of the feudal rights that formed part of their income.[1] This process had been to some extent restrained by the monarchy whose intendants, whether from humanitarian or fiscal motives, had protected peasants whose solvency was a matter of royal concern. Towards the end of the reign of Louis XV Physiocratic theories inclined the intendants to look more favourably on the interests of the bigger landowners, while the social ties of the intendants and the aspirations of their deputies (sub-délégués) made it more painful for them to challenge the local aristocracy. The decline of royal power under Louis XVI further strengthened local interests. The protection of the courts, never very reliable so far as the peasants were concerned, probably suffered from the tendency of the judges to acquire estates for themselves. The seigneurs, possibly spurred on by the pressure of rising prices, were determined to exploit their rights to the full. Even when the noble landowner derived the greater part of his profit from the sale of produce, feudal privileges were still valuable, as an additional source of income, a means of controlling village communities and a weapon for expropriating peasants whose accumulated arrears left them hopelessly indebted to their seigneurs. The combined resources of broad acres and manorial rights could enable their beneficiaries to establish virtual control over the neighbouring countryside.[2] Feudal rights were often farmed out to individuals or companies whose income depended on their enforcement and, if possible, extension. The *terriers*, which listed the rights of the seigneur, were kept up to date to prevent old claims falling into disuse and on occasion to transform past usage into legal precedent. Grazing rights which had not needed precise definition when the lord of the manor kept a few cattle and sheep became a matter of serious concern when he leased them to a stockbreeder. The employment of lawyers specializing in feudal jurisprudence enabled some seigneurs to discover rights that had not been enforced for many years, on which they could

[1] M. Bloch, *Les Caractères originaux de l' Histoire Rurale Française* (Oslo–Paris, 1931), p. 137; P. de Saint Jacob, *Les Paysans de la Bourgogne du Nord au dernier siècle de l'Ancien Régime* (Paris, 1960), pp. 405–35.

[2] Forster, *op. cit.*, chap. i–ii.

claim retrospective payment. This increased 'feudal' pressure gave rise to a spate of recrimination, litigation and peasant violence that aggravated the social tensions of the country-side.[1]

In these various ways the nobility was being driven to emphasize its isolation from the urban middle class and from the peasantry. It has consequently fared badly at the hands of recent French historians, whether liberal or marxist. It was indeed in the invidious position of defending obsolescent privileges and its own hierarchical view of society against utilitarian and liberal theories. Nevertheless, the way of life, with all its imperfections, which it personified, however necessary its demise, could not be destroyed without loss to the community at large. The aristocracy left a memorable legacy of fine architecture, handsome furniture and civilized living. In the society which it dominated the domestic arts attained to standards of taste unequalled before or since. Its cosmopolitan world was marked by a restraint wholly absent from the fanaticism of succeeding ages. Montesquieu, defending the conquests of science in his *Lettres Persanes*, affirmed that even if scientists made possible the production of more cruel and destructive weapons these would at once be banned by international law. This was not the naïve optimism of a political innocent, for there was some historical truth in Montesquieu's argument that an independent hereditary aristocracy restrained the State in its tendency to seek power at any price. Saint-Simon and his less articulate peers, with their exalted view of the rights and obligations of their birth, were not merely concerned to preserve their material privileges. Their argument that social equality went hand in hand with the enslavement of all by a despotic sovereign is not to be dismissed as mere interested antiquarianism.[2] French society was also becoming increasingly humane and tolerant: it was during the reign of Louis XVI that torture was abolished and the Protestants obtained limited religious toleration. The twentieth century is scarcely qualified to underestimate such achievements. Many members of the aristocracy regarded themselves as

---

[1] See the article on the murder of the comte de Dampierre reprinted in G. Lefebvre, *Études sur la Révolution Française* (Paris, 1954).

[2] See, for example, M. Lewis, *Napoleon and his British Captives*, (1962) chap. i–iii.

personally responsible for the well-being of their communities. It was not simply political calculation that led the marquis de Ferrières to write in 1789, 'So long as Marsay is mine I will never allow anyone to be short of bread or clothing.' The writers who played so important a part in this civilizing process, if they were not themselves noble like Montesquieu and d'Holbach, were launched by noble salons, supported, and when necessary protected by members of the aristocracy. Without the salons there might well have been no 'enlightenment'. Bearing all these things in mind, it was not surprising if the aristocracy equated its own values with those of civilization itself and tended to regard them as inseparable from the privileged and hierarchical society in which they flourished.

People who lived in the towns had at least one thing in common: municipal charters shielded them, to a greater or lesser extent, from the full impact of feudal burdens and even from some royal taxation. Orleans, for example, was exempt from the poll tax *(taille)* and from the obligation to produce recruits for the militia, one of the most hated impositions in the country areas. In other respects the townsmen, like the nobility, were divided amongst themselves by barriers of wealth, education, way of life and conflicting economic interests. However the modern division between capital and labour was not yet clearly marked and the distinction between aristocracy and 'people' was not the same thing as the division between 'gentlemen' and 'lower classes'.

The bourgeoisie, in the sense in which the term 'bourgeois' was used in the late eighteenth century—corresponding more or less to the English 'gentleman'—was recruited in the main from two sources: business and the professions.[1] The legal and administrative middle class had been developed by the monarchy for its own purposes and had in the past often been its ally against the feudal nobility. The ancien régime, with its innumerable law courts and extensive bureaucracy, had provided such men with employment and the chance of wealth and even-

---

[1] See E. G. Barber, *The Bourgeoisie in Eighteenth-Century France* (Princeton, 1955), *passim*; P. Leuilliot, 'Réflexions sur l'histoire économique et sociale à propos de la bourgeoisie en 1789', *Revue d'Histoire Moderne et Contemporaine*, I (1954), p. 131.

tual entry into the nobility.[1] On the whole, the lawyers and royal servants had accommodated themselves to the social order and their attitude to the aristocracy was one of aspiration rather than of hostility. Two such lawyers, ignorant of the destinies ahead of them, changed their names from Danton and Derobespierre to d'Anton and de Robespierre. Unable to aspire to such typographical nobility, Brissot called himself Brissot de Warville, after the small estate that he owned at Ouarville, and similar examples could be quoted. These people, often with more education than capital, were perhaps more concerned with status than with fortune, and they were particularly affected by the closing of so many openings, in the parlements, the Church and the army, to themselves and their families. Always closely linked to the machinery of royal Government, their dissatisfaction assumed a political character and they were to become the most bitter opponents of the aristocracy which had rejected them, and were to lead the struggle for reform in 1789. Nantes, for example, chose its six representatives in the Estates General from the legal profession, electing businessmen and bankers as reserve candidates only.[2]

The businessmen had made their own way in the world, helped on occasion by royal favours, licences or monopolies, but on the whole outside the feudal framework of king, government, aristocracy and peasantry. Nevertheless the highest ranks of the business world, the financiers, had been brought into closer and closer contact with the royal Government, which had come to depend on their support. As far back as 1708 Saint-Simon had denounced the 'prostitution' of Louis XIV before Samuel Bernard, when the king personally conducted the banker round the château of Marly in order to extract a loan from him. By the mid-eighteenth century things had been put on a more systematic basis.[3] The farming of indirect taxation had been resumed in 1726 and the *fermiers généraux* who contracted to raise these taxes gradually became almost a branch of Government itself. From 1750 onwards the Crown was unable to repay their deposit

[1] There were 53 law-courts in Angers, a town with a population of 34,000. J. McManners, *French Ecclesiastical Society under the Ancien Régime: A study of Angers in the Eighteenth Century* (Manchester, 1961), p. 4.
[2] Gaston Martin, *Carrier et sa Mission à Nantes* (Paris, 1924), p. 16.
[3] See G. T. Mathews, *The Royal General Farms in Eighteenth-Century France* (New York, 1958), *passim*.

to the *fermiers* when their contract expired and the *fermiers généraux* became creditors to whom the Government was permanently in debt. They exploited the Crown's weakness, in typical eighteenth-century fashion, by buying the *survivance* of their posts, which allowed them to nominate their own successors. In 1780 the succession was restricted to the sons of the *fermiers*, which made the group almost a closed caste, closely linked with the Government and marrying its daughters into the highest ranks of the aristocracy. As the financial situation worsened the resources of the *fermiers généraux* were supplemented by loans on the international money market which brought into close contact with the Court a number of international bankers of whom the most conspicuous was Necker. The marriage, in 1786, of Necker's daughter to the Swedish diplomat, de Stael, was a matter of State policy and the marriage contract was signed by the king and queen and by all the princes of the blood.[1] In 1789 the great financiers might therefore have been expected to stand by the monarchy, but their fortunes were exposed to a repudiation of the Debt by the Government. The revolutionaries were to emphasize the sanctity of the Debt, which could only be effectively guaranteed by the nation, and so the bankers found themselves being drawn into the revolutionary movement, in which some of them participated in person.

Below the financiers who were close to the Government and wealthy enough to be more or less immune from aristocratic hauteur, came the substantial businessmen, who were especially powerful in the seaports. Although the ancien régime had not prevented the rapid expansion of the French economy in the eighteenth century, these merchants and shipowners were far from satisfied. A disastrous and apparently irresponsible foreign policy had lost them Canada and their privileged position in India. An aristocratic navy, believing 'that our ships of the line should fight for the honour of the flag and not for merchants'[2] had tended to subordinate convoy protection to the pursuit of glory, in marked contrast to the British navy's solicitude for 'the trade'. At home these merchants were exposed to humilia-

[1] J. C. Herold, *Mistress to an Age: the Life of Madame de Stael* (1958), pp. 58–59.

[2] De Curt in the Constituent Assembly, 26 June 1790.

tion by the nobility and vulnerable to the bias of the parlements if they went to law against members of the privileged orders. Merchants and manufacturers alike suffered from internal customs barriers and tolls for some of which the aristocracy were directly responsible and which parlements and provincial Estates defended against royal attempts to impose uniformity. Although they were by no means immune from the temptation to retire from business, build country houses and *vivre noblement*, they were perhaps less inclined than the lawyers to see in the acquisition of noble status the only possible conclusion to a successful career. This perhaps helps to explain the revolutionary temper of the ports, which impressed Arthur Young when he visited Nantes in 1788. The contrast in mood between Nantes and the 'county town' of Brittany, Rennes, home of the parlement and of the Breton Estates, was particularly striking in 1789. But the wealthy merchants were far from being indifferent to the values of an aristocratic society and Necker deplored the diversion of their capital to the purchase of noble titles: 'I do not hesitate to affirm that this disposition checks the whole development of French commerce and is one of the main causes of the superiority in many fields of nations where distinctions of social status are less marked.'[1]

All branches of the upper middle class had therefore been inclined, to a greater or lesser extent, both to criticize the aristocracy and to aspire to noble status. The growing exclusiveness of the nobility united their 'inferiors' in bitter opposition to an aristocracy that Creuzet-Latouche, a lawyer elected to the Estates General and a man far removed from revolutionary extremism, roundly denounced as 'anti-social'. But the situation was complicated for the middle class by the fact that they were concerned not merely with social status but also with civil liberty and freedom from arbitrary government. They were inclined to agree with the parlements that such safeguards implied representative government. But in the ancien régime representative government seemed to rest on the parlements and provincial Estates which were centres of aristocratic reaction. The middle class therefore found itself in a dilemma: to attack absolutism was to enthrone aristocratic privilege and

[1] Quoted in J. Lough, *An Introduction to Eighteenth-Century France* (1960), p. 84.

particularism, while the way to the economic unity of the country seemed to lead also to royal despotism. On this issue the *philosophes* were divided. When Maupeou virtually abolished the parlements Voltaire came to his support, while the majority of his fellow writers protested against royal despotism. It was not until the middle class was prepared to enter the political field itself that it could put forward a programme which combined civil liberty with social equality.

Economic conditions in eighteenth-century France varied from one region to another and all generalizations are subject to caution. Between 1750 and 1775 the value of industrial production doubled, that of trade increased threefold and colonial trade fivefold. Prices were rising steadily and there was every incentive to invest and to increase production. Le Havre, Nantes, Bordeaux and Marseilles in particular enjoyed a period of exceptional prosperity. 'Much as I had read and heard of the commerce of this city,' wrote Arthur Young at Bordeaux in 1787, 'they greatly surpassed my expectations. . . . We must not name Liverpool in competition with Bordeaux. . . . The new houses that are building in all quarters of the town mark, too clearly to be misunderstood, the prosperity of the place.'[1] Nevertheless there are signs that, outside the field of colonial trade, this expansion suffered a check during the reign of Louis XVI. C. E. Labrousse has suggested that a period of depression set in about 1776–7 and continued until the Revolution, intensified in the case of the textile industry by the imports from England that followed the commercial treaty of 1786.[2] At Lyons in 1788, 5,442 of the 9,335 silk looms were idle.[3] Present evidence is inadequate to determine the extent and severity of this crisis but it seems unlikely to have appeared to contemporaries as more than a localized and temporary, though severe setback. Viewing the century as a whole, French trade was

[1] A. Young, *Travels in France and Italy* (ed. *Everyman*, 1915), p. 56.
[2] C. E. Labrousse, *La Crise de l'Économie Française à la fin de l'Ancien Régime et au début de la Révolution* (Paris, 1944), Introduction; see also his contribution to vol. V of the *Histoire Générale des Civilisations* (ed. Crouzet, Paris, 1953). For a different view of the effects of the Commercial Treaty see W. O. Henderson, 'The Anglo-French Commercial Treaty of 1786', *Economic History Review*, X (1957), p. 104.
[3] R. Fuoc, *La Réaction Thermidorienne à Lyon* (Lyons, 1957), p. 26. See also, L. Trénard, 'La Crise sociale Lyonnaise à la veille de la Révolution', *Revue d'Histoire Moderne et Contemporaine*, II (1955).

enjoying a period of unprecedented expansion and industry was following in its wake.

As yet this expansion had not led to any dramatic change in methods of production. Factories and mines using steam existed —there were a dozen steam engines working in the Anzin mines in 1789—together with other large factories such as those at Sedan, where the complete processing of wool was undertaken, and the muslin factory at le Puy-en-Velay, which employed 52 looms.[1] But these remained exceptions and the fact that French coal production in 1789 was only about one-twentieth that of England is suggestive of the slower pace of industrialization across the Channel. Most of the town industries were still organized on the guild system, and, in theory at least, the working man was a journeyman who could hope to become a master craftsman and an employer of labour. But the guild system was being outflanked by the growing tendency of entrepreneurs to take their cotton or wool into the country districts for it to be spun and woven by the free labour of the peasants. In the northeast and Normandy in particular large areas practised a dual economy of this kind. Partly as a result of this development, the textile manufacturers in particular were emerging from their old position as master craftsmen employing a few journeymen and the more successful were becoming wealthy merchant-manufacturers owning the looms of the peasants or artisans who worked for them. This process had gone farthest at Lyons, where the silk industry was under the control of a few hundred wealthy merchants. Here a veritable class war opposed masters and journeymen on the one hand to an alliance of aristocrats and merchants on the other. There had been a serious insurrection in 1744 and widespread strikes in 1786 were suppressed by the army.

The merchant-manufacturers demanded the abolition of the guilds and the freeing of the labour market. Faced with this threat to their traditional way of life, the master craftsmen, like the aristocracy, demanded the reinforcement of the traditional safeguards of a relatively static society. But they themselves were simultaneously trying to perpetuate their own privileged position at the expense of their journeymen and to confine

[1] See G. Martin, *La Grande Industrie en France sous le Règne de Louis XV* (Paris, 1900), *passim*.

recruitment to their own families. The journeymen's attempts to organize themselves and to resort to strike action found the Government on the side of the masters and the municipal authorities—royal edicts of 1749 and 1760 prohibited the association of workmen for collective bargaining. The journeyman therefore found his prospects of advancement declining at a time when wage increases were failing to keep pace with the cost of living. Labrousse has estimated that the latter rose by nearly two-thirds in the fifty years before the Revolution, while wages increased by no more than a quarter. There was still, however, no clear division between capital and labour. The master craftsman was no bourgeois, although he might be a man of considerable substance, and there was a strong sense of *esprit de corps* between the master and his journeyman—often living under his roof— and between the various members of the same guild. When food prices rose the journeyman was more disposed to blame the baker, the farmer and the speculator in foodstocks than to demand higher wages. Journeyman and master craftsman therefore joined forces in an economic struggle that divided the town from the countryside, demanding State control of the grain trade and of the price of food. They were also united in defending their traditional monopoly against the spread of manufacturing into the country districts and the claims of outsiders to invade the town markets. These issues tended to set them against the wealthy bourgeoisie, converted to the principles of free trade and often themselves gentlemen farmers who stood to profit from an increase in food prices.

The urban population was therefore a prey to deep internal divisions, with some of the wealthier merchants aspiring to become large-scale industrialists, the master craftsmen and journeymen united in resisting the pressure to reduce them to a mere proletariat, but at the same time at loggerheads with each other. Until 1789 these divisions were to some extent obscured by the general hostility towards the aristocracy. It is tempting to equate this anti-aristocratic feeling with the self-confidence of a rising generation of capitalists impatient to overthrow a system of government and a social order that stood in the way of their advancement. This was the outlook of the socialist historian, Jaurès: 'The bourgeoisie is not merely a force of prudence and economy; it is a bold and conquering force that has already in part revolutionized the system of production and exchange and is about to revolutionize the political system.'[1] The revolutionary statesman, Barnave, seemed to suggest a similar interpretation: 'The whole of the French Revolution can be attributed to the progress of civilization, enlightenment and industry, for it is this cause which, raising up the Third Estate and augmenting its wealth, education and self-respect, made a democratic revolution inevitable.'[2] There is obviously something to be said for this view. The spokesmen of the bourgeoisie had read the works of the physiocrats and of Adam Smith.[3] Liberal economic theories had conquered the intellectual world and were to dictate the policies of all the revolutionary Assemblies. There are indeed some hints that far-sighted liberals had glimpsed the vast possibilities that lay ahead, but it would be very rash to assert that the revolutionary temper of much of the urban bourgeoisie was due to a sense of *economic* frustration. In the prosperous seaports the bourgeoisie was more conscious of the remarkable progress of the previous fifty years than of the possibilities of the future; what they demanded was not so much new opportunities for economic expansion as the social recognition of the position they had already won. Elsewhere, the burgesses of clerical Angers or the humble corn-merchants of Toulouse would have been astonished to learn that they were a 'bold and conquering force'. Of the former, a Government official wrote in 1783, 'The present generation vegetates just as that which preceded it vegetated, and as the succeeding one will vegetate.'[4] It is clear that the wealth, independence and aspirations of the bourgeoisie varied enormously from one town to another. Moreover, the urban population as a whole was by no means sympathetic to the progress of capitalism. Master and journeyman feared for their status and standard of living. The former in particular had reason to cling to a system of production which often brought him relative security and responsibility, rather than to venture

---

[1] *Histoire Socialiste*, I. 47.

[2] A. Barnave, *Réflexions Politiques* (*Oeuvres*, ed. Béranger, Paris, 1843), II. 28.

[3] When the Minister of the Interior sent observers to report on the state of the countryside in 1793, each was provided with copies of the *Wealth of Nations* and of the works of Arthur Young. P. Caron, *Rapports des Agents du Ministre de l'Intérieur dans les Départements* (Paris, 1913, 1951), I, Introduction.

[4] McManners, *op. cit.*, p. 3.

on to the high seas of economic liberalism where ten would founder for every one who made good. Sharing the hostility towards the aristocracy felt by their social superiors, these men might join the bourgeoisie in an attack on the superstructure of the ancien régime, but they were sceptical of the brave new world of free enterprise and suspicious of its advocates.

What does seem to have been common to a great many of the town-dwellers was a dislike of the aristocracy which increased as one mounted the social ladder. The causes of this hostility were social rather than economic. It was not that the middle class could not expand and prosper, but that it was increasingly excluded from the social status and privilege that prosperity had previously been able to buy more easily. Barnave himself, in the passage quoted above, insists that the Revolution was intended to bring 'democracy' to the affluent, not to enable the ambitious to grow more wealthy. Elsewhere he explains himself more clearly, in describing the reign of Louis XVI, 'Since a corrupt Government had struck down the aristocracy, it was held that a paternal Government should restore it. The parlements were recalled, birth reinstated in all its privileges, the Third Estate progressively excluded from the pursuit of arms, laws brought into conflict with habits, with the natural progression of events. Everything was done to arouse the jealousy of one class and to exalt the pretensions of the other.'[1] When Barnave used the word 'class' he really meant 'order'. The Third Estate was not an economic class; to borrow the language of 1789, it was 'ninety-six hundredths of the nation', stretching from the poorest labourer to the *fermier-général*. Its more educated members were, however, aware of its social unity as the lowest order of the State. It was this preoccupation with social rather than economic grievances that enabled them to lead the order as a whole into battle against the aristocracy.

In the late eighteenth century over twenty million of the French population of twenty-six million lived on the land. Besides being by far the most important occupation, agriculture tended to set the pace for the economic life of the whole country. As the intendant at Rouen wrote in 1768, 'the price of bread is

[1] A. Barnave, *Introduction à la Révolution Française* (*Oeuvres*, ed. Béranger, Paris, 1843), I. 84.

the manufacturer's compass'. The problems of the farming community, intimately connected with the evolution of French society since the Middle Ages, were extremely complex.[1] We have already seen something of the burden that seigneurial privileges imposed on the peasant. Theoretically distinct from this relationship, although often overlapping, was the question of land ownership.

France was unique in Europe in that seigneurial privilege co-existed with a free peasantry owning a good deal of the land. Conditions varied, but taking the country as a whole, the peasants probably owned between a third and a quarter of the land.[2] This fact had important social consequences, but it did not prevent the peasants from forming an impoverished section of the community, since few of them owned enough land to support their families throughout the year. Most farming was still based on the two-field or three-field system and it took 20 acres of good arable land to feed a family. Some were able to rent land which, together with their own holdings, made them self-supporting, but the majority worked for part of the year as labourers. In the more prosperous parts of the country, notably to the north and east of Paris, short leases and rents in money were customary. Elsewhere the peasants were often too poor to make solvent tenants and unable to afford their own livestock and equipment. The majority were therefore *métayers* or share-croppers. The landlord provided them with animals and equipment, normally in return for half of the crop and a certain amount of labour-service. Tithes and some manorial dues were shared, but the *métayer* was responsible for the royal *corvée*. In years of bad harvest he was left with a pitifully small surplus when he had paid his various contributions and set aside

[1] See Bloch, *op. cit.*, chap. vi. On the agrarian question see the following works by G. Lefebvre: *Questions Agraires au Temps de la Terreur* (La Roche-sur-Yonne, 1954), *Études sur la Révolution Française* (Paris, 1954), *Les Paysans du Nord pendant la Révolution Française* (Paris–Lille, 1924), and *Documents relatifs à l'Histoire des Subsistances dans le District de Bergues* (Lille, 1914); and C. E. Labrousse, *Esquisse du Mouvement des Prix et des Revenus en France au Dix-huitième Siècle* (Paris, 1933).

[2] For example, 25% around Toulouse, 30% in the Nord, rather more in the District of Saint-Pol in the Pas-de-Calais. Forster, *op. cit.*, p. 35; G. Lefebvre, *Les Paysans du Nord pendant la Révolution Française*, p. 11; G. Sangnier, *L'Évolution de la Propriété rurale dans le District de Saint-Pol pendant la Révolution* (Blangermont, 1951), pp. 26–84.

as much as one-fifth of his total harvest for seed. Once his own stocks were exhausted he found himself competing with other *métayers* and with landless labourers for such poorly-paid employment as was available on the bigger farms. In many parts of France the poorer peasants were only able to survive by the help of domestic industry. The majority were thus, for part of the year, wage-earners. The high food prices that meant prosperity for the wealthy farmer were disastrous to the bulk of the peasantry who bought far more food than they sold. It is easy to convey too sombre a picture of the peasant's life which, hard as it was, compared favourably with that of the serfs of central Europe. French agriculture had risen a little above subsistence level and during the eighteenth century the population rose by about six million. This increase accentuated the competition for land and perhaps helped to keep wages low, but at least the extra mouths were fed.

One important effect of the traditional agricultural system was to foster a strong community-feeling in the village. The management of the open fields required uniformity of cultivation and the commons were administered by the village as a whole. Direct taxation was imposed on the community as a unit and the allocation of taxes was a matter of common concern. The village shared rights which it might have to defend in the courts—in which case the church formed a central meeting-place for the village assembly and the *curé* might provide local leadership. In a system both traditional and partly communal there was little scope for individualism, and the peasants, while recognizing the private ownership of land, were inclined to regard the harvest as the property of the community. When such theories were publicized in 1792–4 the economic liberals took fright and some subsequent historians have interpreted as 'socialism' what was, in fact, the traditional collectivist psychology of the village.

During the second half of the eighteenth century such habits of thought were challenged by the economic ideas of the Physiocrats. Agrarian reformers hoped, by freeing the corn trade, to increase the price of grain, attract capital to agriculture and thereby expand the production of food. The growth of more fodder would permit an extension of herds and the increase in animal fertilizer would augment the grain harvest and allow of the suppression of the extravagant fallow fields. Such scientific agriculture implied enclosures, the division of common land and the curtailment or abolition of traditional grazing rights. A movement in this direction was launched soon after the middle of the century, but failed to acquire the momentum of the agrarian revolution in England.[1] Various reasons have been advanced to explain the limited effectiveness of the agrarian reformers in France: the depression of 1775–80 which discouraged experiment; the feudal privileges of the seigneurs which, together with the scattered nature of their holdings, often gave them little incentive to enclose; the fact that enclosures would interfere with hunting, which accounted for their prohibition in the royal hunting preserves; the existence of large numbers of peasant freeholders who could not be evicted. Since some of these factors apply to the seigneur rather than to the landowner as such, the relics of feudalism that pressed so hard on the peasant may have helped to shield him from some of the consequences of the agrarian revolution.

Nevertheless, the new forces did have some effect, even if they were not carried far enough to satisfy an Arthur Young. A sharp increase in grain prices about 1770 led to a period of speculation in land. Many small tenancies were united into large farms and some enclosures were made, even though full advantage was not taken of the possibilities which they offered. Rents rose even more sharply than prices and the smallholder who relied on finding land to rent was soon in difficulties. The result of this tendency towards capitalist farming was sharply to accentuate the tensions within the village. A small minority of independent farmers, growing for the market, made substantial profits, while peasants of moderate means often found themselves on the road to insolvency and eventual expropriation. The poor, unable to afford to renew their leases and often deprived of grazing for their cattle, were reduced to a rural proletariat on the margin of mendicity. The bad forage harvest and epidemic of murrain in the summer of 1785 completed the ruin of the less fortunate farmers. The peasants of north Burgundy in 1789 were bitterly aware of the sudden deterioration in their fortunes. 'How different things are now from what they

[1] See A. J. Bourde, *The Influence of England on the French Agronomes, 1750–1789* (Cambridge, 1953).

were 25 or 30 years ago. We are perishing before our own eyes!' 'Thirty years ago the parish contained only good landowners and good farmers . . . everyone had a modest but sufficient living. . . . Those happy days are no more, those good landowners have lost everything; the local people do not own a quarter of the land, which has been sold to the seigneurs and the bourgeois of the towns, who are of no help to us.'[1] Around Toulouse and Bordeaux also the nobility were acquiring considerable amounts of peasant land in the second half of the century.[2]

In periods when grain was scarce and prices high it was customary for the Government to intervene on the side of the consumer by restricting the circulation of grain, obliging farmers to sell on the open market and if necessary enforcing controlled prices.[3] The Physiocrats might lament that such measures discouraged the investment of the capital that alone would permanently remove the danger of famine. Faced with more immediate problems, the intendants, even when sympathetically disposed towards the free-traders, did not hesitate to enforce controls in order to keep the peace. For the economists tended to overlook the fact that the high cost of inland transport prevented the establishment of a national market. A journey of 300 miles doubled the cost of grain, while the variation in local prices rarely exceeded 50 per cent. Moreover the peasant resented any attempt to convey grain outside his locality in times of scarcity and did not hesitate to arrest and pillage the grain convoys.

In normal times, however, the Government was neither willing nor able to reverse the economic trend in favour of capitalist agriculture, despite its pressures and tensions within the village. The inevitable consequence, since the French peasant was no serf, was an increase in rural litigation and violence. Villages that lost lawsuits against their seigneurs—and very few won them—found themselves crushed under a new

[1] P. de Saint Jacob, op. cit., pp. 498, 571; Part III contains an excellent survey of the agrarian re.orm movement in North Burgundy and a description of the village community on the eve of the Revolution that is probably valid for much of France.

[2] Forster, op. cit., chap. ii; Forster, loc. cit., p. 18.

[3] See A. Mathiez, La Vie Chère: le Mouvement Social sous la Terreur (Paris, 1927), pp. 7–13.

burden of debt. Tempers rose, enclosures were invaded and by 1789 much of the countryside was ripe for revolt. The real enemy of the majority of the peasants was the large landowner, noble, bourgeois or *laboureur* (yeoman farmer), whose acquisitiveness was threatening them with expropriation. But the main landowner in the village was often the seigneur, who was also responsible for the growing burden of seigneurial dues. It was not difficult to lay most economic grievances at the seigneur's door. Royal taxation would have been lighter if the nobility had paid its full share. The unjust allocation of the *taille* often made it even more burdensome—and its assessment frequently lay in the hands of the *coq du village*, a relatively wealthy *laboureur* who might be the steward of the seigneur, mayor of the village and purchaser of the right to collect tithes and *champart*, whose power as lender of draught animals and source of employment put much of the village at his mercy. The *feudist*, whose professional exploitation of feudal dues pressed rigorously on the peasantry, was buttressed by the manorial court, while the complaining villagers found the royal administration deaf to their clumsy *patois*. The tithe, in very many cases, went not to the local *curé*, but to maintain the aristocratic abbot of an almost empty monastery in luxury at Versailles, while the impoverished contributors had to make supplementary grants to maintain the village church. The countryman thus found himself locked in a circle of frustration of which privilege seemed to hold the key to every door. Consequently, the village was able, for a time, to submerge its internal divisions in a common assault on the privileges of the nobility. Here, as in the towns, the predominant issue of social privilege partially obscured underlying economic rivalries that were only later to come into the open. This was evident in 1789, when the insurgent peasants made not for their seigneur's valuables but for their feudal title-deeds.

The Church in eighteenth-century France shared many of the characteristics of the lay society with which it was closely integrated. The enforcement of religious uniformity after the revocation of the Edict of Nantes in 1685 apparently guaranteed for all time the predominance of the Roman Catholic religion, in perpetual alliance with His Most Christian Majesty. When the position of the Church seemed assured there was a natural tendency for the clergy to concentrate their attention on the trimmings of religion—the 'improvement' of their churches, which more historically-minded generations were to deplore; the cultivation of religious music; research into ecclesiastical history—and on the pursuit of power and office. Contemporaries were thereby led to underestimate the genuine religious vocation of the majority of the clergy, which was none the less sincere for being overshadowed by more secular preoccupations. The organization of the Church mirrored that of lay society in the sense that there was a fairly sharp distinction between a ruling hierarchy and an impoverished rank and file, a distinction based essentially on noble birth. The religious superstructure was more obviously top-heavy than that of the laity: in Angers there were 72 canons to 17 parish priests. All of the bishops were noble. Many chapters and religious houses for men and women were similarly the exclusive preserve of the aristocracy, abbots, abbesses and deans being frequently appointed while still very young. Pluralism was rife and rich prebends and accumulated benefices assured a comfortable living to noble clergymen. Privilege was not entirely limited to the aristocracy, for some of the canons of the more humble chapters were placed in office by their powerful bourgeois families, although the more conspicuous prizes were beyond their reach. Tithes had often been alienated in favour of abbeys or cathedral chapters, the *curé* being left with an allowance *(portion congrue)*, officially increased in 1786 to the still inadequate sum of 700 livres. In practice, there were ingenious ways of paying even less. Many *curés* supplemented this pittance by a little humble pluralism of their own, but their *vicaires*, denied such compensation, lived in real poverty.[1]

The Church was a semi-autonomous body which intervened in the political, social and economic life of the community at all levels while itself escaping from secular control. Although the clergy amounted to no more than 100,000, they owned about one-tenth of the land, in addition to enjoying a substantial income from tithes. Secure in their economic independence, they governed themselves by Assemblies, meeting every five years, in which the upper clergy monopolized all power. The Church had its own administration and was responsible for its own

[1] McManners, *op. cit.*, pp. 6, 166, 140.

finances. Exempt from taxation, it voted a quinquennial grant to the Crown and could therefore exert financial pressure on the Government by threatening to withhold or reduce its contribution to the exchequer. In spite of its great wealth it was heavily burdened with debt since it had contracted the habit of raising its grant to the treasury by loans, instead of drawing on its own revenues. The Church was not merely autonomous; it also exercised much of the authority that has subsequently been claimed by civil governments. Education was almost wholly under its control. Information was also partly in its hands, since the pulpit provided the only means of publicizing Government policies to a largely illiterate mass audience. In addition, the Church was able to censor publications which it considered dangerous to faith or morals. It was the main source of public assistance and religious orders staffed most of the hospitals. Its control over the registers of births, marriages and deaths gave it considerable influence in the field of civil law. The local predominance of the First Estate was often striking. At Toulouse and Angers ecclesiastical buildings and their gardens occupied about half of the area of the town. The Church, besides being a great landowner, was also an important source of employment in the towns. Aristocrats and bourgeois had been educated in its schools, the entire population observed its religious festivals and the artisan and peasant regulated their working day by the church bells. Ties of family and economic interest bonded it into every course of the social fabric and assured its influence at every level.

Too much has been made of the degeneracy of the Church under the ancien régime. There were, of course, dissolute aristocrats like Talleyrand, bishop of Autun, whose life suggested that disbelief was enthroned in the highest ranks of the clergy, and Louis XVI is alleged to have remarked of his chief minister, Brienne, archbishop of Toulouse, that he would have preferred his prelates to believe in God. But such exceptional cases were mainly confined to the small minority of absentees at Versailles. The overwhelming majority of the clergy led respectable if secular lives that would have entertained a contemporary Trollope without striking him as being particularly reprehensible. Nepotism, preoccupation with aristocratic connections and touchiness about claims to precedence were to be found everywhere in eighteenth-century society, and if they appeared more incongruous in ecclesiastical than in lay society they were not necessarily more vicious. What does seem to have made an unfavourable impression on contemporaries was the contrast between the wealth and the decay of the religious orders. The secular clergy were busy men in their own way and many of the bishops were active in administration. The abbots, on the other hand, were mostly absentees, using their abbeys merely as sources of income. There was an extraordinary proliferation of religious houses in the French towns—Angers (17 parishes) had 27, Toulouse (10 parishes) 52, and Nantes (16 parishes) 36. Although the convents were often well populated, most of the monasteries were almost empty. At Angers, where there were about 60 monks and 40 friars, the 8 Benedictines of Toussaint shared 25 rooms between them. The whole trend of the eighteenth century was against a life of religious contemplation. The fifteen noble families of the Toulouse area studied by R. Forster had put five sons and five daughters into the Church between 1730 and 1760. From 1760 to the time of the Revolution they sent none.[1] Since the monasteries were often very rich and their buildings and gardens stood in the way of municipal town-planners, they offered an obvious target for anti-clericalism.

The Church had been affected in various ways by the 'feudal reaction' of the second half of the century. As a great landowner, often by seigneurial tenure, it participated in the more business-like management of its assets, which appeared to the peasantry as hard-fisted avarice. The nobility's appropriation of the episcopate and its attempts to create still more noble chapters discredited both the First and Second Estates. The pious Louis XVI obviously failed to realize that his concessions to the aristocracy debased the quality of the Church to which he was genuinely attached, and won it new enemies. On the other hand, the clergy might find themselves threatened by the revival of ancient claims on behalf of the nobility, as happened at Angers in 1774. When the comte de Serrant claimed ownership of all roadside trees within the bounds of his seigneurie, in 1784, it was the Angevin clergy, led by one of its canons, that organized resistance. Serrant retaliated in 1789, when he aspired to become

[1] McManners, *op. cit.*, pp. 4–5, 79; Forster, *op. cit.*, pp. 22, 129; *The Gentleman's Guide in His Tour Through France* (1788), p. 252.

leader of the local nobility, by raising the cry of anti-clericalism. In Angers, therefore, the advent of the Revolution found the clergy as a whole aligned with the Third Estate and suspicious of the nobility.[1]

The 'enlightenment' had been characterized by a noisy assault on the Church, the consequences of which it is difficult to assess. The salon society of Paris was often inclined to agree with men like Condorcet that the historical rôle of Christianity had been one of persecution and obscurantism. Voltaire's attack on contemporary examples of intolerance like the iniquitous condemnations of Calas and the chevalier de la Barre also contributed to discredit the Church as a whole. Atheism was still rare and dangerous to profess, but the prevailing belief in intellectual circles was a vague deism that ranged from Voltaire's divine watchmaker to the emotional vision of Rousseau's *vicaire savoyard*. Reason and sensibility both accommodated themselves to violent onslaughts on the organization and theology of the Roman Catholic Church—the Calvinists, whose republican city-state of Geneva was more to the tastes of the age, had a better Press. To a limited extent the Church was able to adapt itself to the changing atmosphere. In 1762 a pastor had been executed for the crime of preaching to a Protestant congregation, but the last Assembly of the Clergy, in 1788, while still demanding the exclusion of Protestants from public office, declared its sympathy for them as individuals with a warmth that would have scandalized previous generations.[2] The Benedictine monastery of Saint Aubin, at Angers, was in possession of busts of Voltaire and Rousseau, and several of the local clergy belonged to masonic lodges.[3] But there were obvious limits beyond which concessions could not be made.

How far scepticism had penetrated the provinces it is difficult to say. In Poitou the marquis de Ferrières was busy writing on Deism and attacking the monastic orders, and if one is to judge from similar writings by several of the men who were to play an active part in the Revolution, scepticism may have been

---

[1] McManners, *op. cit.*, pp. 119, 216–18.

[2] J. Égret, 'La dernière assemblée du clergé de France', *Revue Historique*, CCXIX (1958), 1; M. Péronnet, 'Les Assemblées du Clergé de France sous le Règne de Louis XIV', *Annales Historiques de la Révolution Française*, XXXIV (1962), 8.

[3] McManners, *op. cit.*, pp. 44, 39.

widespread amongst the aristocracy and the more restless members of the urban middle class. The bourgeoisie as a whole, however, remained more than nominally Catholic. Civil society assumed that all Frenchmen were members of the Church and for a great many religion was much more than a matter of superficial conformity. This was especially true in the country-side, where illiterate peasants were unlikely to challenge the curé's theology. Popular religion contained a large element of superstition—a witch was put to death near Angers as late as 1780 some of which the Church was able to harness in support of Christianity.

The clergy were themselves divided on important questions of doctrine and ecclesiastical organization. By the reign of Louis XVI the fire had gone out of the Jansenist controversy. One or two influential deputies to the Estates General, such as the curés Grégoire and Saurine, and Camus and Lanjuinais from the laity, could be classified as Jansenist, but the lower clergy were more influenced by Richerist ideas of a return to ecclesi-astical democracy, to which secular political theory and their treatment by the Church hierarchy both inclined them.[1] They therefore began to attack what they called the 'aristocratic ascendancy of the nobility within the clergy', to demand more influence within their quinquennial Assemblies and eventually to challenge the theological basis of the hierarchy with the radical argument that bishops and parish priests were essenti-ally equal as pastors, while chapters and monastic orders were of human, not divine institution.[2] The 'insurrection of the curés' of 1780, demanding greater representation in diocesan bureaux, led to a royal declaration forbidding them to 'form any union or league and to deliberate in common'—another instance of the king's readiness to subordinate his genuine concern for religion to the interests of the aristocracy. Since the parish priests had retained the ear of their parishioners and often enjoyed the sympathy of the educated critics of the upper clergy, this breach within the ranks of the Church was all the more danger-ous to the hierarchy. A local movement by the Angevin clergy

[1] See E. Préclin, Les Jansénistes du Dix-huitième Siècle et la Constitution Civile du Clergé (Paris, 1928), passim.

[2] M. G. Hutt, 'The curés and the Third Estate: ideas of reform in the pamphlets of the French lower clergy in the period 1787–1789', Journal of Ecclesiastical History, VIII (1957), 75.

in 1785 provided them with a dress rehearsal of the tactics that four years later enabled them to secure for the *curés* all four seats in the Estates General. It is significant that three of the leaders of this opposition movement were later to lead the tiny minority of the local clergy that accepted the revolutionary church settlement.[1]

The latent tensions within the Church came to a head in 1788, when the Assembly of the clergy broke its traditional alliance with the Crown and joined in the aristocratic offensive against the monarchy. Such an attempt by the higher clergy to use the Church as a political weapon could only aggravate internal conflicts and incite the *curés* to ally in their turn with the Third Estate. In so doing they were to provide valuable reinforcements for an assault on privilege in which the corporate interests of the Church would not be spared.

The France of the ancien régime was therefore an extremely complex society marked by great local variations at every level. For a number of reasons, political, economic, social and religious, tensions were increasing during the second half of the eighteenth century and it had become commonplace for writers to predict an imminent revolution, although none of them had any clear conception of the cataclysm ahead. The monarchy's abdication of the rôle created for it by Louis XIV had allowed the aristocracy to reassert itself in every field. The developing economic power of the middle class, its growing awareness of its importance in the life of the community and the sceptical and utilitarian temper of the age ensured that this aristocratic offensive would be vigorously resisted by those whose dignity and social aspirations it offended. The peasantry, feeling the pinch of economic trends that worked against the small producer, were incensed by the additional burden of the 'feudal reaction'. A major social crisis was imminent, irrespective of the political manoeuvring of the royal Government and the aristocracy. On the outcome of this crisis would depend not merely the nature of the future régime, but the whole question of whether French society would be integrated into a more or less united structure or whether the whole fabric would be torn apart by new and even more bitter divisions.

[1] McManners, *op. cit.*, pp. 201–3.

II

∞∞∞∞∞∞∞∞∞∞∞∞∞∞∞∞∞∞∞∞∞∞∞∞∞∞

The Victory of the Aristocracy

∞∞∞∞∞∞∞∞∞∞∞∞∞∞∞∞∞∞∞∞∞∞∞∞∞∞

Alors (in 1787) *commença un combat qui, jusqu'à la convocation des états- généraux, n'offre plus que le tableau de l'agonie du pouvoir.*

BARNAVE

The catalyst that fused the social tensions of France in a tremendous explosion was the bankruptcy of the monarchy. Royal finances, inadequate since the reign of Louis XIV, finally succumbed under the burden of the war of American Independence. The Swiss banker, Necker, who had been at the head of the economy from October 1776 to May 1781, won easy laurels by raising loans to defray war expenditure without increasing taxation to provide for their servicing and redemption. His misleading *compte-rendu* of 1781, claiming that there was a 'normal' annual surplus, exclusive of war expenditure, of the order of ten million livres, embarrassed his successors by implying that no increase of taxation was necessary. The end of the war, in fact, left the monarchy with a burden of debt in the region of 3,400 million livres and an annual deficit of about 80 million. As the debt increased so did the proportion of the public revenue devoted to servicing it, on which no economy was possible without a breach of faith with the State's creditors. The scope for retrenchment in the remaining sectors of the economy was inadequate to balance the budget. The level of taxation could not be materially increased in a period of

34

declining real wages. Louis XVI, unlike some of his royal predecessors, regarded a partial repudiation of the Debt as dishonourable. In these circumstances the only course left open to him was to increase the taxation of the privileged orders. This provided the latter with an excellent opportunity to win a final victory over what was left of royal absolutism by using the power of the purse to force the king to accept some form of aristocratic constitution.[1]

The first move lay with the monarchy. Calonne had been appointed Controller-General of Finance in November 1783. Whether with a view to strengthening credit by a show of affluence, or in the hope of securing the support of the influential courtiers on whom his survival would depend, he inaugurated his period of office by a display of munificence for which further loans supplied the means. The fact that the third *vingtième*—a tax introduced for the redemption of the American debt—was due to expire at the end of 1786 put an end to such easy liberality. In August 1786, therefore, Calonne presented Louis XVI with far-reaching plans for restoring the solvency of the royal Government. His programme offered the Bourbon monarchy its last opportunity to recover the power that was slipping from its hands and to consolidate its finances on a basis that would guarantee its independence of the parlements.[2]

Calonne's proposals went beyond the immediate needs of the monarchy to include a general overhaul of much of the financial system. The abolition of internal customs barriers, the commutation of the *corvée* and the reduction of the *gabelle* (salt tax) were calculated to attract the support of the economists and of public opinion in general. An increase in stamp duties, calculated to raise 20 million livres per annum, mainly from the wealthy, would not provoke violent resistance. The crux of Calonne's plan was his attempt to substitute for the *vingtièmes*, whose assessment tended to favour the privileged orders and

[1] For more detailed accounts of this aristocratic revolt see A. Goodwin, *The French Revolution* (1953); A. Cobban, *A History of Modern France* (1957), I; G. Lefebvre, *The Coming of the French Revolution* (Eng. trans., Princeton, 1949); A. Chérest, *La Chute de l'Ancien Régime* (Paris, 1884), and especially J. Égret, *La Pré-Révolution* (Paris, 1962) which appeared too late for me to benefit from its scholarship.

[2] A. Goodwin, 'Calonne, the Assembly of French Notables of 1787 and the origins of the "Révolte Nobiliaire" ', *English Historical Review*, LXI (1946), pp. 204, 329.

whose renewal required registration by the parlements, a new permanent tax on land, irrespective of the status of its owners. This tax, varying from 2½ per cent to 5 per cent of the annual value of the land according to its fertility, was estimated by Calonne as likely to yield 50 million livres in 1787 and its importance would increase as land values rose. Once the principle of such taxation were admitted it would be comparatively easy to adjust the level of the tax in accordance with the needs of the royal Government. The *noblesse de robe* would thereby lose such limited control over taxation, and hence over royal policy, as had been permitted by the *vingtièmes*, limited in amount and in duration. Financially secure, ministers would now be free to disregard the remonstrances of the *parlementaires* and 'ministerial despotism' might become much more of a reality. The provincial Estates and the parlements had therefore valid constitutional reasons for raising the alarm. Moreover Calonne was threatening the privileged orders in both purse and principle. If the land tax were accepted the clergy would have more to pay and the thin end of the fiscal wedge would have prised a crack in their corporate autonomy. The lay nobility, besides a natural reluctance to submit to increased taxation that might strengthen the monarchy at their expense, were also threatened by the levelling principle that treated all land as merely more or less fertile soil. If the fiscal distinction between noble and ordinary land (*terres nobles* and *terres roturières*) were abolished, the way would be open for the gradual extinction of seigneurial privileges of every kind, since all rested on the common assumption of a special relationship between the noble and the king.

Fears of this kind were reinforced by Calonne's plan for the assessment of taxation by new district assemblies where voting power would be proportionate to land ownership and not to social status. In the *pays d'élection*—those parts of the old monarchy that had no provincial Estates—new provincial assemblies were to be created, subject to the close control of the intendant. These provincial assemblies were to be elected by the district assemblies from their own members or from other wealthy landowners. Once again membership would be determined solely by land ownership and birth would confer no privilege.

The combined effect of the land tax and the new assemblies would therefore be to reinforce the fiscal and administrative authority of the Government while introducing a new concept of the social order in which landed wealth alone would be the criterion of civic rights and fiscal liability. Calonne's scheme thus seemed to the parlements to confirm their argument that a privileged aristocracy was the last bastion against royal absolutism. For the time being, constitutional principle, aristocratic exclusiveness and fiscal self-interest created a curious coalition in opposition to the minister. His adversaries were probably not clearly aware of which motive was uppermost in their own minds and many of those who united against him in 1787 were to find themselves on different sides two years later.

Calonne may not have been fully aware that the implication of his policy was the substitution of a bourgeois for an aristocratic conception of society, but he was under no illusions as to the strength of the resistance he could expect from the privileged orders and especially from the Paris parlement. He therefore took the rash but understandable decision to summon a meeting of 'notables'—leading members of the clergy, the *noblesse de robe* and the Court aristocracy—to advise him on the implementing of his policy. Calonne presumably hoped that discreet pressure would allow him to confine the notables to matters of detail, while he would subsequently be able to present their conclusions to the parlement as proof of the acceptance of his policy by representatives of the aristocracy. But the acceptance of the notables would not necessarily commit the parlement, while their rejection of his plans might encourage its members to imitate them. Calonne, in fact, revealed the weakness of the Crown by stooping to consult where he did not dare to command. Once the decision had been taken it was of the utmost importance that all the advocates of royal authority should present a common front in support of Calonne. But the Court nobility seemed unaware of the issues involved and the elder of the king's two brothers, the comte de Provence, tried to win influence and popularity by encouraging those who challenged the king's minister.[1]

Spurred on by Loménie de Brienne, archbishop of Toulouse, who aspired to replace Calonne, and by the partisans of Necker,

[1] *Journal de l'Assemblée des Notables de 1787* (ed. Chevallier, Paris, 1960), p. 26.

committed to their hero's assertion that he had left France solvent in 1781, the notables at once adopted a critical attitude.[1] They asserted the parliamentary argument that the redress of grievances came before the voting of supplies, accused Calonne of dilapidating the national finances and demanded access to the Government's accounts. The harassed finance minister confirmed them in their belief that he was hostile to the privileged orders, by appealing to public opinion in a pamphlet distributed free of charge all over France and read from parish pulpits, which Augeard, an official in the queen's household described as 'a terrible diatribe against the clergy and the nobility'. This ended the possibility of any compromise between Calonne and the notables and could only lead to the humiliation of the latter or the capitulation of the Government.

It was at this point that the Court revealed its lack of any coherent policy and its inability to think beyond personal terms. In the assembly of the notables Provence and Orléans had joined in the attack on Calonne, while Artois, the king's youngest brother, had given him only tepid support. Marie Antoinette was perhaps more aware than most of the Court of the extent to which royal authority was endangered, but she had no sympathy with any policy of enlisting popular support, such as that implied by Calonne's *avertissement*, and strongly disapproved of this appeal to public opinion. Unable to see beyond personalities, she found nothing illogical in denouncing the opposition of the notables while simultaneously using her influence to have Calonne replaced by her own candidate, Brienne, the leader of the opposition. Louis XVI, vacillating and unsure of himself, was therefore persuaded to dismiss Calonne, whose place was soon taken by his main opponent. The king did, however, reject the conditions that the archbishop tried to impose: the recall of Necker as financial adviser and the convocation of the Estates General.[2]

Louis might deceive himself that the question was merely one of personalities, that Calonne's plan would go forward under his successor; Brienne might support the illusion by defending a watered-down version of the proposals he had previously helped

---

[1] See the diaries of Loménie de Brienne and his brother reprinted in *Journal de l'Assemblée des Notables de 1787* (ed. Chevallier, Paris, 1960).

[2] *Ibid.*, p. 123.

to reject; the king might dismiss the notables, who saw no reason to accept from Brienne what they had refused from Calonne: nothing could conceal the fact that the privileged orders had won the first round in their conflict with the royal Government. The notables, summoned to advise Calonne, had overthrown him, and the Paris parlement was soon to open proceedings against him that drove him to flee to England. The baron de Besenval, who had regretted the convocation of the notables, observed when he came to write his memoirs that the sacrifice of Calonne was certainly the worst course that the king could have adopted, and he was probably not alone in drawing a parallel with Strafford.

Brienne now had to face a Paris parlement encouraged by the success of the notables, who had included some of its own members. To defeat the land tax the parlement adopted the radical position that it was not competent to authorize new taxation, which required the assent of the Estates General, a consultative body that had not met since 1614. After months of confused skirmishing the parlement eventually won the consent of the Government to the convocation of the Estates. Friction continued, however, until Brienne, in a desperate *fuite en avant* prepared to take violent action against the magistrates. In anticipation of this action one of the leading *parlementaires*, d'Eprémesnil, induced his colleagues on 3 May 1788 to appeal for public sympathy with the issue of a manifesto defining the rights alleged to be implicit in the traditional constitution of the kingdom: all taxation to be voted by the Estates General; all subjects to be entitled to trial by judges who could be neither dismissed nor arrested without due process of law; the privileges of the French provinces to be inviolable.

The expected blow fell on 5th May, when the Government surrounded the parlement's meeting-place with troops and attempted to arrest d'Eprémesnil and de Montsabert. After a tense session of twenty-three hours, during which the magistrates defied the troops and were blockaded in their hall, the two men surrendered themselves and were led away to imprisonment. On 8th May a *lit de justice* enforced the registration of six edicts prepared by the Chancellor, Lamoignon, which drastically modified the entire judicial system. The registration of royal decrees was henceforth to be entrusted to a *Cour*

Plénière, which was to include the princes of the blood, the *pairs de France* (a much more limited body than the English peerage) and Grand Officers of the Crown, in addition to magistrates. The parlements were also to lose much of their purely judicial work by the creation of 47 appeal courts *(grands bailliages)* which would give a final verdict in all but the most serious cases. Seigneurs who failed to maintain proper courts, prisons and trained legal officers were to lose their right to administer justice and they were, in any case, to be debarred from taking cognizance of cases which had already been submitted to the royal courts. To prevent any further reaction from the Paris parlement its session was suspended as soon as the new decrees had been registered.

The situation had probably deteriorated too far for these desperate remedies to have much hope of success, especially since they extended the conflict to all who enjoyed the privilege of seigneurial jurisdiction. The key to the situation remained financial. If the Government could not raise loans or impose new taxes its apparent triumph over the parlements would prove but a Pyrrhic victory. Brienne's last hope of financial relief lay in an extraordinary meeting of the Assembly of the Clergy, which he hoped would provide him with a subsidy of eight million livres.[1] But the Assembly's proceedings were dominated by the prelates, who associated themselves with the dissent of the privileged orders. They protested against the *Cour Plénière*, upheld the parlement's contention that the Estates General alone could authorize new taxation, and offered only 1,800,000 livres, to be spread over two years. Brienne's comment is alleged to have been: 'Since the nobility and the clergy abandon their natural protector, the king, he will have to take refuge in the arms of the commons.'[2] The position of the Government was now untenable. Its fate was finally sealed by an outbreak of opposition in the provinces where action was limited neither to legal circles nor to legal methods. Hitherto the crisis had not appeared much worse than earlier storms that Louis XV had weathered, but the provincial revolt was something new, for the

---

[1] J. Égret, 'La dernière Assemblée du Clergé de France', *Revue Historique*, CCXIX (1958), p. 1.

[2] De Pradt, *Les Quatre Concordats* (Paris, 1818), I. 449–50; quoted in J. Égret, *art. cit.*

privileged orders now showed themselves ready to resort to violence, and their position in the army and the administration meant that the Crown could not rely on the loyalty of its servants. In August 1788 the *chargé d'affaires* at the British Embassy reported, 'In Dauphiny and other Provinces, no Taxes whatever can be collected, and accounts of some fresh act of Revolt and disobedience arrive every day from different parts of the Kingdom.'[1] As the agitation of the privileged orders in Brittany and Provence provoked a retort from the middle class there appeared the first signs of the conflict between the nobility and the Third Estate for the spoils of expiring absolutism that was to dominate the political scene during the first months of 1789.

The aristocracy in the provinces had first been roused to action in opposition to the new assemblies created by Calonne. Some of the provinces that had formerly enjoyed the privilege of their own Estates countered the Government's proposals with a demand for the revival of these ancient bodies and were allowed to have their way. The result was not merely to weaken the power of the Central Government but to transfer local influence into aristocratic hands, since these ancient Estates were dominated by the nobility. In Provence many of the municipal officers, who in most parts of France constituted a self-perpetuating oligarchy, were still elected by the townsfolk, and the province as a whole had an *assemblée des communautes* which met for a few days each year. The nobility took advantage of the Government's weakness to demand the replacement of this predominantly bourgeois assembly by the ancient provincial Estates which had not met since 1639. In spite of protests from the Third Estate, Brienne gave way and in December 1787 the Estates reassembled. The privileged orders outnumbered the representatives of the Third Estate in the proportion of more than two to one, and some of the latter were themselves members of the *noblesse de robe*. This victory of the privileged was challenged by the more radical leaders of the Third Estate in the winter of 1788-9, when there were outbreaks of rioting in Aix, Marseilles and Toulon.[2]

[1] *Despatches from Paris, 1784-1790*, II. 98.

[2] J. Égret, 'La Pré-révolution en Provence (1787-1789)', *Annales Historiques de la Révolution Française*, XXVI (1954), p. 98.

In Franche-Comté the Third Estate demanded the convocation of a consultative assembly to draft a constitution for the province. The nobility countered this with a request for the revival of the Estates that had not met since 1678. In the seventeenth-century gatherings the Third Estate had had a strictly circumscribed membership, the Church had been represented by the upper clergy only, while all nobles owning fiefs had had the right to attend. The nobility conceded that some reform of the old institutions was necessary, but insisted that their amendment must itself be the work of an assembly of the traditional pattern. When the Government complied and convened the Estates for November 1788 the nobles of Franche-Comté took their attachment to the seventeenth century a stage further by excluding from attendance such of their order as did not possess four quarterings and a full century of nobility. The *anoblis*, supported by the intendant, protested to the king, but without success. Moreover, the majority of the representatives of the Third Estate consisted of members of the *noblesse de robe*.[1]

In the Hainault and the Dauphiné there were also demands by the privileged that the new territorial assemblies should give way to the old provincial Estates, while the Bordeaux parlement tried to prevent the convocation of the assembly of the Limousin. The provincial aristocracy was on the move, especially in the peripheral areas, with the demand for decentralization and for the local predominance of the privileged orders. The ground was well prepared for an alliance between the *noblesse d'épée* and the parlements when the latter took up a similar stand against the edicts of 8 May 1788. The specifically aristocratic objectives of this movement were obscured by the fact that its leaders genuinely considered themselves to be defending the cause of the 'Nation' against 'ministerial despotism' and the privileges of the Court aristocracy.[2] The proclamation of Lamoignon's judicial reforms led to minor outbreaks of violence in Toulouse and Dijon, where the wealthy heiress of a leading magistrate struck a blow for her father's cause by breaking off her engagement to Lamoignon's son, but once again the most serious

[1] J. Égret, 'La Révolution Aristocratique en Franche-Comté et son Échec', *Revue d'Histoire Moderne et Contemporaine*, I (1954), p. 245.
[2] L. Hartmann, 'Les Officiers de l'Armée Royale à la veille de la Révolution' *Revue Historique*, C, CI (1909).

trouble came from the periphery—Béarn, Brittany and the Dauphiné.

At Pau the parlement of Béarn refused to register the new edicts and on its expulsion the courts appealed for local support. The battle cry of provincial privilege roused the local aristocracy, whose farmers and shepherds came down from the Pyrenees, blockaded the intendant and the military commander and reinstated the parlement. The latter launched a proclamation in which it protested against the application of uniform rules to a region 'which has never become a French province'. Brienne, who probably did not take this manifesto of local particularism too seriously, tried to induce the parlement to apologize. His emissary was greeted by a picturesque procession carrying the cradle of the local hero, Henry IV. Brienne failed to get his apology, but nevertheless took no action against the defiant parlement.

The situation in Brittany was more serious.[1] The province was economically backward and abounded in country squires whose contempt for Versailles was matched by their aloofness with regard to the *roturiers*. There were no less than 2,500 courts of seigneurial jurisdiction in Brittany alone. The powerful local Estates had also been engaged in a running fight with the royal administration throughout the greater part of the eighteenth century.[2] The reaction of the Breton nobility to the May edicts was therefore likely to be violent. The intendant at Rennes, Bertrand de Molleville, foreseeing trouble, reluctantly returned from Versailles in May 1788 with a substantial packet of sealed orders. Had he known that these contained the new edicts, together with blank *lettres de cachet* for use against the parlement, he would probably have refused to set out at all. The parlement had taken the precaution of getting representatives of the nobility, the university and the legal profession to join it in an anticipatory protest against any infringement of its own liberties. On behalf of the nobility the comte de Botherel brought forward the separatist argument that was also used at Pau: the association of Brittany with the French Crown was

[1] J. Égret, 'Les Origines de la Révolution en Bretagne', *Revue Historique*, CCXIII (1955), p. 191; B. de Molleville, *Mémoires Secrets pour servir à l'Histoire de la Dernière Année du Règne de Louis XVI* (1797), I. 36–37.

[2] H. Fréville, *L'Intendance de Bretagne, 1689–1790, passim*; G. T. Mathews, *The Royal General Farms in Eighteenth-Century France*, pp. 106–9, 127–8.

declared to be a contractual one which would cease if the king violated the terms of the sixteenth-century union. The parlement naturally refused to register the decrees that Molleville had brought with him. The lawyers' clerks and their allies who had surrounded the *Palais de Justice* then began a riot from which the intendant and the military commander escaped with some difficulty. According to Molleville the parlement was ready for compromise, but was intimidated by the crowd—in which the nobility's servants were well represented—into defying his ban on its reassembly. Its members were then sent into exile, but the conflict between the aristocracy and the king's representatives persisted. Molleville, believing his life to be in danger, fled to Paris. Illegal gatherings of the nobility led to a deputation being sent to Versailles, where their attempts to enlist support eventually drove the Government to put them in the Bastille.

Since the Breton troubles were to continue throughout the winter it will be expedient here to follow them to their conclusion. Hitherto the conflict had been essentially between the royal authority, the parlement and the *noblesse d'épée*. With the king's release of the deputation and agreement to the convocation of the local Estates the Third Estate began to intervene. Significantly, the initiative was taken by the prosperous commercial port of Nantes, whose self-confident middle class was less dependent on the aristocracy than the lawyers of the 'county town' of Rennes. A bourgeois group at Nantes produced a revolutionary programme for the local Estates that foreshadowed the later demands of the bourgeois deputies to the Estates General: the representatives of the Third Estate should be equal in numbers to the combined forces of the clergy and the nobility and all voting should be in common. This group then put through a municipal revolution in Nantes and appealed to the other Breton towns to displace their ruling oligarchies in the same way—a course of action that was also to be taken up on a national scale during the following year. The few liberal nobles were silenced by the squirearchy and when the Estates met the two sides were sharply divided. The more cautious representatives of the Third Estate were intimidated by pressure from the public galleries into taking no part in proceedings until they had been granted enlarged representation, voting in common and the agreement of the privileged to pay their full share of taxation.[1] The ensuing deadlock led to recurring violence which provided the young Chateaubriand with a dramatic début to his political career. Four hundred youthful members of the bourgeoisie of Nantes marched to the defence of their colleagues in Rennes, where the nobility were blockaded for three days in their place of meeting. When the Estates resumed in February after a period of suspension the Government authorized the trebling of the representatives of the Third Estate, whose members now formed a municipal union binding the Breton towns together. The nobility appealed to the countryside for support against the townsmen, but to no great effect. The session ended on a note of anti-climax with the Third Estate reluctantly agreeing to prolong the existing taxes on the understanding that the constitution of the Estates would shortly be reformed. By this time the imminence of the Estates General was directing all eyes to Versailles.

The Breton revolt, which had begun with the joint action of the parlement and the nobility in defence of privilege had therefore produced a vigorous ·reaction from some of the urban middle class. Neither side had been much helped or hindered by the weak and vacillating intervention of the Government and both had relied in the main on their own resources. The Breton conflict, significant in itself as an indication of the depth of social divisions in 1788–9, was also to have an important effect on the subsequent course of the Estates General. As J. Égret remarked, 'it is in their struggle with the stubbornness of the *épées de fer* that the leaders of the Breton movement, who were to become the deputies of the Third Estate, acquired that rigidity that was to win them fame in the early sessions of the Estates General'. He might have added that the same experience taught them their tactics as well as their resolution.

The situation in the Dauphiné, which had initial points of similarity with those elsewhere, evolved in a different and rather more hopeful direction.[2] This was perhaps influenced by the fact that Dauphiné was a relatively industrialized province,

[1] The British Ambassador, Lord Dorset, described as 'preposterous' the demand of the Breton *Tiers* for access to military commands and the highest posts in the Church. *Despatches from Paris, 1784–1790*, II. 140.

[2] J. Égret, *La Révolution des Notables; Mounier et les Monarchiens* (Paris, 1950), pp. 7–47.

the most thoroughly industrialized in the whole of France, according to Roland in 1785. Here an important section of the nobility was prepared to think in terms of the social and national unity of France rather than in those of aristocratic exclusiveness and provincial privilege. Such views were, however, by no means universally held even in Dauphiné, and it required both skill and concessions on the part of Mounier to maintain a coalition between the different orders. The crisis at Grenoble began in the usual way: in August 1787 the parlement declared itself unable to authorize new taxation and demanded the convocation of the Estates General; it went on to call for the restoration of the local Estates (which had last met in 1628) and was exiled in June 1788 for the violence of its protests against the new *Cour Plénière*. In the ensuing riot the municipality for a time prevented the magistrates from complying with the royal command. It was at this stage that Mounier, a lawyer who had purchased an office which conferred on him personal but not transmissible nobility, succeeded in obtaining the signatures of 9 of the clergy, 33 nobles and 59 commoners to a petition to the king for the recall of the parlement and the convocation of provincial and national assemblies. The lack of local opposition allowed Mounier and his associates to defy the Government's ban and to organize municipal assemblies. These assemblies, together with the rural parishes, were invited to send representatives to a meeting of the whole province. The governor, unable or unwilling to prevent this meeting, contented himself with demanding that it should not be held in Grenoble. The delegates therefore met at Vizille, in the château of 'Périer milord', a wealthy merchant who had married into the *noblesse de robe* and bought the château with the intention of establishing a cotton mill there—a most suitable rendezvous in every respect. At Vizille assembled about five hundred representatives of the clergy, nobility and Third Estate. The meeting began on 21 July 1788 by refusing to accept new taxes unless these were voted by national and provincial Estates. It went on to demand that in the local assembly the Third Estate should have as many members as the two privileged orders combined, a proposal notable for the fact that it was accepted by the clergy and the nobility. The latter agreed to pay their share of a new tax that was to take the place of the *corvée*. Finally, and most strikingly, the assembly declared that it took its stand on the traditional privileges of Dauphiné only so long as there existed no National Assembly. When the latter should be convened the *Dauphinois* would abandon their local privileges to become one with the nation as a whole.

Brienne now accepted the *fait accompli* and agreed to the official election of a 'Preparatory Assembly' which should draft a new constitution for the provincial Estates. This Preparatory Assembly was in session from 1 December 1788 to 16 January 1789. Its proposals showed that the unity of the three orders rested on a fragile basis. The clergy insisted on excluding their humbler members and the nobility on imposing an electoral qualification of four quarterings. It was this assembly which jointly elected the Dauphiné representatives to the Estates General and drafted the statement of grievances (*cahier de doléances*). Mounier succeeded in getting the meeting to impose on himself and his fellow deputies the imperative mandate to accept only voting in common, but for this he had to pay a high price—the preponderance of the upper clergy amongst the clerical deputies and a guarantee that the Third Estate would uphold the claims of the nobility to their feudal privileges and would indemnify them for the special status of the lands they held by seigneurial tenure in return for their acceptance of fiscal equality. Even so a group of nobles and clergy refused to accept the compromise and petitioned the Estates General to invalidate the elections. The opposition to Mounier's policy of conciliation did not come entirely from one side, for some of the lower clergy addressed a pamphlet to the Breton *curés* in which they denounced their bishops in the most violent terms.[1]

Dauphiné was the only province in which there was any serious attempt at concerted action by the privileged orders and the Third Estate, and even here the agreement was both limited and precarious. Elsewhere the aristocracy rushed in to exploit the opportunity offered by the decline of royal power in the hope of resuming the authority which they had wielded until the seventeenth century. The course of the offensive in the provinces throws a sharp light on the extraordinary collapse of royal power. The ministers offered little effective opposition, in part perhaps because they had no longer the means of making

[1] M. G. Hutt, 'The *Curés* and the Third Estate', p. 75.

themselves obeyed. In Rennes, Pau and Grenoble, intendants and military governors were insulted or ignored. None showed any great readiness to challenge the local aristocracy, and had they attempted to do so the allegiance of their troops was by no means certain. On the other hand, the provincial revolt had revealed a breach between the aristocracy and the Third Estate which suggested that the monarchy might be able to provide itself with allies.

At the centre, Brienne was driven from one admission of failure to another. In July 1788 he agreed to the convocation of the Estates General in 1789. By August the Government was on the verge of bankruptcy. Treasury payments were suspended for a month and would henceforth be made partly in banknotes of the *Caisse d'Escompte* which was relieved of the obligation to redeem its notes on demand. The city could scarcely be expected to remain indifferent to the danger of a partial repudiation of the Debt, and Madame de Chastenay's lament that her family was impoverished by the fall in Government securities is a reminder that some of the aristocracy were important rentiers as well as landowners.[1] Brienne was burned in effigy and there was disorder in Paris. Late in August the archbishop accepted the inevitable and handed his resignation to the king.

The immediate need for credit left Louis with no alternative but to call on the financial experience of Necker, probably the only man who could avert a complete breakdown, and even Necker had to bring his considerable private resources to the rescue of the Treasury. His advent made a significant change in the disposition of the Government. His wilder critics at Court, who were inclined to blame him for the subsequent course of the revolution, were very wide of the mark in suggesting that he wanted to humiliate the king and attack the Church and the aristocracy. Nevertheless, as a citizen of the republic of Geneva, a banker and a Protestant, Necker could not be expected to share Brienne's acceptance of both autocracy and aristocratic privilege. If he was less concerned about Divine Right he was also less inhibited in calling on the Third Estate to check the offensive of the privileged orders. The change of political emphasis threw Versailles into confusion. Court society was

[1] See also R. Forster, *The Nobility of Toulouse in the Eighteenth Century*, chap. v.

often incapable of distinguishing between the interests of the monarchy and those of the aristocracy, and Necker's half-hearted attempt to draw on the support of the Third Estate in order to buttress the Crown against the attacks of the privileged orders was viewed by some as being in the royal interest and by others as treason. On the one hand 'liberals' like Madame de Chastenay and Madame Campan attributed the collapse of royal authority to 'the successive ministries, and above all the parlements, the aristocracy, the whole army', and complained that 'to speak of the English constitution at Court . . . seemed as criminal as if one had suggested dethroning the king'.[1] On the other, Augeard urged the Parisian lawyer Target to attack the ministers—by whom he presumably meant Necker—as 'the real cause of our misfortunes and those of the king'.[2] The king's two brothers changed sides. Provence, who had encouraged the notables in their opposition to absolutism, now found himself supporting Necker, while Artois, hitherto the king's most reliable ally, henceforth identified himself with the opposition of the privileged orders.

The king, as usual, was uncertain and incapable of adopting any resolute policy, but on the whole he appears to have approved of Necker's tentative alliance with the Third Estate, whatever he felt about its author. Such at least was the opinion of those in contact with the Court. Madame de Chastenay thought that if the king had been alone all might have gone well, and regretted that the *noblesse* as a whole had not followed the example of the Breton aristocracy and boycotted the Estates General. The princesse de Lamballe, whose political insight left a good deal to be desired, virtually accused Louis of hostility to the royal family because of his support for the *parti populaire*![3]

Marie Antoinette's attitude, which became increasingly important as the development of the crisis brought the need for action, seems to have been less single-minded than is generally supposed. She was painfully aware of her unpopularity at Court and had no reason to be particularly affected by the tribulations of courtiers who had been libelling her for years in anonymous

[1] Campan, *Mémoires sur la Vie Privée de Marie Antoinette* (2nd ed., 1823), II. 418–19; Chastenay, *Mémoires* (3rd ed., Paris, 1896), I. 98.

[2] J. M. Augeard, *Mémoires Secrets* (ed. Bavoux, Paris, 1866), p. 185.

[3] Princesse de Lamballe, *Mémoires relatifs à la Famille Royale de France pendant la Révolution* (Paris, 1826), I. 334.

pamphlets. Moreover, she resented the aristocracy's attack on royal absolutism, which probably meant more to her than to her husband. She had opposed the convocation of the Estates General with an instinctive fear of its revolutionary consequences, and in conversation with Augeard she put the blame for its summons squarely on the shoulders of the clergy and the parlements. She told him that the comte d'Artois was 'driven by an infernal faction that will destroy us all', and at the second meeting of the notables she supported Louis against the princes of the blood. But like many at Versailles she lived in a blinkered world and could not conceive of a society in which the Court would not be the summit of an aristocratic pyramid. When the Third Estate declaimed against the extravagance of the Court nobility she knew herself to be one of their targets. She was perceptive enough to be more aware than Louis of the danger of their situation, but when it came to deciding on a policy she could only lament: 'The nobility will destroy us, but it seems to me that we cannot save ourselves without it.'[1] Her sense of the social hierarchy no less than her automatic rejection of the idea of a constitutional monarchy prevented her from considering the unknown lawyers of the Third Estate as more than the faithful subjects whose rôle was to frighten into obedience the great families of France. Her policy would be decided by what she conceived to be the interests of royal authority and she could only visualize this in terms of a traditional order that was already obsolete.

It was against this background that Necker had to prepare for the Estates General. He began by repealing the edicts of 8 May 1788 and recalling the Paris parlement, a final concession to the aristocracy that was perhaps motivated by the need to restore confidence if the Government were to be able to raise new loans. From the summer of 1788 onwards the impending Estates General dominated the political scene. But the rôle of the assembly would be largely dependent on its composition and method of voting, for which there was no fixed precedent. The Paris parlement tried to settle these questions by its own authority: when registering the edict for the convocation of the Estates General it added, 'in accordance with the forms observed in 1614'. In essence this implied that the three orders,

[1] Augeard, op. cit., p. 156; Campan, op. cit., III. 111.

clergy, nobility and commons, would meet and vote separately, each having a veto on the decisions of the other two. The parlement obviously expected that all three would combine to create some kind of constitutional monarchy while the Third Estate would be incapable of implementing any motions unfavourable to aristocratic privilege, even though it might enjoy the support of the Government. The *vote par ordre* meant the triumph of the aristocracy. The Third Estate was quick to take up the challenge in Paris and during the winter of 1788–9 its campaign slowly spread into the provinces. The battle was fought primarily between the Second and Third Estates and did not immediately concern the relations between the monarchy and the Estates General. Necker, while no extreme advocate of levelling measures, was ready to use the Third Estate to check the privileged orders. This implied strengthening its representation and enforcing voting in common whenever the Government considered this to be appropriate. Faced with many controversial issues relating to the election of the Estates General, Necker turned to the notables for advice, re-assembling them in November 1788.[1] Although he accepted their opinion on most of the minor questions, on the fundamental issues of representation and method of voting he found them no more co-operative than in 1787. Only one bureau out of the seven was prepared to advocate the double representation of the Third Estate—significantly enough, by the casting vote of its president, the comte de Provence—and even this deprived its action of any significance by insisting on the *vote par ordre* throughout. However, the advice of the notables was disregarded, for Necker had the support of the queen, who took the exceptional step of attending in person the meeting of the Council of Ministers on 27th December which agreed to the *doublement* of the Third Estate. Nothing was said about the method of voting.

In these circumstances the *Mémoire* which the princes of the blood, with the exception of Provence and Orléans, presented to the king on 12th December makes significant reading. Its argument against the double representation of the Third Estate indicated the ground on which the aristocracy was subsequently to take its stand. After threatening a boycott of the Estates

[1] See J. Égret, 'La Seconde Assemblée des Notables', *Annales Historiques de la Révolution Française*, XXI (1949), p. 103.

General by the privileged orders and even an appeal to the parlements, reinforced by a tax-strike, the *Mémoire* went on to make the extraordinary assertion, in view of the events of the past two years, that the Crown's natural defenders were 'that brave, ancient and respectable Nobility, who have shed so much blood for their country and for their Kings'. Even the parlements became 'the Magistrates who in times of difficulty have always been the props of the Throne'.[1] The argument may have lacked plausibility, but the tactics were clever enough: to maintain pressure on the throne by presenting the equalitarian demands of the Third Estate as an attack on the monarchy. If the king could be convinced, the aristocracy would be able to break off its assault on the royal Government, which the growing agitation of the commons made increasingly dangerous. The king would then surrender his absolute power into the hands of the privileged orders, who would be able to mobilize the resources of the Central Government—and notably the army—against their new rivals. Necker was unlikely to accept this policy or to respond to the emotional and aristocratic interpretation of French history on which it was based. The nobility's alleged crusade in defence of the monarchy had therefore to begin with an attack on the chief minister, in whom the king professed his confidence. Artois' acceptance of this disingenuous policy led to his temporary estrangement from Marie Antoinette.

The elections to the Estates General assumed very different aspects in the different constituencies. In the Dauphiné the three orders met together in relative harmony, while in Brittany the privileged boycotted the elections altogether and refused to be represented in the Estates General. In Franche-Comté clever manoeuvring by the Third Estate induced the majority of the local nobility to leave and made possible the election of members of the liberal minority.[2] Madame de Chastenay has left a vigorous account of the meeting at Châtillon-sur-Seine which elected her father.[3] Of the 280 nobles who attended she recognized only 150 at most as being *hommes de qualité*. Some of these, 'almost ashamed to find themselves treated as equals by

[1] B. de Molleville, *Annals of the French Revolution* (1800), I. 7–18.

[2] J. Égret, 'La Révolution Aristocratique en Franche-Comté et son Échec', *Revue d'Histoire Moderne et Contemporaine*, I (1954), p. 245.

[3] Chastenay, *op. cit.*, I. 75–86.

nobles so far beneath them and their way of life, thought to create another distinction between them by steering clear of their prejudices'—or in other words a profession of liberalism was a hall-mark of 'upper-class' nobility! This phenomenon was far from being limited to Châtillon. The same author pointed out that the liberal nobility in general represented 'not the provincial gentry and those least qualified, but the most brilliant youth, men whose families had been the most loaded with gifts and honours at the Court'. The liberal camp was indeed well endowed with great names: the dukes of La Roche-foucauld, Montmorency-Laval and Aiguillon; Talleyrand, the marquis de Lafayette, hero of the American war, and his brother-in-law, the vicomte de Noailles. These men resembled each other in age as well as distinguished birth. La Roche-foucauld was the only one above 40, Aiguillon was 28 and Montmorency only 22. The contrast was striking between this array of titles and the relatively humble origin of the main spokesmen on the aristocratic side, such as Cazalès and the *abbé* Maury. The apparent paradox should not be overemphasized, but it is clear that a section of the Court nobility was prepared for some sacrifice of aristocratic privilege in return for a constitutional form of government in which they might hope to play an active part. Such men had little in common with the 'wretched nobles, reduced to living by the labour of their hands and distinguished only by an ancient borrowed sword', who surprised their neighbours by appearing at the elections at Châtillon. On the whole, Madame de Chastenay found the Third Estate less disorderly and more attached to the person of the king than her own order—an interesting comment on the thesis of the *Mémoire* of the princes of the blood.[1]

The *cahiers* which the nobles drafted for the guidance of their representatives offer a good indication of the demands of the order and indicate the field in which the battle with the Third Estate was to be fought. They contain a strange jumble of anticipation and archaism, demands for representative government standing by the side of requests for the establishment of an official genealogist in each province to verify the titles of claimants to nobility. On the constitutional issue the nobility advocated the creation of some form of legislative assembly that

[1] Chastenay, *op. cit.*, I. 101, 75–76, 78.

should control taxation. The royal Government, deprived of legislative initiative, was also to lose part of its hold over the provinces, where its powers would be shared by local assemblies. Here there was at least room for initial co-operation between the aristocracy and the commons. On the issue of civil rights— the freedom of the Press, abolition of *lettres de cachet*, *habeas corpus*, etc.—they were in general agreement. Since the king had neither the desire nor the means to oppose an unyielding resistance on these fronts profound conflict was unlikely. With regard to taxation, the aristocracy was not disposed to challenge the Government and the Third Estate on the principle of fiscal equality, although many of its members hoped to find ways of interpreting their concessions to their own advantage. The fundamental conflict between the aristocracy and the commons was neither political nor economic but social. The nobility were determined to preserve their existence as a separate order in a hierarchical society. They valued privilege perhaps more as an indication of status than as a source of wealth. Seigneurial rights, including that of justice, the virtual monopoly of military and naval commissions, the provision of noble chapters for titled ladies, were not so much specific claims as illustrations of a concept of society. There were frequent demands for a return to the social practices of the past, such as the abolition of those royal offices which conferred nobility on their purchasers, a ban on the purchase of fiefs by commoners, even on their wearing swords. The Third Estate were determined to overthrow the whole conception of society to which the nobility were committed. They demanded the substitution of 'merit' for birth, a society in which all doors should be open to talent and education. Each side was fighting for a principle which admitted of no compromise—as the liberal nobles and the more conservative deputies of the Third Estate were to find to their cost. Their recent successes against declining absolutism had probably led the 'orthodox' nobility to overestimate their strength. Their determination to strike for the victory that seemed within their grasp was to provoke an equally vigorous reaction from their adversaries and the ensuing conflict was to tear France apart.

When the Estates General met on 5 May 1789, the privileged orders were by no means united. There was a strong majority of parish priests in the First Estate, where the upper clergy accounted for no more than 83 deputies out of a total strength of 291. Clerical opinions were not merely a reflection of social status, but none the less it soon became clear that the aristocracy could not count on the unconditional support of the clergy.[1] Within the Second Estate the 'liberal' nobility were in the minority—about 50 out of 270. The remainder, however, were neither unanimous nor easily organized. The magistrates had taken longer than Marie Antoinette to realize that the convocation of the Estates General would constitute a mortal danger to the parlements, but they were now eager for the dismissal of the assembly which they had done so much to bring into being. The impetuous d'Eprémesnil was said to have urged the king to have the parlement try the duc d'Orléans in secret and hang him at the palace gates before dissolving the Estates General.[2] Artois and his supporters, who still hoped to use the assembly for their own purposes, were effusively welcoming the obscure provincial gentry in the hope of enlisting their support. It was not merely his characteristic moderation that led the marquis de Ferrières to fulminate against the intrigues of the Court nobility, but also his provincial distrust of Versailles. He observed of the behaviour of those whom he termed *'les grands'* that 'the external forms of a civility which they now realized to be necessary replaced their arrogance and hauteur'. But even Ferrières had taken some time to overcome his natural pleasure at finding himself dining between the comtesse Diane de Polignac and the comte de Vaudreuil, in the presence of the comte d'Artois. His provincial colleagues for the most part allowed themselves to be won over. 'D'Eprémesnil, Bouthilier, Lacqueille, took it upon themselves to guide the chamber of the aristocracy. They had no difficulty in inducing it to commit all the follies which they intended. . . . Thèse gentlemen proposed (to found) a club. . . . Once the club was established the fanatics were immediately in the majority.'[3]

When the Estates General met the Government had given no decision as to the manner of voting. The Third Estate

[1] See M. G. Hutt, 'The Rôle of the *Curés* in the Estates General of 1789', *Journal of Ecclesiastical History*, VI (1955), p. 192.

[2] D'Allonville, *Mémoires Secrets* (Brussels, 1841), I. 147A.

[3] Ferrières, *Mémoires* (Paris, 1821), I. 34–35, 37; *Correspondance Inédite* (ed. Carré, Paris, 1932), p. 51.

adopted the delaying tactics that some of its members had already employed in Brittany and refused even to constitute itself as an assembly unless all credentials were verified in common. From the verification of credentials it was only one step to voting in common. In the ensuing conflict between the orders the Government remained neutral. The clergy temporized, but the nobility hastened to present the *Tiers* with a *fait accompli* and declared themselves constituted. The vote on this issue—188 to 47—gives a good indication of the state of opinion within the order. Necker, who found the rigidity of the nobility 'truly incomprehensible', condemned their provocative tactics when he came to write his memoirs, and it seems quite likely that in May 1789 he and the king still regarded the main danger as coming from the aristocracy.[1]

By 9th June the deadlock was complete and the Estates General had made no progress after five weeks of argument. The Third Estate now declared that it would make a last summons to the privileged orders, verify its returns and proceed to business. By so doing, as Mirabeau was uneasily aware, it appeared to play into the hands of the aristocracy. For its assumption of the title of National Assembly on 17th June implicitly denied the king's right to decide the shape that the Estates General should take. When the self-styled National Assembly went on to declare that it authorized the collection of the existing taxes only so long as it remained in session, the aristocracy—who would have been quite ready to proclaim as much if they had succeeded in organizing the Estates General to their own liking—could turn to the king and pose with some plausibility as the defenders of the royal authority against the rebellious commons. Unfortunately for the tactical position of the privileged orders, the First Estate now broke up under the stress of its internal tensions. From 13th June onwards a trickle of *curés* had been making its way to the Third Estate to present their credentials for verification and on the 19th the clerical order voted by a small majority to join the National Assembly. At this point Necker intervened in the hope of regaining the initiative, suspended all meetings and announced that the

---

[1] J. Necker, *De la Révolution Française* (Paris, 1797), I. 171–3; see also J. Flammermont, 'Le Second Ministère de Necker', *Revue Historique*, XLVI (1891), p. 1.

king would address a joint session of the three orders. Necker's intention was to present the deputies with a royal programme outlining the concessions the king was prepared to make and specifying how the assembly should conduct its business. Now that the Government was at last taking the initiative it had to reveal its own sympathies. Necker's proposals were cautious enough, since they would have guaranteed the feudal privileges of the aristocracy, although not its monopoly of 'noble' occupations.[1] But the finance minister was losing ground at Versailles, where the Court nobility succeeded in winning over first the queen and then Louis XVI. How and when this happened is to some extent a matter for conjecture, but Marie Antoinette was certainly the first to be converted. The king's opinions were rarely proof against sustained lobbying. Bombarded with advice by the princes of the blood, representatives of the parlement, the cardinal de la Rochefoucauld, head of the First Estate, the archbishop of Paris and the queen herself, who interrupted a meeting of the Council that was about to accept Necker's proposals, Louis eventually gave way, and the proposals were amended. The Austrian ambassador reported that the resignations of Necker and Montmorin, the foreign minister, were rejected and that Artois told Necker he would be held as a hostage, and even pressed for his arrest. Necker therefore absented himself from the royal session when the modified royal programme was communicated to the Estates General.

The new proposals constituted a veritable charter of the aristocracy.[2] The king undertook to become in effect a constitutional monarch, raising no loans or taxes without the assent of the Estates General. He offered to consider the abolition of *lettres de cachet* and to take steps towards the removal of the censorship of the Press. This was the effective end of Bourbon absolutism in France. The provisions with regard to local government were rather less satisfactory to the nobility, since they envisaged the creation of provincial assemblies, voting in common, comprising equal numbers of the Third Estate and the privileged orders. But the aristocracy

[1] Necker, *op. cit.*, I. 187–211.
[2] For text see J. M. Thompson, *French Revolution Documents* (Oxford, 1933), pp. 41–51; for a commentary on the *Séance Royale*, A. Brette, 'La Séance Royale du 23 juin 1789', *La Révolution Française*, XXII, XXIII (1892).

could hope that their local prestige and influence would enable them to control the new bodies which seemed destined to absorb much of the power of the intendants. The king's offer of penal and fiscal reform and of internal free trade were likely to meet with general approval. From the viewpoint of the privileged orders the vital clauses were elsewhere. The decrees of the 'National Assembly' were declared void. 'The king wills that the ancient distinction of the three orders of the State be maintained in its entirety as essentially bound up with the constitution of his kingdom.' This was an echo of d'Eprémesnil's own language in the Chamber of the nobility. 'The following will be specifically excepted from the subjects which may be discussed in common: those which regard the ancient constitutional rights of the three orders, the form of constitution to be given to the next Estates General, feudal and seigneurial property, the material rights and honorary prerogatives of the two first orders.' 'The particular consent of the clergy will be necessary for all dispositions which may affect religion, ecclesiastical discipline, the régime of religious orders and of the secular and monastic corporations.' The privileged orders were invited voluntarily to surrender their exemption from taxation, which might allow them to impose their own views of the nature of fiscal equality. 'All forms of property without exception will be continually respected, and His Majesty includes specifically under the name of property, the *dîmes, cens, rentes, droits et devoirs féodaux et seigneuriaux* and in general all rights and material or honorary prerogatives attached to lands, fiefs or persons.' The king even agreed to consult the Estates General on the appointments which should in future confer personal or transmissible nobility. The privileged orders might therefore hope to close many of the roads by which the bourgeoisie could attain to nobility.

The tone of the royal proclamation must have provided the majority of the nobility with lively if short-lived satisfaction. Ferrières considered that the king spoke 'more like a despot who commands than a monarch who discusses'; Creuzet-Latouche, a deputy of the commons, described the proposals as 'the most bizarre, the most despotic and the most self-contradictory of which history offers an example'. More acutely, Bailly, the president of the Third Estate, complained that the effect of the royal programme would be 'to establish the first two orders as sovereign judges of their own cause'.[1] This was the objective they had been seeking since 1787. Not merely had they driven the king to comply with their demands; they had induced him to adopt them as royal policy, for Louis was subsequently to take his stand on the programme of the royal session as the last important act of his unfettered will. The king had finally committed the resources of the monarchy to the aristocratic cause. The question now was whether they would prove sufficient.

[1] Ferrières, *Mémoires*, I. 58; J. A. Creuzet-Latouche, *Journal des États Généraux et du début de l'Assemblée Nationale* (ed. Marchand, Paris, 1946), p. 138; J. S. Bailly, *Mémoires* (Paris, 1821–3), I. 212.

III

<><><><><><><><><><><><><><><><><><><><><><><><><><><><><><>

The Victory of the Third Estate

<><><><><><><><><><><><><><><><><><><><><><><><><><><><><><>

The deficit would not have produced the Revolution but in concurrence with the price of bread.

ARTHUR YOUNG

THE deputies of the Third Estate were far from forming a social cross-section of the commons of France. Two-thirds of them came from the legal profession or the royal service, the majority of these having previously been agents of the Crown: judges, barristers and mayors. Business and banking accounted for no more than 13 per cent, while landowners, farmers and gentlemen of independent means provided another 10 per cent.[1] This heavy predominance of the law and the administration at the expense of industry and agriculture probably accentuated the speculative and theoretical bias of the Assembly, but had less importance than might have been expected since the drafting of the *cahiers* had revealed a great measure of unanimity within the ranks of the upper middle class.

Each constituency had produced a general *cahier* from the various *cahiers* of its subdivisions and at the level of the constituency, or *bailliage*, the demands of the electors were surprisingly uniform throughout the country.[2] There was a widespread

[1] *Archives Parlementaires* (Paris, 1868–1912), I. 601 *et seq.*
[2] See A. Vialay, *Les Cahiers de Doléances du Tiers-État aux États-Généraux de 1789* (Paris, 1911), *passim.*

demand for the abolition of the royal right of administrative arrest *(lettres de cachet)*, for freedom of the Press, for fiscal equality and the abolition, or at least reduction, of indirect taxation. The general request for more uniformity in such matters as legal codes and weights and measures posed problems of application rather than of principle. What was more impressive was the unanimity with which the *bailliages* demanded revolutionary political and social changes. They were agreed on a constitutional monarchy in which the king's ministers should be responsible to an elected assembly in control of the public purse. The emphasis in social policy was primarily on the destruction of the barriers that separated the nobility from the upper middle class: equality of access to appointments and royal commissions, the abolition of *franc-fief*, a tax paid by commoners who acquired seigneurial lands, the abolition or reduction of feudal burdens and of seigneurial justice. The middle class also showed signs of a widespread impatience with the organization of the Church. Some of its demands—for the abolition of pluralism and the residence of bishops in their sees—were in accordance with the views of clerical reformers, but the frequent demand for the total or partial sale of Church lands, for the cessation of payments to Rome and for the reduction or abolition of monastic orders, were more far-reaching in their implications. The general *cahiers* were least unanimous on questions of economic policy. Apart from seeking to protect local interests such as the slave trade or the privileged position of Lyons in the silk market they diverged in their attitude to the new doctrines of economic liberalism. There was general agreement on the abolition of internal customs barriers and also a widespread dislike of the edict of 1784 which allowed foreigners access to French colonial trade, and of the 1786 commercial treaty with England. But whereas some *bailliages* favoured the abolition of the guilds others advocated the extension of the corporate system to all urban manufactures. The *cahiers* devoted comparatively little space to agriculture. On the whole, they tended to support the new methods of farming, but they were more concerned with the feudal privileges of the seigneur than with the agrarian problems of the village.

To appreciate the extent to which the *cahiers* reflected 'public opinion' it is necessary to bear in mind the circumstances of their composition.[1] This may be illustrated by the example of le Havre.[2] The various corporations first drafted their individual petitions and elected representatives to a town gathering. Even at this level some of the *cahiers* were essentially political, but others concentrated on purely professional grievances such as quarrels with rival guilds and the desirability of excluding outside traders from the local market. The town *cahier* not merely disregarded these sectional interests but called into question whether the guilds would be preserved at all. It was significant that, while the humble *cahiers* of shoemakers and tailors, some of them illiterate, received such short shrift, that of the merchants was judged important enough to be annexed *en bloc* to the town *cahier*. Le Havre then chose twenty citizens to represent it at the meeting of the *bailliage*: seven merchants, five lawyers, two aldermen, two serving or retired naval officers, one gentleman (bourgeois), one shopkeeper, and two others. The 'little men' had already been virtually eliminated. These twenty were joined by seventeen representatives of the rural and suburban neighbourhood, each described as a *laboureur* or yeoman farmer. Although the social composition of the thirty-seven *bailliage* electors was now weighted in favour of the farmers, the *cahier* of the *bailliage* was drawn almost entirely from those of the town and the merchants of le Havre. The *bailliage* chose to represent it at the meeting of the *grand bailliage* of Caudebec, of which le Havre formed a part, three merchants, three lawyers and two aldermen from le Havre and only two of the farmers from the surrounding districts. At the Caudebec meeting were chosen the deputies to the Estates General. These consisted of three lawyers in the royal service, two farmers and one merchant. The only man from le Havre to go up to Versailles was the merchant, Bégouen, a very wealthy man and the owner of plantations in the West Indies.

A similar situation obtained elsewhere—at Orleans, for example, the general *cahier*, representing the interests of the wealthy and privileged merchants, called for the abolition of the

[1] See B. Hyslop, *A Guide to the General Cahiers of 1789* (Columbia University Press, 1936), *passim*; there is a good account of the electoral meetings in Paris in J. S. Bailly, *Mémoires*, I. 9–59.

[2] E. le Parquier, *Cahiers de Doléances du Bailliage du Havre* (Épinal, 1929), *passim*.

guilds which the artisans wished to preserve; Paris *intra muros*, where the voting qualification was relatively high, concentrated on political demands while the *cahiers* of the extra-mural areas, where the electorate was wider, also demanded a reduction in the price of bread[1] Thus the multiple electoral process of 1789, although democratic in the sense that, except in Paris, all tax-payers were entitled to vote, tended to eliminate from final representation both the humbler citizens of town and country and the demands which they had put forward. In this way the relative homogeneity of the commons at Versailles, which was to constitute an important element of their strength, was achieved at the expense of relegating the great majority of their order to a purely passive rôle.

The deputies of the Third Estate had therefore a fairly similar view of their collective aims. Broadly speaking, their intention was to replace the ancien régime by a society based on the political and economic ideas of the Enlightenment, the experience of representative government in Britain and the social and economic realities of late-eighteenth-century France. They stood for the abolition of all privileges conferred by birth and the unlimited enjoyment of the ownership of property. They aspired to a share in political power for themselves and the protection of all against arbitrary government. They wished to replace the archaism, particularism and arbitrariness of the ancien régime by a society that would be efficient, national, orderly and humane. Convinced that a new era of progress had already begun, most of them held that the abolition of the controls devised for the protection of both consumers and producers in a relatively static economy was the necessary prelude to rapid social and economic advance. Their creed combined principle and self-interest in explosive proportions and they felt themselves, not without reason, to be the vanguard of a crusade, with the eyes of all Europe upon them.

These objectives were to remain those of the majority of the bourgeoisie throughout the Revolution. With only individual exceptions the deputies of the Convention in 1793–4 aspired to much the same sort of society as those of the Third Estate in 1789. They were often the same men and the experience of four

[1] C. Bloch, *Études sur l'Histoire Économique de la France (1760–1789)* (Paris, 1900), pp. 161–223.

years of revolution affected their tactics rather than their principles. It would be very difficult to prove the evolution of a new social conscience after 1792, under the stimulus of *sans-culotte* pressure, for many of the deputies had always tempered their *laissez-faire* principles with a humane concern for the victims of a competitive economy. Malouet was regarded in 1789 as belonging to the Right, but he produced, on 3rd August, a draft Bill for the creation of a nation-wide system of employment and public assistance bureaux, to be supported in part by public funds, quite as audacious as the social clauses which Robespierre tried to write into the Constitution of 1793.[1] Conversely, neither the *Tiers-État* of 1789 nor the *Montagnards* of 1793 intended to share political power with the artisan and the peasant. As the deputy, Duquesnoy, wrote of the 'people' in June 1789, 'its happiness must be assured, but not by its own efforts'.[2] We shall see later that this was very much the opinion of the Committee of Public Safety, although it might not have cared to say so in so many words.

The divisions within the political spokesmen of the Third Estate in 1789 and throughout the Revolution were therefore less concerned with final objectives than with the means of achieving them. In particular they disagreed as to the risks that were worth running, the need for compromise and the direction in which allies should be sought. The specific issue in the summer of 1789 was whether the ends of the commons could be achieved with the consent of the king and the privileged orders or whether their attainment necessarily involved a more or less violent conflict. The conciliators held that it would be better to be content with a compromise that secured the essentials, rather than to press for total victory at the price of discord and disorder. The radicals took the opposition of the aristocracy, if not of the Court, for granted, and their main concern was to maintain contact with the masses whose support they would need in an eventual trial of strength.[3]

In the first days of the Estates General, when the deputies

[1] For all references to debates in the Assembly see *Archives Parlementaires*. A summary, adequate for most purposes, is available in P. J. B. Buchez and P. C. Roux-Lavergne, *Histoire Parlementaire de la Révolution Française* (40 vol., Paris, 1834–8).

[2] R. de Crèvecoeur, *Journal d'Adrien Duquesnoy* (Paris, 1894), 1. 147.

[3] On this subject see F. Braesch, *1789, l'Année Cruciale* (Paris, 1941), *passim*.

of the Third Estate tended to meet in provincial groups to avoid losing themselves in the anonymity of a House of 648 members, political attitudes often reflected the recent past. The men of Dauphiné, under Mounier's leadership, pursued a moderate course, while the Breton deputation earned a reputation for intransigeance and could generally rely on the support of the deputies from Franche Comté and Provence—all areas of conflict in 1787–9. The Breton Club formed the nucleus of what was later to become the Jacobins. As the *Tiers-État* gradually found its leaders, questions of individual temperament became more important. Mounier and Malouet emerged as the chief partisans of conciliation while the *abbé* Siéyès and the Breton, le Chapelier, led the radicals. Mirabeau, as usual, was in a class apart. By temperament a radical and by conviction a conciliator, he was suspected by most of his colleagues of being primarily concerned to secure a patron wealthy enough to pay his debts and see to his considerable needs. Since his two possible sponsors, the king and the duc d'Orléans, were on opposite political sides, this still left him with some room for manoeuvre. A similar division obtained within the nobility where Noailles, d'Aiguillon, Clermont-Tonnerre and others of the Court aristocracy followed a policy of compromise, while the fiery d'Eprémesnil had now become one of the most violent partisans of royal authority. Amongst the clergy the violence of the 'radical' Grégoire and the 'reactionary' Maury contrasted with the moderation of the archbishops of Vienne and Bordeaux.

The conventional picture of the Estates General as divided into the Third Estate plus roughly half of the clergy and one-sixth of the nobility versus the remainder of the privileged orders is therefore inadequate. There was also a second cleavage between those in all three Houses who were prepared for compromise and those who hoped to impose their full programme on their defeated opponents. If the Revolution were not to shatter French society the Third Estate had not merely to implement its *cahiers*, but to do so with the assent, or at least without the violent hostility of the privileged orders. It was presumably with this in view that Malouet, and to a lesser extent Mounier, tried to preserve contact between the orders in May. In June the radicals took the initiative—it was Siéyès who proposed that the *Tiers-État* should constitute itself as the sole representative of the nation and who eventually won the adoption of the title of National Assembly, against the opposition of Malouet, Mounier, Mirabeau and Barnave. The threat from the Court once more united the *Tiers*: the Tennis Court Oath of 20th June, not to separate until France had a constitution, was proposed by Mounier and only one member refused to sign. After the king's declaration at the *Séance Royale* the Third Estate unanimously refused to leave the hall as ordered, and Mirabeau's motion that the deputies should declare themselves immune from legal prosecution was carried by 493 votes to 34. After his brief show of resolution at the *Séance Royale* the king appeared to capitulate. He made no attempt to expel the commons, who were joined by the majority of the clergy on the 24th and by 47 members of the nobility on the following day. When, on 27th June, the king ordered the remainder of the clergy and the nobility to meet with the commons, Arthur Young wrote in his diary, 'The whole business now seems over and the revolution complete.' This would seem to have been the opinion of the nobility also, for their spokesmen challenged the king's interpretation of the situation and 80 of them were at first reluctant to obey the royal command. Cazalès produced the argument to be expected from an aristocratic radical, that saving the monarchy had priority over saving the monarch, but the resistance of the nobles was overcome by an emotional appeal to them to sacrifice their private interests to the defence of the king.[1] It was characteristic of the French nobility in 1789 that it was more affected by an appeal to its generosity than by threats of danger or counsels of prudence.

The nobility might have been less recalcitrant if they had realized that the king was merely playing for time. He seems to have given way temporarily because of his fear of immediate violence in Paris and Versailles, but the Court had no intention of accepting defeat and orders had already been given for the concentration of troops. The defiance of the Third Estate had, in fact, produced the first major crisis of the Revolution, which could only be decided by a trial of strength. The subsequent policy of the Court is obscure, probably because those in charge had no clear idea of what they intended to do. The troop movements were on a scale that suggested some sort of *coup d'état*.

[1] See B. de Molleville, *Annals of the French Revolution* (1800), I. 134–40.

Whereas few soldiers had been brought into the Paris area when the Estates General were convened, six regiments were ordered up on 26th June and ten more on 1st July, the majority consisting of German and Swiss troops relatively immune to revolutionary propaganda. These forces were expected to take up their positions in the vicinity of Paris between 5th and 18th July. How they were used would probably depend on the outcome of a struggle for influence at Court, about which little evidence has survived. It seems improbable that the Court's plans provided for a military offensive, such as the occupation of Paris. The Commander-in-Chief, the maréchal de Broglie, was a confirmed royalist, but both he and his field commander, Besenval, were anxious to avoid bloodshed.[1] This was certain to be the attitude of the king and the most likely explanation of the Court's policy, and the one circulating in the corridors of Versailles, was that Louis would dissolve the Assembly, either with or without a reaffirmation of the *Séance Royale*, and that the troops would ensure the execution of the royal commands and prevent violent reactions in Paris or Versailles. The signal for action would be the dismissal of Necker and those ministers who would be unlikely to accept an open breach with the Assembly.

The deputies were in real danger of seeing all their hopes destroyed. They had no means of knowing how far the Court was prepared to go and they felt their liberty, if not their lives, to be in danger. By the end of June they were aware of the appointment of Broglie and of the first troop movements and they must have realized that events were building up to a climax. But the union of the three orders had altered the balance of forces in the Assembly. Although those who had come over merely in compliance with the king's orders appear to have abstained from speaking and voting, the prestige of the 'moderate' nobility and upper clergy allowed them to dominate proceedings. On 7th July the archbishop of Vienne was elected president by 700 votes out of 793 and three of the six secretaries elected were also moderates. In contrast with its resolute attitude before the *Séance Royale*, the Assembly seemed to have lost its bearings, presumably because its leaders were unwilling to

[1] P. Caron, 'La Tentative de Contre-Révolution de juin-juillet 1789', *Revue d'Histoire Moderne*, VIII (1906–7), pp. 7, 650; Besenval, *Mémoires* (Paris, 1821), II. 352–67.

recognize the open conflict with the Court. This policy brought the danger of losing touch with Paris, where middle-class opinion was becoming more radical.

On 8th July Mirabeau induced the Assembly to petition the king to recall the troops that were beginning to appear in the neighbourhood of Paris. Although his motion was carried with only four opposing votes, it had previously been weakened by the deletion of a clause recommending that the city be authorized to raise its own militia. The king did not reply until the 11th, when he rejected the petition. The Assembly then took refuge in a debate on the text of a declaration of rights that seemed increasingly unlikely to see the light of day. On the same evening the dismissal of Necker and all but two of the ministers and the formation of a 'reactionary' Council under the baron de Breteuil seemed to indicate that a *coup d'état* was at hand. The move was well timed, for the 12th was a Sunday, when the Assembly did not meet. This time there was no repetition of the emergency meeting that produced the Tennis Court Oath. On the 13th the debate on the change of ministers was interrupted by news that Paris had risen, the municipal customs houses were in flames, the armourers' shops emptied and fighting between troops and citizens expected every moment. The Assembly reacted with horror rather than indignation and during the next two days the conflict in Paris gave its proceedings an unreal and legalistic air. It declared the ministers responsible for their actions, guaranteed the Debt, in order to keep the city on its side, and reaffirmed the motions of the Third Estate of 17th, 20th and 23rd June. Even after the fall of the Bastille a motion by the Orleanist noble, Sillery, to petition the king to dismiss his ministers, was defeated by the conciliators, Lally-Tollendal, Clermont-Tonnerre and Mounier, as likely to antagonize the king. Barnave, who broke with them on this issue, denounced their attempt to compromise between 'a force which was all-powerful and one which had ceased to exist'.

During the crisis of 11th–15th July the Assembly therefore remained on the touch-lines and even gave the impression that it regarded the revolt of Paris as a lamentable breach of public order. Radical deputies such as Siéyès, Grégoire, le Chapelier and Barnave, who tried to commit it to the support of those who were fighting its battles for it, had no success. The deputies would certainly have reacted violently against any attempt to disperse them by force. They might have won a civil war, but they would not have forestalled one. They were saved by the spontaneous action of the middle class in most of the French towns, and notably in Paris.

Irrespective of political events, there would have been widespread rioting and disorder in France during the summer of 1789. The harvest of 1788 had been devastated by hail and bread remained dear throughout the winter.[1] As supplies became exhausted in the spring of 1789 prices reached their highest level since 1709. In spite of the Government's imports, supplies were uncertain, and the grain often barely fit for human consumption. Since rye-bread was the basic, indeed almost the sole, food of the poor, there was widespread hunger. Grain merchants were suspected of hoarding, food convoys were pillaged as they tried to make their way through famished villages, there were riots in the markets and the troops brought to the Paris area in the early spring were mainly employed in maintaining order in the countryside. Conditions worsened in the critical period before the new harvest. A royalist newspaper wrote, 'The nearer one got to July 14th the more serious the food shortage became. Each baker's shop was surrounded by a crowd that received a very parsimonious ration and the next day's supply was never sure. The complaints of those who had queued all day without getting anything increased the alarm of the rest. There were frequent fights for bread. The workshops were empty; workmen and artisans wasted so much time in fighting for a meagre ration of bread that they lost the means of paying for the next day's supply.' [2]

At any time in the eighteenth century such a situation would have led to disorder. There was serious rioting in Provence in the spring and as prices tended to rise—even the bread sold in Paris and made from imported grain which the Government sold at a loss cost $3\frac{1}{2}$ sous the pound—the early summer brought innumerable minor outbreaks in many parts of the country. As the critical period of the *soudure* approached, when there was

---

[1] See the description of the damage caused by hailstones 'sixteen inches in circumference' in *Despatches from Paris, 1784–1790*, II. 75–76, 82.

[2] *Ami du Roi*, quoted in Buchez and Roux, II. 40.

liable to be a gap between the exhaustion of last year's harvest and the gathering of the next, tension rose in the countryside, where the ripening crops were increasingly vulnerable to storms, pillage and wanton destruction. On this tense atmosphere was superimposed the political excitement of 1789. A country unused to any form of constitutional debate was inundated with pamphlets promising better conditions, attributing present suffering to unjust privilege, denouncing the plots of the aristocrats and the *pacte de famine* which linked grain-hoarding with the counter-revolution. Poor communications— Arthur Young was scathing in his comments on important French towns where there was not a newspaper to be seen— gave credence to the wildest rumours and magnified them in the process of distribution. It was widely believed, for example, that the queen and the comte d'Artois were following in the footsteps of Guy Fawkes and intended to blow up the entire National Assembly. When the critical period of the year from the point of view of food supplies coincided with the political crisis of July 1789, those who might wish to enlist popular support for an insurrection were not likely to lack followers.

There was a serious outbreak in Paris in late April, when the house of a prosperous wallpaper manufacturer, Réveillon, was plundered.[1] This arose from a remark attributed to Réveillon, probably incorrectly, that working men should be able to live on 15 sous a day. His own employees, who were paid the relatively generous sum of 25 sous, took no part in the insurrection, which therefore cannot be classified as a strike. It was more in the nature of an explosion of fury on the part of men driven to the limits of endurance by the high cost of living. The movement was not political, nor does it seem to have been organized from above. But the fact that the rioters shouted political slogans in support of the Third Estate showed that the political and economic crises had become associated in the minds of the Parisian working men.

After the Réveillon riots there was a period of relative calm in Paris, although political feeling was running high. The pleasure gardens of the Palais Royal, owned by the duc d'Orléans, were the focal point of this activity. The concentration of troops in the Paris area and the establishment of a camp in the

[1] See G. Rudé, *The Crowd in the French Revolution* (Oxford, 1959), pp. 34–44.

Champ de Mars just outside the city raised tempers still further and there were widespread rumours that a *coup d'état* was imminent. On the night of 11th–12th July before the news of Necker's dismissal reached Paris, 40 out of the 54 customs houses surrounding the city were attacked and burned to the ground. Although the men directly responsible were artisans and workmen, the movement was presumably planned from above and there is some evidence to suggest that the Orleanist headquarters at the Palais Royal was responsible. Paris was therefore in a state of excitement bordering on insurrection when the news arrived, about noon on the 12th, that the counter-revolutionaries at Versailles had struck. Since the 12th was a Sunday, the wage-earners were free to manifest their political opinions without jeopardizing their livelihood. Once again the Palais Royal took the lead. Desmoulins and other orators inflamed the crowds with violent speeches, culminating in a call to arms. From this time onwards the insurrection became general, as large crowds broke into the armourers' shops, paraded busts of Necker and Orléans about the streets and skirmished with the royal troops. The first reaction to the news of Necker's dismissal was therefore popular, tumultuous and confused. Lacking organization and a clear purpose, it was likely to burn itself out. Moreover the eclipse of the police and the appearance of armed bands in the Paris streets on the night of 12th–13th July were perhaps more alarming to the peaceable citizens than to the troops in the Champ de Mars. The deputies of the Third Estate at Versailles certainly regarded the first news from the capital as catastrophic.

What transformed the movement from a riot into a revolution was the readiness of the bourgeoisie to take control instead of turning to the king for protection against the threat to property. The marquis de Ferrières commented that the capitalists and rentiers rallied to the support of the Assembly and employed in its defence all the powerful weapons of money, influence and connections.[1] This hostility of the city meant that the king would be unable to float a loan if he dismissed the Assembly. One of the decisive steps in the insurrection was the winning over of the French Guards, and considerable financial resources were presumably required to feed, house and pay the

[1] Ferrières, *Mémoires* (Paris, 1821), I. 76.

zealots, if not to bribe the more hesitant. The bourgeoisie provided organization as well as funds. Paris had been divided into 60 Districts for the election of deputies to the Estates General and these Districts continued to hold meetings after the elections. The 407 Electors who had finally chosen the Paris deputation to the Estates General had also formed themselves into a political club which on 4th July had already been discussing the formation of a Parisian militia. When the crisis broke the Electors had their programme ready. They themselves came in the main from the wealthier strata of the middle class. The 379 who were present at the Hôtel de Ville on 14th July included two members of the Academy, five deputies, four bankers, 26 merchants, 154 lawyers, and 13 doctors and surgeons.[1] At the lower end of the social scale came the 43 retailers and 18 masters of various crafts, but some of these were probably men of substance, if not gentlemen in the contemporary sense. Socially there can be no doubt that the prosperous and cultivated upper middle class predominated amongst the Electors.

On the Sunday evening, 12th July, the Electors began to make their way to the Hôtel de Ville without any formal summons. There they found an impatient crowd clamouring for arms. Before midnight a quorum had assembled and the meeting then took the first steps towards bringing the insurrection under control. The old municipal officers were provisionally confirmed in their posts, but absorbed into a committee of 24 in which the Electors had a majority. The Districts were ordered to assemble and Electors sent out to put a stop to any violence in the streets. It was also decided to begin the creation of a militia by enrolling and arming an initial quota of 200 from each District. On the afternoon of the 13th detailed plans for the creation of this militia, now raised to 48,000, were approved—ostensibly to maintain order within Paris. The National Guard, as it was christened on 16th July, was the perfect weapon for the bourgeoisie. Composed of civilians and French Guards who had rallied to the Revolution, its political reliability was assured. At the same time, since it was drawn only from respectable citizens with settled addresses, was subject to military discipline

---

[1] P. Robiquet, *Le Personnel Municipal de Paris pendant la Révolution* (Paris, 1890), pp. 43–64.

and kept under the control of the Districts, it made possible the disarming of the people at large and formed a police force that could maintain order and protect property. In its early days the Guard had perhaps a more popular character than it was to assume after the exclusion of the poorer citizens and the adoption of a uniform that cost the guardsmen nearly £5 each, but from the start the obligation to serve one day in four probably excluded most of the wage-earners. The deputy Duquesnoy, alarmed by events in Paris, comforted himself with the thought that the new militia contained 'a great number of really respectable people, some of the best citizens of the town, knights of St. Louis, knights of Malta, very well-established bourgeois, financiers, priests, lawyers, monks'.[1]

As early as 13th July the Electors, helped by the defection of an entire regiment of French Guards and various other troops, had begun to impose some sort of order on the revolt. But if the Hôtel de Ville had seized the tiller it still had to run before the storm. So long as royal troops occupied the Champ de Mars, Paris would be virtually ungovernable and the Electors themselves, personally committed to the success of the insurrection, would not dare to loosen their links with the populace on whom their safety depended. The crowds were still in the streets, the debtors' gaol of la Force was emptied, barricades were going up, trenches being dug to repel cavalry and paving stones carried to the upper floors of the five- and six-storey buildings that dominated the narrow streets. The executive committee of the Electors itself authorized the distribution of powder to the popular forces. By the 14th, with the Guard in the process of formation, the shortage of arms and powder became acute. A mass deputation, led by one of the royal officers of the old municipality and including a company of lawyers' clerks and the priest of Saint Étienne-du-Mont at the head of his parishioners, marched to the Invalides to demand the muskets in the arsenal there. The governor, who had no intention of making a forcible resistance, failed to hold off the crowd by fair words, his arsenal was ransacked and 28,000 muskets and 20 cannon went to reinforce the revolutionaries. It was now the turn of the Bastille, the towering medieval fortress in the populous East end of Paris which had won a European reputation as a place of confinement

[1] R. de Crèvecoeur, *op. cit.*, I. 229.

for state prisoners. The prime motive for the move against the Bastille was to obtain access to its powder magazine, but the governor, de Launay, had run out his guns and reinforced his slender garrison with Swiss mercenaries earlier in the month and the Bastille was a potential royal strongpoint in the heart of the capital. If de Launay had followed the example of Sombreuil, the governor of the Invalides, the occupation of the Bastille would have been little more than another incident in the Parisian insurrection. But although conciliatory he refused to open his gates to the Parisians besieging them and his little garrison of not much more than a hundred pensioners, and the Swiss, possibly intimidated by the gathering crowds, eventually opened fire. It was this act, together with the garrisons firing on a deputation that later advanced under a white flag, that infuriated the besiegers, who convinced themselves that de Launay had tried to mislead them by peaceful pretences so that he could shoot them down more effectively. Their blood was now up and nothing less than the storming of the fortress would satisfy them.

The Electors appear to have been horrified by the turn of events—whether because they feared disorder or because they expected the attack to fail—but the initiative was no longer in their hands. The attackers, drawn mainly from the working-class population of the neighbouring Faubourg Saint-Antoine, were reinforced by detachments of French Guards with light artillery.[1] After five hours' resistance, with his main defences still intact, de Launay capitulated. His forces had lost only one man killed as compared with 98 killed and 73 wounded on the attackers' side. However limited its tactical significance, the storming of the Bastille was a major feat of arms that resounded throughout Europe. The very image of medieval oppression and royal absolutism had yielded to the blows of the all-conquering Third Estate. There could be no doubt now that the people of Paris had the will and the means to turn their narrow streets into a citadel of revolution, and the Electors, however alarmed at the violence around them, would swim with the tide rather than call on the monarchy for help. Besenval was already withdrawing to Sèvres when he received his Commander-in-Chief's order for a general retreat.

[1] G. Rudé, op. cit., pp. 56–59.

For a time it appeared that the Electors had lost control. Furious crowds murdered de Launay and his second-in-command and the French Guards with difficulty prevented a massacre of the entire garrison. De Flesselles, the *prévôt des marchands*, or mayor, who had tried to sabotage the insurrectionary movement from within the executive committee at the Hôtel de Ville, was exposed, allegedly by the discovery of one of his letters in de Launay's pocket,[1] expelled from the committee and shot down as he left the Hôtel de Ville. His severed head joined that of de Launay at the end of a pike and was paraded through the streets to the horror of the less sanguinary citizens. Even when order had been precariously restored, a second outbreak of mob violence proved too powerful to be controlled. On 22nd July Foulon, who had been appointed to ministerial office on the 11th, and his son-in-law Berthier, the intendant of Paris, were murdered outside the Hôtel de Ville. Both were accused of speculating in the grain trade as well as abetting the counter-revolution. When Berthier was murdered a fanatic tore out his heart and thrust it at the horrified municipality. The ferocity of these scenes, only equalled in Paris by the massacres of September 1792, shocked and alarmed many, but a public accustomed to seeing criminals broken on the wheel was inclined to think that Foulon and Berthier had received no more than their deserts. In other respects Paris was returning to normal. Bailly, a distinguished Parisian deputy, was elected mayor and Lafayette put in command of the National Guard. Shops and theatres, closed since the 12th, were reopened and on 18th July the municipality ordered all back to work, shrewdly offering six livres to those who produced a certificate of attendance from their employer and three more to any who surrendered a fire-arm. There could be no real peace until the harvest, but at least the fury of the people had been contained, and all who were not suspected of food-hoarding or counter-revolutionary activities were safe.

In the meantime the king had capitulated to the Revolution. When it became impossible to conceal from him that what was happening in Paris was very much more than a bread riot he

---

[1] Molleville (*Annals of the French Revolution*, I. 247) denies the existence of this letter, quoting Bailly in his support. Bailly himself (*Mémoires*, I. 382) claims that the committee tried to save Flesselles.

agreed to send away the troops whose inactive presence exasperated the city without conferring any advantage on the Court. On the same day, 15th July, the new ministers resigned and Louis had to suffer the humiliation of recalling Necker. The next night the more extreme members of the Court party, the comte d'Artois, Marie Antoinette's favourites the Polignacs, Vaudreuil and others, fled from Versailles and out of France.

The crisis had transformed the balance of power and it was henceforth impossible to arrest the Revolution by force of arms. Effective power had passed into the hands of the Third Estate. The July crisis was as decisive as a military victory, but the fact that there had been no large-scale fighting, that the king did not regard himself as estranged from his people and that the Assembly had not been identified with the revolt meant that appearances could still be saved and a compromise between the old order and the new was still possible.

The importance of the events in Paris which were the immediate cause of the Court's defeat lent plausibility to Arthur Young's contention that the provinces were waiting for a lead from the capital, but in fact this was far from being the case. Had the municipal revolt been confined to Paris, the king might well have accepted the suggestions of his advisers and escaped to the provinces, and marshal Broglie would not have killed the scheme with the pessimistic comment, 'We can get to Metz all right, but what are we to do when we have got there?'[1] As impressive in its way as the dramatic events in Paris was the comparable rising in one after another of the French towns. The extent of this movement and its general similarity to the course of events in the capital show clearly enough that both were part of a vast popular reaction whose most striking events, even the storming of the Bastille itself, were no more than isolated waves in a great storm.[2]

In the provinces as in Paris the combination of a famished populace and a middle class resolute in support of the Assembly produced a powerful revolutionary force. This first expressed itself in the form of addresses of solidarity presented to the

[1] P. Caron, *loc. cit.* (1906–7), 673.
[2] See D. Ligou, 'A propos de la Révolution Municipale', *Revue d'Histoire Économique et Sociale*, XXXVIII (1960), 147.

Assembly. The first such address, from Paris, on 26th June, was followed by a trickle of similar declarations from the provincial towns during the following days. Brittany took a leading part, perhaps because the municipality of Ploërmel circularized its neighbours inviting them to follow its example. Before the dismissal of Necker brought the crisis to a head there had been more than forty such addresses from towns which included Rennes, Nantes, Metz, Bordeaux, Poitiers, Colmar, Dijon and Montpellier—county towns, trading ports and garrison towns in all parts of the country. Another score, including Strasbourg, Marseilles, Nîmes, Cahors, Nancy and Besançon, expressed their support of the Assembly before they could have heard of the Parisian victory. From 20th July these addresses poured in from every side and about 150 were received in the ensuing ten days.

When the crisis broke many of the towns took action without waiting for the capital. When Rennes heard of Necker's dismissal the *Tiers-État* ransacked the arsenal and the troops refused to fire. At Caen a similar movement seized the citadel and attacked the hated *tribunal de sel* (the court which enforced the salt tax). The frightened municipality reduced the price of bread and formed a militia which was soon in conflict with the local garrison. At le Havre the naval arsenal was seized and troops sent from Honfleur prevented from landing. Arthur Young witnessed the pillage of the Hôtel de Ville at Strasbourg while the garrison looked on. The citadel of Bordeaux was handed over to the insurgents with whom the troops fraternized. The local pattern and the timing of the revolt varied a good deal, and the revolutionaries were not always successful, but in most cases an insurrection, led by the bourgeoisie, encountered no resistance from the army. Commanders showed little inclination to fight, and if they had done so their troops would have mutinied. The formation of *milices bourgeoises* maintained order and created a military force whose enthusiasm would have more than made up for its lack of training if confronted by regiments whose sympathies were on its side. In many towns the old municipal oligarchies were swept aside and replaced by committees drawn from the electors to the Estates General. The process was more or less violent and the change more or less complete in proportion to the promptitude with which concessions had been offered to the starving poor and to the impatient electors, but the general result was to transform the appearance of the country. Many of the intendants abandoned their posts and the machinery of royal centralization broke down. The new municipalities were virtually autonomous and were driven to assert their authority over the surrounding countryside to protect their grain supplies and maintain order. They quickly established fraternal relationships with each other—Nantes, for example, offered to send 2,000 men to Brest where the Third Estate was at odds with both the old municipality and with the naval authorities. Within the space of a few weeks the royal government lost control over the provinces, for in matters of importance the towns henceforth took their orders only from the Assembly.

From the viewpoint of the commons at Versailles the municipal revolution was entirely satisfactory. They soon forgot the alarm that they had felt at the news of the rising in Paris. The danger of mob violence was so swiftly overcome by the creation of the National Guard that the more radically-minded deputies, who had never been face to face with the crowds, unlike Bailly and Lafayette, soon convinced themselves that they had never had any hesitations about the course or outcome of the insurrection. Not for the last time during the Revolution men justified past violence from which they had profited, reserving their condemnation for those whom they suspected of seeking to renew it. As Duquesnoy put it, 'Personally I think that . . . [a period of anarchy] was necessary, but I also think it has got to stop.' The comment of Barnave apropos of the murder of Foulon and Berthier is well known—'Was their blood, then, so pure that we should so much regret spilling it?' More significant perhaps was the easy consolation that the moderate marquis de Ferrières offered to his sister, 'I should never have thought that a good and easy-going people would have been carried to such lengths; but the justice of heaven often uses the hands of men.' Lafayette, whose appeal for Foulon's life had been disregarded, offered his resignation, but according to Bailly he neither intended nor expected that it would be accepted.[1]

[1] R. de Crèvecoeur, *op. cit.*, I. 232, Ferrières, *Correspondance Inédite* (ed. Carrè, Paris, 1932), p. 97; J. S. Bailly, *op. cit.*, II. 127.

But the satisfaction of the deputies and of the urban middle class was soon destroyed by an insurrection of a different kind. The sporadic rural violence that had continued throughout the spring was fanned by the political crisis into a series of major revolts. Leaders who were aware of the resistance of the aristocracy to the demands of the Third Estate found little difficulty in convincing the ignorant peasants of the existence of an aristocratic plot—in which they themselves probably believed—to starve the revolutionaries into submission. The seigneur's feudal dues bore heavily on the rural population in times of famine. It was tempting to assume that his hoarding of grain was the main cause of the food shortage and that his motives were as much political as economic. Many were persuaded that they were fulfilling the wishes, even executing the orders of the 'bon Louis' in striking at his enemies and those of the people. In the Normandy bocage, in Franche-Comté, Alsace and the Mâconnais, the news of fighting in Paris led to widespread revolts in late July. The peasants made for the châteaux, burned the feudal charters that provided the legal evidence of the seigneur's rights, and, except in Normandy, frequently burned the château itself for good measure. In actual fact there was little if any loss of life, but rumour naturally magnified events beyond recognition, and even the level-headed Young reported 'the seigneurs hunted down like wild beasts, their wives and daughters ravished'. Such rumours naturally left more fortunate seigneurs little inclined to press for the payment of the dues owing to them.

Hard on the heels of the agrarian revolt, and covering a much wider area, came the Grande Peur, lasting roughly from 20th July to 6th August.[1] The large numbers of beggars who roamed the country in intimidating bands, the default of prompt communications and the growing political tension had produced a crop of rumours of brigands, who had been reported at Montpellier in May, at Beaucaire in June, and at Bourg in early July. The characteristic activity of the 'brigands', defined by Ferrières as early as 22nd June, was that they threatened to cut or burn the corn ripening in the fields, a form of wanton destruction which, had it existed in reality, would have fully justified the peasants in their anger and also in their belief in the existence of a 'pacte de famine'. Ferrières further reported on 17th

[1] See G. Lefebvre, La Grande Peur de 1789 (Paris, 1932), passim.

79

July, 'The Paris militia has driven out of the town a horde of brigands who will take refuge in the provinces.'[1] Opinion was therefore prepared, with the political crisis at its height and the harvest at its most vulnerable, for the outbreak of the *Grande Peur* in late July. The main characteristics of this phenomenon were the conviction that the brigands had arrived and the rapid diffusion of the rumours over great distances. The peasants gave picturesque shape to their imaginary tormentors—English, Imperial or Spanish troops, Piedmontese, even Poles. Educated opinion, while rejecting these higher flights of fancy, was virtually unanimous in its belief in the existence of the brigands, especially since it was impossible to distinguish between the mythical bandits and the real, if exaggerated, reports of the agrarian revolt. The *peur* was less of a panic than an alarm. Everywhere preparations were made to resist the shadowy menace, towns and villages stood to arms, warned each other and sent out offers of help. The confusion, excitement and gathering of armed groups led to a renewal of the agrarian revolt in the Dauphiné, where the peasants turned against the seigneur the forces prepared for the brigands. As it gradually became clear that the latter were not coming and had, in fact, never existed, there was a universal readiness to believe that so widespread an illusion must have been deliberately fostered by plotters whose motives were as elusive as the brigands themselves. The aristocracy suspected the middle class of raising the countryside against it, while the bourgeoisie was convinced that the nobility was trying to discredit the Revolution by a campaign of violence. The whole country was swept by a wave of suspicion, as Arthur Young found to his cost when travelling in a frontier area without a passport.

The Assembly was taken by surprise by the uprising in the countryside, which it viewed with undisguised dismay. Having disposed of the Court's attempted *coup d'état*, it was settling down to the drafting of a constitution, which it regarded as its primary *raison d'être*, when it found itself brought face to face with the peasant grievances which had often been passed over in the general *cahiers*. The urban middle class had nothing to gain and much to lose from the assault on the châteaux. Its victory was already assured and it saw in the agrarian revolt a

---

[1] Ferrières, *Correspondance Inédite*, pp. 73, 92.

potential threat to property. The deputy Salomon reported to his colleagues on 3rd August a general refusal to pay tithes, seigneurial dues and even rents. 'Property of every kind is a prey to the most criminal brigandage.' An anonymous member exclaimed: 'It is a war of the poor against the rich!' Conciliators, such as Malouet, emphasized the threat to property, while radicals tended to attribute the disorders to the plots of the aristocracy.

The deputies now found themselves saddled with an awkward situation. The only forces available for the control of the riotous peasantry were the royal troops and the newly-formed National Guards of the towns. The employment of the latter, as happened in the Dauphiné and the Mâconnais, threatened to split the *Tiers-État*, while a petition to the king to use regular troops would have offered him a chance to recover some of the authority he had lost during the July crisis in Paris. When moderates such as Lally-Tollendal and Dupont de Nemours stressed the need to restore order, Robespierre and some of the Breton deputies reminded the Assembly that it was in danger of repudiating the popular insurrection to which it owed its own salvation. As the disorder in the countryside continued, pressure mounted within the Assembly for some sort of intervention. But even the most inoffensive proclamation inviting the peasants to respect the rights of property was liable to prejudge the question of whether or not seigneurial privileges were a legitimate form of property. Any attempt to curtail these privileges by legislative action was liable to be defeated by the clergy, afraid for their tithes, the great majority of the nobility and many of the more conservative deputies of the Third Estate. The Breton Club therefore decided on an ingenious tactical move: members of the liberal aristocracy were to propose the voluntary *renunciation* of some of their feudal privileges in the hope of sweeping away the Assembly on a wave of emotional generosity whose consequences would appease the countryside and remove the need for repression.

When the scheme was put into effect, at the evening session on 4th August, its success was jeopardized by the vicomte de Noailles, who had apparently got wind of it and sprang up before the spokesman of the Breton Club. The proposal by Noailles for the suppression without compensation of personal services, the option to buy out feudal payments related to land ownership and the equality of all before the tax-collector, was liable to misfire, since the viscount himself had little to lose. However, he was promptly replaced by the greatest landowner in France after the king, the duc d'Aiguillon, said to have enjoyed an annual income of over 100,000 livres from his feudal rights, who made his prepared speech in which he invited his fellow nobles to sacrifice their rights on the altar of justice, in return for compensation for *all* of their feudal privileges.[1] The pre-arranged applause that greeted this proposal was somewhat marred by a sour demand from Dupont de Nemours that troops and militia be employed to restore order in the countryside. But the Bretons had another speaker ready, an obscure deputy who mounted the rostrum in peasant costume and proceeded to describe the feudal burdens of the village in terms more pathetic than accurate. So far the session had probably gone more or less as planned. The Breton Club had perhaps not expected that Le Guen de Kerengal would be followed by the marquis de Foucault, who came out with a vigorous attack on the Court nobility and suggested, presumably with one eye on Noailles and d'Aiguillon, that they might well give up their pensions. From this time onwards the session became more and more excited as one speaker after another renounced his own—or his neighbour's—privileges. When the nobility, the clergy and the legal profession had abandoned hunting rights and seigneurial justice, occasional payments to the clergy and the levying of tithes in kind, the privileges of the parlements and the venality of judicial offices, it was the turn of the provinces and privileged towns to surrender, sometimes with reservations, their particular rights and immunities. Renunciations flowed so quickly that the secretaries could not keep pace with them. All these motions were voted with acclamation and the Assembly dispersed at two o'clock in the morning.

This extraordinary session had probably far exceeded the expectations of those who launched it. The caustic Mirabeau, who had stayed away, commented, 'How like our Frenchmen. They spend a whole month quarrelling over syllables [with regard to the Declaration of the Rights of Man] and within one night they overthrow the whole traditional order of the mon-

[1] J. Droz, *Histoire du Règne de Louis XVI*, p. 326B.

archy.' Even the impressionable Ferrières, when he came to look back in his memoirs, said that 'a sentiment of hatred, a blind desire for vengeance and not a desire for good seemed to animate people's spirits'. He claimed that at the height of the session Lally-Tollendal sent a note to the unheeding president, le Chapelier, 'They have all lost control of themselves. Suspend the session.' Ferrières himself said that the Assembly was like a band of drunkards.

It would certainly seem that some of the motions on the 4th were motivated by a desire to punish others for the losses they had inflicted. Moreover the adoption of the reform programme allowed Mounier to push through the Assembly a motion authorizing the municipal authorities to requisition troops and disarm vagrants, which might otherwise have been defeated by the Left. And yet the temptation to easy cynicism must be resisted. Foucault, when he attacked Court pensions, was not necessarily disapproving the concessions proposed by d'Aiguillon; on 6th August he was to prove himself a violent opponent of the personal services claimed by the seigneurs. In the generous intoxication of the night of 4th August it is perhaps not too naïve to assume that the readiness to see abuses elsewhere did not necessarily imply a refusal to recognize those from which the speaker himself profited. Even Molleville, who strongly disapproved of the proceedings, admitted the sincerity of the participants. The main charge against the memorable session is not that it went too far but that it did not go far enough, especially after the initial fervour had abated and the drafting debates of 5th–11th August allowed of modifications to the original decisions. Various minor amendments preserved to the seigneurs their fishing rights and the right to keep their dovecotes, subject to certain restrictions. The clergy in particular showed signs of alarm and in their concern over tithes questioned the validity of all the proceedings on the 4th. This ill-advised attitude led to an anti-clerical majority deciding on the total abolition of tithes. While superficially a victory for the reformers, this was, in fact, a concession to the landowners—and hence to a substantial proportion of the aristocracy.[1] But the clergy were the object of so much suspicion and dislike that

[1] See P. Massé, 'Survivances de la Dîme à Bonneuil-Matours (1790–1834)', *Annales Historiques de la Révolution Française*, XXX (1958), 1.

when Siéyès pointed this out, in a brilliantly-argued speech, the only effect was to destroy his own popularity.

The final version of the Assembly's work was a good deal less radical than its preamble suggested: 'The National Assembly destroys in entirety the feudal system.'[1] Feudal burdens allegedly incurred in connection with the transfer of land were not abolished. Their extinction by purchase was not unknown before the Revolution and the right to buy them out was of no interest to the vast majority of peasants who had not the necessary capital.[2] Moreover, the vital question of which services were abolished without compensation and which guaranteed as property, was left for future definition. Until such time as the necessary legal and administrative measures had been taken, the *status quo* was maintained in all respects except that personal services were abolished forthwith.

The new regulations conferred great benefits on the wealthy and educated middle class, whose members were alone likely to derive much advantage from the facility to redeem feudal dues and from the nominal admissibility of all citizens to all appointments and commissions. Nevertheless a great deal had been done for the poorer peasants. The abolition of personal services and of seigneurial justice affected them at least as much as the bourgeoisie, while they also stood to benefit from the abolition of fiscal privilege. The night of 4th August was marked by more genuine self-sacrifice than has sometimes been conceded; it is difficult, for example, to ascribe any ulterior motive to the clergymen who renounced the plurality of benefices which some of them enjoyed. The debates of 5th–11th August were not wholly devoted to whittling away concessions offered in a moment of enthusiasm. Duquesnoy, neither an extremist nor given to displays of emotion, wrote to his correspondents: 'What a nation, what glory, what an honour to be a Frenchman!' Bailly commented nostalgically, a few years later, '*Beaux moments, qu'êtes-vous devenus?*'[3]

The events of July and August provided the answer of the Third Estate to the *Séance Royale*. Their victory over the king

---

[1] For text see J. M. Thompson, *French Revolution Documents* (Oxford, 1933), pp. 58–61.

[2] P. Massé, 'Les Amortissements de Rentes Foncières en l'An III', *Annales Historiques de la Révolution Française*, XXXIII (1961), 351.

[3] R. de Crèvecoeur, *op. cit.*, I. 267; J. S. Bailly, *op. cit.*, II. 216.

in July had ensured that France would have a constitution and the 4th August proclaimed the civil equality that Louis had rejected on 23rd June. One after another the clauses of the royal *diktat* had been reversed and the claims of the vast majority had prevailed over those of the privileged few. Ferrières wrote to his wife on 7th August, when he had had time to reflect on what he had to lose: 'If the result will lead to any advantage to the general good I will console myself easily enough for what I lose as a nobleman and the seigneur of a fief.' To his sister he wrote three days later: 'The best thing the nobility can do is to join forces with the *Tiers* and raise to its own level the wealthy and respectable bourgeoisie . . . after all, I had sooner have Coucaud think himself my equal than a Grandee regard me as his inferior.'[1] The events of July and August had not wholly destroyed the links between the majority of the Assembly on the one hand and the king and the majority of the nobility on the other. Their previous conflict could be blamed on Artois and his friends, who were safely out of the country, and an attempt be made to restore on a new basis of conservative equality the fabric of French society which had been shaken but not torn apart. Having seen their programme triumph, it was to this end that the conciliators now bent all their energies.

[1] Ferrières, *Correspondance Inédite*, pp. 110, 120.

IV

<hr>

The Failure to Compromise

<hr>

Les chefs de la majorité se persuadaient que, s'ils travaillaient sérieusement au rétablissement de l'autorité royale constitutionnelle . . . on s'en servirait pour les écraser. . . . D'un autre côté, la majorité de la noblesse et du clergé ne pouvait s'accoutumer à regarder comme définitifs les décrets rendus.

MALOUET

During the second half of August 1789 the advocates of compromise tried to form themselves into an organized political party. Their leaders, a committee of fifteen led by Malouet, Mounier, the bishop of Langres and the comtes de Virieu and de Lally-Tollendal, claimed the support of about half the deputies of the Third Estate.[1] From 17th August to 28th September they won every one of the fortnightly elections to the presidency of the Assembly. Masters of the influential committee charged with the preparation of a draft constitution, the *monarchiens*, as they were known, hoped to dictate the form that political institutions were to take. At Lafayette's house they met the leaders of the more radical deputies to discuss the formulation of a common policy.[2] The radicals, Duport, Lameth and Barnave, were prepared to accept an Upper House, provided that it had no absolute veto over legislation, and an absolute royal veto, provided that the king were not authorized to dis-

[1] Malouet, *Mémoires* (Paris, 1874), I. 301 *et seq.*
[2] A. Mathiez, 'Étude Critique sur les Journées des 5 et 6 octobre 1789', *Revue Historique*, LXVII, LXVIII, LXIX (1898–9).

solve the Assembly. Confident of their majority, the *monarchiens* refused these terms and negotiations were broken off on 29th August. It was probably no coincidence that a violent meeting at the Palais Royal on the following evening proposed taking the law into its own hands and was with difficulty restrained from marching on Versailles in order to bring the king back to Paris. In the face of this popular hostility the *monarchiens* drew towards the aristocratic Right and after a meeting with some of the leading royalists urged the king to withdraw farther away from Paris—advice which Louis rejected. The constitutional debate in the Assembly therefore opened somewhat ominously, with the Third Estate divided, the radicals looking to popular forces in Paris to intimidate the Assembly and the *monarchiens* turning towards an aristocracy whose intentions they had good reason to suspect.

The aim of the *monarchiens* was to establish a conservative constitutional monarchy. The king was to be appeased by the right to veto legislation, and the nobility by the creation of an Upper House. Both of these moves were intended to restrain the impetuosity of the Assembly in the interests of social conservatism; as the comte de Clermont-Tonnerre explained, union had been necessary in order to overthrow the 'feudal' order, but now that all sacrifices had been made, precautions had to be taken against what he described as *'oscillations populaires'*. The *monarchiens* were mistaken on every count. There is no reason to suppose that Louis XVI would have accepted the rôle they assigned to him. On the issue of the Upper House the radicals enlisted the support of many of the provincial nobility, from moderates such as Ferrières to ultra-royalists like Mirabeau's younger brother, who were afraid that the Senate would be filled by the Court nobility or the 'liberal' nobles.[1] Even on the question of the royal veto the *monarchiens* had overestimated their strength and their motion was defeated by 673 votes to 325 in favour of a suspensive veto only. On 12th September, the day after this division, Mounier, Lally-Tollendal and Bergasse resigned from the constitutional committee. The new committee, elected on the 15th, contained no influential members of their party. This was the point at

[1] See the comments of the British Embassy in *Despatches from Paris, 1784–1790*, II. 261.

which the historian, Droz, concluded the 1839 edition of his *History of the Reign of Louis XVI*, on the ground that the failure of the *monarchiens* marked the end of the attempt to reshape French institutions by agreement. Contemporaries were less disposed to regard the defeat as final and Mounier and his allies apparently hoped to maintain their influence, although they were now driven to turn to the Court after their rebuff by the Assembly.

As in June, the victory of the radicals produced a conflict with the king. Louis XVI indicated his attitude by refraining from promulgating the Declaration of the Rights of Man and the decrees of 4th August, and thereby raised the issue of whether his veto might be applied to the provisions of the constitution itself. To have acknowledged any such right would have left the king in final control of the work of the Assembly and only the more violent members of the aristocracy were prepared to go so far. In the face of Louis's reservations the Assembly was virtually unanimous in demanding an unequivocal royal confirmation of its decrees. The ensuing deadlock recalled that of June and July and was resolved in the same way: the king summoned troops whose arrival provoked an insurrection in Paris.

On this occasion only one regiment was involved and the royal position had deteriorated too far for there to be any question of a *coup de main* against the Assembly. It was therefore all the more imprudent of the Court to let the arrival of the Flanders Regiment be the occasion for a banquet offered to the newcomers by the Household Guards, and at one point favoured by a visit from the royal family, since the festivities degenerated into drunken demonstrations of royalist enthusiasm. The Court ladies, who were thereby encouraged to manifest their own hostility to the Revolution, acted with their customary ignorance of the world outside the palace walls. The celebrations at Versailles goaded Paris into action. For weeks journalists, pamphleteers and popular orators had been calling for a march on Versailles to remove the king from the corrupting influence of his Court and bring him to Paris for safe custody. Bailly and Lafayette had with difficulty maintained order and now they allowed themselves to swim with the popular tide. The insurgents who stormed the *Hôtel de Ville* on 5th October were mainly women, but the uprising, which showed evidence of previous planning, was not merely prompted by the scarcity of bread. From the *Hôtel de Ville* the women set out for Versailles, followed during the afternoon by a substantial detachment of National Guards with the more or less reluctant Lafayette at their head. The first result of the Parisian invasion was political: Louis XVI promptly signified his assent to all the decrees that the Assembly had voted. But Lafayette was accompanied by two representatives of the municipality, whose demands included the king's return with them to Paris. This Louis refused to accept, and when Lafayette went to bed, about three in the morning, after providing for the safety of the château, the question was still unresolved. About 5.30 on the morning of 6th October some of the crowd forced their way into the palace, apparently making for the queen's apartments. Marie Antoinette, roused in haste, fled to the king's chamber, and Lafayette and the National Guards were eventually able to restore order, although not before some of the royal bodyguard had been murdered. The crowd in the courtyard greeted the royal family on the balcony with cries of 'To Paris!' and the king had no alternative but to submit. In the afternoon the French monarchy left Versailles for ever and an interminable cortège took the royal family in triumph to Paris.

Henceforth there could be no compromise between the Court and the Revolution. Marie Antoinette was never to forgive Lafayette for the terror of her last night at Versailles. Louis XVI sent secret messages to Vienna and Madrid repudiating all the concessions that he had made since 15th July. All hopes of compromise were ended although the royalist cause itself was far from lost. For the *monarchiens*, however, and their policy of revolution by consent, the defeat was final. On 7th October they decided to withdraw from an Assembly whose legitimacy they no longer recognized and whose freedom of action they were not the only ones to suspect. Mounier and Lally-Tollendal left at once on a fruitless mission to raise the provinces against Paris. Over 300 deputies were induced to ask for their passports, but only 26 actually withdrew from the Assembly. The *monarchiens* had never been very successful in their parliamentary manoeuvres and even their resignation proved to be an anticlimax. Those who remained, like Malouet and Clermont-Tonnerre, henceforth inhabited an unhappy limbo, suspected by the Left and despised by the Right. They had, on the whole, tended to self-righteousness, obsequiousness to the aristocracy and suspicion of the poor. Their faulty political insight had led them to seek a compromise where none was possible, since both the king and the Assembly were determined to impose the constitution of their own choice. But they were men whose honour even their opponents respected, and with them disappeared the last hope of domestic peace for France. Henceforth the Revolution was to pursue a more passionate and tragic course than that which they had mapped out for it with so much moderation and self-assurance.

The deputies were still recovering from the October crisis, which brought the Assembly to Paris in the wake of the king, when they involved themselves in a new conflict that was to establish new lines of bitter division. During the debates that followed the night of 4th August voices had already been heard demanding that some at least of the possessions of the Church should be sold by the State in order to reduce the national debt. Such proposals were also present in some of the *cahiers*. After the failure of Necker's various financial expedients, the clergy were prepared for the blow, but they scarcely expected the initiative to be taken by one of themselves, the unscrupulous Talleyrand, bishop of Autun, whose disgust with the vacillating policy of the Court led him to offer this gage of loyalty to the Revolution. The ensuing debate demonstrated what became a truism of French politics—that the anti-clerical issue split the nation along different lines from its political and economic divisions. The Left, eager for the sale of Church property, was joined by conservatives such as Dupont de Nemours, by some of the aristocracy and even by priests such as Grégoire and Dillon. The deputy Duquesnoy asserted that about twenty parish priests voted in favour of the Bill—perhaps influenced by its proposal to increase their incomes to 1,200 livres a year.[1] On 2nd November the Bill passed the Assembly by 568 votes to 346, a majority indicative of the relative isolation of the clergy.

The implementation of this decision of principle was bitterly but unsuccessfully contested. On 20th December the Assembly

[1] R. de Crèvecoeur, *Journal d' Adrien Duquesnoy*, II. 11.

voted to sell Crown lands and Church property to the value of 400 million livres, using these assets as security for the issue of *assignats* or State credit notes, which eventually became the currency of the Revolution. When it was further proposed on 11 April 1790 that the entire property of the Church should be put under the administration of the new local authorities, pending its sale, Grégoire parted company with the anti-clericals on the ground that the clergy should not be mere salaried officials of the State, and some of the more influential leaders of the nobility, such as Cazalès, came to the support of the clergy. The debate was more acrimonious than usual and the extreme Right boycotted the division—perhaps the first sign of the coming alliance between religion and counter-revolution. On 16th June the Assembly approved the conditions of sale and threw on to the market an immense agglomeration of land, farms, forests and urban buildings.[1]

So far the revolutionaries had concerned themselves only with matters temporal and the main motive for the expropriation of the Church was financial. But some of the deputies had spoken of the evil effects of the corporate organization of the Church and the need to purify the morals of the clergy in terms which suggested that the Assembly would go on to invade fields that the clergy themselves regarded as spiritual. To some extent the 'reform' of the Church was implicit in the secularization of its property, for the State, as paymaster, now had a direct interest in reducing ecclesiastical expenses. Moreover the Assembly as a whole was impatient of any limitations on its authority and was inclined to 'regenerate' the Church as a logical corollary to its secular reforms. The lead was taken, not by the Left, but by men of moderate political views, eager to restore the Church to what they imagined to have been its pristine purity, and some of them perhaps looking forward to repaying the harsh treatment inflicted on the Jansenists throughout the previous century. Of the leading anti-clerical deputies, Thouret had voted against the 'National Assembly' motion of 17th June, and Treilhard had supported the proposal to give the king an absolute veto. But if the reform movement was led by conservatives, extremist members of the aristocracy came to the support

[1] For an examination of the consequences of the sale of Church property see below, pp. 251–53.

of the established Church, whose interests they prejudiced by
their embarrassing and ineffective intervention. In the Assembly
itself the immediate effect of the religious question was to reinforce the Right by the majority of the votes of the clergy. More
important was the possibility that in the country at large the
counter-revolution would for the first time be able to draw on
widespread popular support.

In February 1790 the contemplative orders were abolished
and on 29th May Martineau introduced a Bill for the complete
reorganization of the Church. The main provisions of this Civil
Constitution of the Clergy were a reduction in the numbers of
the ecclesiastics, to be achieved partly by eliminating all except
bishops and parochial clergy and partly by redistributing dioceses and parishes on more rational—and economical—principles, and the election of bishops and curés by their congregations. Bishops were henceforth to inform the Pope of their
election, but not to ask him for canonical institution.[1] In spite
of the revolutionary nature of these changes, the upper clergy
adopted an accommodating attitude, but insisted on the need
for their confirmation by a spiritual authority, either the Pope
himself or a national synod. When the Assembly, jealous of its
own authority, refused to accept a synod, the Archbishop of
Aix declared that the clerical deputies could not recognize the
authority of a lay assembly in this field and would abstain from
the debate. The deputies were probably under a genuine mis-
apprehension, believing that the Civil Constitution of the
Clergy, as its name implied, dealt with temporal matters only.
But the ensuing conflict was based on something far more fundamental than a disputed interpretation of a point of canon law.
Behind the attitude of the Assembly lay an assumption of
secular sovereignty that could not co-exist for long with the
claim of a corporate Church to dictate its own terms of association with the State. 'Rousseau had defeated Richerism.'[2]

The Civil Constitution was voted on 12 July 1790 and received the royal assent on 24th August. The French clergy, in

[1] For text see J. M. Thompson, *French Revolution Documents*, pp. 67–79. On
the religious question as a whole see A. Mathiez, *Rome et le Clergé Français sous la
Constituante* (Paris, 1911), *passim*.
[2] McManners, *French Ecclesiastical Society under the Ancien Régime*, p. 260;
chap. xiv contains an excellent survey of the implications of the Civil Constitution
from the viewpoint of the clergy.

the hope of averting the impending schism, appealed to the Pope to authorize them to accept the Civil Constitution. When Pius VI delayed his reply the Assembly, losing patience, voted that all the clergy in positions of public responsibility—primarily the bishops and parish priests—should take an oath of loyalty to the constitution. On 27 December 1790 the Assembly ordered its own clerical members to lead the way. Grégoire and 59 others did so, but all the bishops present and two-thirds of the lower clergy refused. The breach was now manifest to all and the clergy of France was split into two hostile factions.

In the country as a whole seven of the bishops and about half of the lower clergy took the oath—although many of the latter withdrew when the Pope condemned the Civil Constitution on 13 April 1791. The response of the clergy varied considerably from one part of France to another: in the Vendée, Brittany, Normandy, Flanders and Alsace less than 20 per cent took the oath; in the Var, 96 per cent. The similarity to present-day religious practice is interesting: the west, the extreme north, the Bas-Rhin and Moselle were bastions of the refractory clergy; the south-east, most of the centre and the Île-de-France supported the *constitutionnels*. The modern reader must share the surprise of the Assembly that an episcopate conspicuous for its secularism in the years before the Revolution should so overwhelmingly have chosen the arduous road of exclusion and persecution. Its principles may not always have been of the most spiritual—the bishop of Narbonne wrote: 'If I had been only a bishop I might perhaps have given way like the others, but I was a nobleman.' Such considerations of aristocratic *esprit de corps*, however, would not account for the painful decisions of over half of the lower clergy to abandon their parishioners for privation, exile and sometimes death. Many of the French clergy responded with an abnegation worthy of the tragic nature of the choice offered to them—it was to be the unhappy destiny of the Revolution to evoke from all sides the noblest responses to the most fratricidal causes.

Having committed the irreparable, the Assembly tried to palliate the consequences of its acts. Those of the parish priests who had rejected the Civil Constitution were given pensions, invited to continue their functions until replaced, and eventually offered the same toleration as any other minority religion. The pacific intentions of the Assembly foundered on Papal anathema and popular prejudice. Local opinion—whether Roman or revolutionary—refused to tolerate the presence of a hostile priest. The logic of events drew towards the counter-revolution those whose consciences could not accept the decrees of the Assembly, while the deputies had no alternative but to lend the support of the secular arm to priests who had committed themselves to the revolutionary cause. And so discord spread throughout the length of France, dividing families and friends and for the first time setting humble villagers against the new régime. From 1791 until Napoleon's Concordat of 1801 the religious civil war was to continue. The aristocratic party acquired passionate popular support in some areas, while the constitutional clergy gradually forfeited the respect and confidence of those who had called them into being.

In France as a whole the period from 1789 to 1791 was one of change and instability. The new system of local government tended to transfer power from the ennobled oligarchies of the towns to wealthy and educated professional people, and in the countryside from the seigneurs to the more prosperous *laboureurs*.[1] In the process the precarious unity of the Third Estate was subjected to a growing strain as latent conflicts of a social and economic nature came into the open. Men of property were alarmed by the tendency of their 'inferiors' to profit from the decline of royal authority and to take the law into their own hands. They would willingly have taken vigorous action in defence of property and order had they not feared that a breach with their embarrassing popular allies would have played into the hands of the aristocracy and endangered all the gains of the Revolution. The attitude of many of the nobility was that expressed in a despatch by the British Ambassador, dated 6 November 1789. 'Birth, fortune and favour are to lose all influence and every man from the meanest station in life is to rise to the highest honours in the State if he has merit sufficient to convey him to them. Such, My Lord, is the total subversion of all things in this country, and so general is the disgust that I can conceive that nothing but a bloody civil war can ever possibly restore matters to any degree of order.'[2] Rather than

[1] See below, pp 113–16.
[2] *Despatches from Paris, 1784–1790*, II. 277.

submit to this sort of 'order' the deputies of the Third Estate were prepared for disorder. They knew the forces of counter-revolution to be formidable, especially after the religious conflict had broken out, and they were reluctantly prepared to tolerate a certain amount of popular violence if the alternative was military repression by aristocratic army officers. But they lived in expectation of a time when the acceptance by the king and the nobility of the fact of the Revolution would allow them to enforce their own 'order' on their own terms.

It would be a mistake to attribute to the revolutionary situation every food riot or attack on municipal customs posts (*octrois*). Such occurrences were commonplace in eighteenth-century France, and if they were more frequent in the early years of the Revolution this was only to be expected in view of the weakness of the Central Government, the inexperience of the new local authorities and the unreliability of the troops. Such outbreaks were almost invariably local and short-lived and rarely led to bloodshed unless aristocratic officers were provocative or the municipal authorities were faced by serious popular movements, as happened at Angers in September 1790, where the quarrymen's protest against the high price of bread was suppressed by National Guards and regular troops. In cases such as this the municipality was generally ready to use force and the Assembly to support it.

Potentially more serious was the unrest caused by the revolutionary upheaval itself, which took a variety of forms. Open attempts to raise the countryside against the Assembly were rare and evoked little popular support, as the bishop of Tréguier found to his cost in October 1789, when his effort to mobilize religious intolerance in support of 'our ancient laws' attracted the interest of some of the Breton nobility, but was easily suppressed by the spontaneous action of the local revolutionaries. The attempt of some of the parlements (Rouen, Metz, Rennes and Toulouse) and provincial Estates (Dauphiné, Languedoc and Cambrésis) to challenge the authority of the Assembly on constitutional grounds was equally unsuccessful in attracting popular support and was repudiated by the king, in whose name the resistance was organized.

More disturbing to the Assembly was the prolongation of the peasant revolt which had caused it so much concern during

the summer of 1789. The riotous peasants drew no fine distinctions between the social status or political opinions of the
landowners against whom they revolted. Even the leaders of
the liberal nobility, Charles de Lameth and the duc d'Aiguillon,
each had a château burned in the Agenais in February 1790.
During the course of the year there were serious outbreaks in
Brittany, the south-west, the centre and Lorraine. These were
essentially peasant movements aimed at extending the concessions won on 4th August by burning feudal charters, refusing
the payment of dues which the Assembly had declined to abolish
and even, in the Bourbonnais and in Berri, claiming to recover
common lands acquired by the seigneurs during the previous
120 years. In most cases the municipal authorities did not hesitate to send troops and National Guards against the peasants,
some of whom were possibly their own tenants, and the
Assembly was ruthless in its suppression of movements which
challenged its own land settlement and seemed to constitute a
threat to property in general.

Attitudes were very different when the conflict lay between
the bourgeois revolutionaries of the towns on the one hand and
the old municipal oligarchies and officers of the royal garrison
on the other. This prolongation of the municipal revolt of July
1789 divided the Assembly. A typical example was the riot at
Toulon in December 1789. Relations between the *Hôtel de
Ville* and the naval authorities were already bad when the
Commander-in-Chief Ashore, d'Albert de Rions, dismissed two
dockyard workers for wearing the revolutionary cockade. This
led to a riot in which Rions and one or two of his officers who
had been wounded were arrested by the municipality, ostensibly
for their own protection. When the news reached the Assembly,
Malouet and the Right stressed the affront to the king's uniform
and demanded the punishment of the municipal authorities. The
Left, embarrassed by the incident, but aware that Rions was a
royalist and the municipality devoted to the Revolution, threw
the blame on the admiral and exonerated the civilians. After
days of acrimonious debate the Assembly finally passed a compromise resolution that commended both sides and satisfied
neither. There were similar disturbances at Briançon, Marseilles
and Montpellier which in each case resulted in the occupation
of the town's defences by the National Guard. The Assembly,

while theoretically advocating the maintenance of order, could not help regarding each municipal citadel as a miniature Bastille. As Ferrières put it, 'The men of the Constituent Assembly, always suspicious of the king's sincerity, feared that if they checked the people too severely they would deprive themselves of the means of employing them when they should need to set them in motion. Hence this alternation of anarchy and order, of sedition and repression.'[1] The situation created a vicious circle—the more the Assembly tolerated insults to royal officers the more the king resented the position to which he had been reduced, and the greater his reservations the more the Assembly distrusted him.

The Assembly's predicament was clearly illustrated by the serious trouble at Nancy in August 1790. A dispute over pay led to the revolt against its officers of the Swiss regiment of Châteauvieux which General Bouillé proposed to repress with the garrison and National Guards of Metz. The Assembly hesitated, suspicious of Bouillé and hoping to avoid an open conflict, but determined to restore military discipline. While the deputies argued, Bouillé marched, seizing Nancy after a pitched battle with very heavy casualties on both sides. Confronted with this *fait accompli* the Assembly first passed Barnave's motion for a full enquiry and then accepted Mirabeau's proposal to vote its congratulations to Bouillé and his troops. Whatever the origins of the conflict, the political consequences of Bouillé's victory became apparent when the conservative Nancy municipality broke up the local Jacobin Club and arrested 40 of its members. In December the uneasy Assembly voted an amnesty for all those involved, but by this time one of the Swiss soldiers had been broken on the wheel and 28 more hanged.

One must not exaggerate the extent of provincial disorder. No other incident approached the seriousness of the Nancy affair, many parts of France had scarcely been affected and in the towns at least the situation was one of insecurity rather than of anarchy. With the help of a good harvest there was reason to expect that the countryside would begin to settle down by the end of 1790. Nor should one underestimate the strength of revolutionary solidarity which often triumphed over other

[1] Ferrières, *Mémoires*, I. 242.

divisions. This was best illustrated on 14 July 1790, when National Guards from all parts of France assembled in Paris to join with Louis XVI in taking an oath of loyalty to the constitution. The *Fête de la Fédération* was perhaps the greatest of all the revolutionary festivals. Certainly it was the most successful in creating an impression of national unity: thousands of volunteers from all classes helped the workmen who were preparing the vast amphitheatre in the Champ de Mars. But revolutionary *fraternité* imposed its own conditions. The *Fédération* served as a pretext for the parliamentary manoeuvre of 19th June which abolished noble titles, armorial bearings and all the trappings of nobility. If Ferrières is to be believed this symbolical gesture had important consequences in alienating many of the provincial gentry who had hitherto resigned themselves to the Revolution.[1] But even though the nobility might find themselves increasingly out of sympathy with the new order, the Revolution retained, until the summer of 1790, the support of the overwhelming majority of the population.

This situation was transformed by the promulgation of the Civil Constitution of the clergy. Already in April and May there had been serious trouble in two of the main Protestant centres, Nîmes and Montauban. At once the political issues became confused. At Nîmes the municipality and the National Guard were divided, Roman Catholic extremists enjoyed much popular support and their adoption of the royalist cockade was a clear enough indication of the reinforcements that religion was to bring to the counter-revolutionaries. With the military garrisons in the area loyal to the Revolution and popular forces mustering under royalist emblems it became difficult for the Assembly to distinguish friend from foe. The religious issue also produced trouble in Strasbourg in January 1791, while in Brittany in February the National Guards of Lorient reinforced those of Vannes, who were defending the town against an attack from the surrounding peasantry, over twenty of whom were killed. There were disturbances at Uzès in February and in June supporters of the recalcitrant clergy seized Bastia, declaring their acceptance of all the revolutionary changes except the Civil Constitution of the Clergy. The eviction of recalcitrant priests led to widespread violence during the spring and

[1] Ferrières, *Mémoires*, II. 76.

summer of 1791. The Assembly, anxious to avoid religious war, was under constant pressure from the local authorities to come to the support of the constitutional clergy and the application of repressive measures against their opponents was merely a question of time.

While the provinces were passing through this troubled period Paris itself was relatively calm. The murder of the baker François, on 21 October 1789, led to the immediate voting of a Bill which empowered municipal authorities to proclaim martial law and inflicted severe penalties on those involved in riots. For the next eighteen months the municipality was able to maintain order and although disturbances occurred from time to time there was virtually no bloodshed. This relative stability was far from implying general acceptance of the *status quo*. One of the most striking developments of this period was the conversion of one group of revolutionary leaders after another to the principle of co-operation with the king. Whether they judged the Court to have been beaten into impotence or whether they became more alarmed at the possible threat to the social order implied by continuing instability, the result was much the same. For to negotiate with the king was to offer him hostages as well as concessions, since the revelation of the negotiations would destroy the political reputation of those concerned, in Paris, if not in the Assembly itself.

This process may be said to have started when the *monarchiens* urged the king to leave Versailles in August 1789. In the following May, Mirabeau, the most able and potentially the most dangerous of the Court's opponents, became a paid royal adviser and directed his considerable talents to strengthening an executive power which he must have known to be counter-revolutionary.[1] The following month saw the creation of the 1789 Club, visibly a reply to the Jacobins. The new club became the political home of many of the revolutionary leaders of the previous year, such as Lafayette, Bailly, Siéyès, Talleyrand, and even le Chapelier. Its outlook was socially conservative and its creation divided the revolutionary movement. Even the radicals of 1789, the Lameths, Barnave and Duport, entered into secret negotiations with the Court in the spring of 1791 and accepted its

[1] See *Correspondance entre le comte de Mirabeau et le comte de la Marck* (ed. Bacourt, Paris, 1851), *passim*.

financial support in order to launch their own newspaper. By June 1791 only a handful of extremist deputies maintained the uncompromising attitude of 1789 and most of the ex-radicals were now intent on finishing the Revolution—which meant conciliating the king. But if the Assembly was now more or less converted to the old views of the compromisers of 1789 that the Revolution could not safely proceed farther than the king was prepared to go, important sections of the public retained their previous enthusiasm and their previous suspicions.

The result, in Paris, was that the leadership of the revolutionary movement passed from the Assembly and the *Hôtel de Ville* into new and humbler organizations. During 1789–90 the District of the Cordeliers, under the guidance of Danton and his friends, challenged the municipality, protected Marat from arrest and signalized its revolutionary zeal on every appropriate occasion. It was perhaps mainly because of the Cordeliers that the Districts were dissolved in May 1790, whereupon the leading Cordeliers founded a club whose emblem was the 'eye of vigilance' and whose special function was to protect the citizen against abuses of authority. Its subscription of only a penny a month opened the Cordeliers Club to almost everyone and both the style and substance of the speeches there were in striking contrast to the lavish dinners of the 1789 Club and the academic oratory of the Jacobins Not long after the foundation of the Cordeliers, in October 1790, the abbot Fauchet opened to the public his Social Circle, at which a mixture of freemasonry and 'social' Christianity was preached. The Circle's membership ran into several thousands and the public enjoyed free admission to its meetings, where Fauchet expounded his views on Rousseau's *Social Contract*, reprinting his lectures in his newspaper, the *Bouche de Fer*.[1] Fauchet's stress on the social basis of property and insistence on the inadequacy of mere political reform were too much for many of the revolutionary leaders, but they commanded the enthusiastic attention of the poorer citizenry of the neighbouring quarters, whose political education probably owed a good deal to his efforts. Women, who were admitted to the Social Circle, were also able to join the new fraternal and popular societies which began to spring up in 1791, primarily with a view to explaining the course of the Revolution and the

[1] V. Alexev-Popov, 'Le Cercle Social (1790–91)', *Recherches Sovietiques*, 1956.

implications of its legislation to a largely uneducated audience. Through these media the Revolution began to send its roots deep into the lower strata of Parisian society. New leaders began to speak to a new public, with results that were to be seen from 1792 onwards, when the concerted action of the revolutionary people contrasted strikingly with the anarchic violence of 1789.[1]

During the first two years of the Revolution the attempts of the Assembly to create order and confidence were impeded by the bitterness and suspicion of part of the Parisian Press. If Loustalot in the *Révolutions de Paris* maintained a sufficiently moderate tone for Ferrières to send the paper to his wife, Desmoulins and Marat were continually proclaiming their distrust of authority and denouncing counter-revolutionary plots. Although they had probably less influence than they imagined, they must have helped to maintain the hatred and suspicion of 1789 by their—often extremely acute—exposure of the pious fictions of the Assembly, and so long as their papers continued to attract a numerous public the situation in Paris could scarcely be considered settled.

Too much has perhaps been made of the conflicts between Parisian workmen and their employers during this period.[2] In August and September 1789 the tailors, wig-makers and shoe-makers had assembled in turn to try to impose minimum wage-rates. In the case of the tailors the masters had supported their journeymen and the municipality had accepted the new wage-rates. The wig-makers and cobblers were less successful but the municipality was probably more concerned to prevent crowds gathering than to intervene in the labour conflict itself. There appear to have been no further labour disturbances of any importance until the spring of 1791, when plentiful employment encouraged the carpenters to press demands for increased pay. The municipality seems to have sympathized with their claim, even to the extent of allowing their representatives to meet in one of its own buildings, but it declared its inability to mediate and as it came to fear for public order its attitude gradually hardened, although it remained neutral on the basic issue of the conflict. Both masters and journeymen appealed to

[1] On this subject see G. Rudé, *The Crowd in the French Revolution*, chap. xiv.
[2] See G. A. Jaffé, *Le Mouvement Ouvrier à Paris pendant la Révolution Française (1789-91)* (Paris, n.d.).

the Assembly. The deputies had voted to abolish the guilds during the tumultuous session of 4 August 1789, but whether deliberately or not, this decision had been ignored during the drafting debates of the 5th–11th. On 14 June 1791 le Chapelier introduced a Bill to prohibit all forms of association by capital or labour, which was passed with virtually no debate. The deputies were probably thinking in general terms and the guilds were anathema to their liberal doctrines. Had their intention been specifically to benefit the masters there would have been protests from some at least of the Left. Although the immediate result of the law was, in fact, unfavourable to the carpenters, even Marat, who two days previously had published a bitter attack on the master-masons, considered le Chapelier's law to be a purely political instrument for preventing working people from assembling together. Although it would almost certainly be a mistake to regard the new law as a piece of deliberate class legislation, the agitation of May 1791 may perhaps have confirmed some of the deputies in their conviction that it was necessary to bring the Revolution to a halt if the continuing instability were not to lead to that ill-defined 'threat to property' that was always at the back of their minds.

Those who, with whatever reservations, accepted the *status quo* of 1791 were correct in suspecting the existence of a hostile underground movement, although the counter-revolutionaries were scarcely more united than their opponents.[1] From his place of exile in Savoy the comte d'Artois negotiated with the Powers and intrigued with the disaffected in France. The objectives of the numerous *émigrés* who were also trying to stir up discontent were on the whole aristocratic rather than royalist. Their main aim was the restoration of the old social order and they were only incidentally concerned with the future of the monarchy and the fate of the king. They openly prepared for civil war and foreign invasion and urged Louis XVI to take an uncompromising stand in order to force a crisis. This advice was taken up by the king's sister and by the more irresponsible courtiers in Paris whose incautious enthusiasm compromised the plans and even the safety of the royal family. The extreme Right in the

[1] See E. Vingtrinier, *La Contre-révolution, première période, 1789–1791* (Paris, 1924), and J. Godechot, *La Contre-révolution, 1789–1804* (Paris, 1961).

Assembly was more concerned with the defence of royal authority, but the allegiance of many deputies was primarily to the *émigrés* whom they hastened to join at the end of the session. All of them found the king's hesitations, withdrawals and eventual acceptance of revolutionary legislation singularly frustrating. The Powers could scarcely intervene to liberate a monarch who repeatedly proclaimed his freedom of action and acceptance of the Revolution, while the concessions he made were all the time helping to establish the new order more securely. This attitude was clearly demonstrated at the time of Artois' most ambitious plot, that of August 1790, which involved two Ministers and the mayor of Lyons. A major revolt was planned for Lyons, to be supported by local troops and National Guards. The king was to escape from the Tuileries and join the insurgents, who would be reinforced by Artois at the head of a Piedmontese army. The whole scheme collapsed when Louis XVI refused to participate in it and the king went so far as to warn the Powers that Artois had no authority to negotiate on his behalf. Throughout 1790 counter-revolutionary plots kept much of the south in a state of continual unrest.

The king, as always, was not prepared to assume the responsibility for starting a civil war and Marie Antoinette had no intention of finding herself the prisoner of an *émigré* Restoration. In other respects the royal family's views of the situation were a good deal less realistic. The king was determined to make no concessions beyond those of the *Séance Royale* and was not prepared to accept any constitution that did not represent his own free choice. He and Marie Antoinette regarded the extremist politicians of Paris as a mere *canaille* whose neutrality could always be bought in time of need. Their main enemies they thought to be the constitutional monarchists and particularly the liberal nobility, whom the queen denounced to Madame Campan as too guilty for royal pardon.[1] Superficially, the king's confidence of eventually recovering his power was not altogether without justification for, as we have seen, the revolutionary leaders of 1789 had begun to seek a compromise with the Court. But during the autumn of 1790 he appears to have lost confidence in his ability to resume control of the Revolution, perhaps because of the Civil Constitution of the Clergy,

[1] Campan, *Mémoires de la Vie Privée de Marie Antoinette* II. 143.

which imposed a heavy burden on his conscience. From this time onwards he began to seek foreign intervention. It is difficult to say with confidence what his intentions were, for he dabbled with a number of mutually conflicting plans, each concerted with a different group of advisers, but his final aim seems to have been to escape to the protection of Bouillé's army on the north-east frontier in order to force the reluctant Austrian Emperor to intervene on his behalf. Louis would then have posed as the mediator between the revolutionaries and the threatening Austrian invasion and concluded peace with the Emperor in return for the right to amend the constitution to his own satisfaction.

It was some such intention that sent off the royal family on the road to the frontier during the night of 20 June 1791. Their arrest at Varennes was entirely due to the initiative of the local authorities, whose suspicions had been aroused by Bouillé's troop movements. The reaction was spontaneous and decisive. National Guards poured into Varennes to resist any attempt at a rescue by Bouillé. All over France defensive preparations were made. In the north-east itself the king's flight led to a minor repetition of the *Grande Peur*, with some château-burning and the close supervision of strangers and recalcitrant priests. The extent of the king's miscalculation in imagining that he could have mastered the Revolution with the threat of an Austrian army was at once apparent. The flight inevitably compromised, humiliated and discredited Louis XVI, and his situation was the more serious in that he had left behind a proclamation repudiating many of the acts of the Assembly he had previously endorsed with expressions of his devotion to the revolutionary cause. The first reactions of the Assembly showed an efficient self-confidence that impressed even Molleville. Ministers were ordered to execute decrees without the customary royal signature, National Guards were mobilized and the Assembly went into permanent session. Louis XVI had succeeded in demonstrating that the monarchy was no longer indispensable. But when it came to drawing the logical conclusion there was an almost universal reluctance to dethrone the king. The Lameths, Duport and Barnave, who might have been expected to lead the attack on Louis XVI, hoped that the revelation of his weakness and isolation would throw him into their hands, and they had no intention of renouncing the policy of compromise with the monarchy on which they had recently embarked.[1] The danger of an Austrian invasion if the Emperor's brother-in-law were dethroned was an additional motive for caution. But the Parisian populace, urged on by the extremist Press and the popular societies, was impatient of such calculations and demanded the trial and punishment of a king who had deserted his post. The point at issue, itself primarily constitutional, in fact divided Parisian opinion along social lines, with the wealthier and more educated supporting the Assembly in its fiction that the king had been 'kidnapped' and those whom their opponents were beginning to call *sans-culottes* demanding the kind of clear and forceful measures that corresponded to their view of the situation. Inevitably, therefore, the pursuit of a compromise with the king led the Assembly to prepare for conflict with the *sans-culottes*, who were organizing petitions against any hasty rehabilitation of Louis XVI. The Jacobin Club, the home of the Left, was torn apart after it voted to petition the Assembly to dethrone the king. The great majority of the deputies seceded, to form the Feuillant Club, leaving only five or six in the Jacobins.

The Assembly and the municipal authorities of Paris were so active in preparing to suppress popular demonstrations that the radical Press could plausibly accuse them of seeking a pretext for a show of force. On 16th July the Assembly criticized the security measures of the *Hôtel de Ville* and again on the following day instructed Bailly to take firm measures to maintain order. The deputies were understandably nervous in view of the continuous popular agitation that accompanied their debates on the king's fate, but in fact there was no danger of insurrection. When the Jacobins abandoned their petition on the ground that its presentation would be irregular after the Assembly had expressed its intention to maintain Louis XVI on the throne, popular leaders less sensitive to constitutional propriety drafted a petition of their own for the dethronement and trial of the king.[2] The result was a new phenomenon in the history of the Revolution,

[1] See G. Michon, *Essai sur l'Histoire du Parti Feuillant: Adrien Duport* (Paris, 1924), chap. x.

[2] A. Mathiez, *Le Club des Cordeliers pendant la Crise de Varennes et le Massacre du Champ de Mars* (Paris, 1910), and F. Braesch, 'Les Pétitions du Champ de Mars', *Revue Historique*, CXLII–CXLIV (1923).

an organized popular movement whose leaders came not from the educated middle class but from the Cordeliers Club and some of the popular societies. All through the Sunday afternoon of 17th July a peaceful crowd on the Champ de Mars was signing a petition that had been drafted on the spot. The petition itself was destroyed when the *Hôtel de Ville* was burned down in 1871, but Buchez and Roux, who saw the original, maintained that most of the six thousand signatories wrote with difficulty and many were illiterate. The most important names which they identified were of men who were to make their mark in 1792–3, Chaumette, Hébert, Hanriot, Santerre. At the *Hôtel de Ville* the municipality, its nerves probably on edge after days of tension, decided on violent measures, either because it was genuinely convinced that the signature of the petition was degenerating into a riot, or because it was glad of a pretext for a display of force. Martial law was proclaimed, a strong body of National Guards with Bailly at its head marched to the Champ de Mars, was greeted by cat-calls and stone-throwing, and opened fire on the crowd. The actual casualties are unknown, but it seems likely that about fifty people were killed. The municipality, stimulated by the Assembly, which on 18th July passed a ferocious law for the maintenance of order, then embarked on a period of general repression. Martial law remained in force for three weeks and an attempt was made to silence the leaders of the *sans-culottes*. Danton fled to England, Desmoulins and Santerre went into hiding in Paris, Marat's presses were seized, and Vincent and Mororo were arrested, together with scores of obscure citizens and one or two royalist journalists.

The 'massacre' of the Champ de Mars marked the end of the period when it was possible to think of the Revolution in Paris as a united movement against the aristocracy. Bailly, at his trial in 1793, described the agitators of July 1791 as 'the people, above all, those who wanted liberty for all, who were determined that the prestige of the two defeated orders should not be annexed by one section known as the bourgeoisie'.[1] It is significant that this sharp class distinction, which impressed contemporary observers, should have arisen over an issue that had no immediate relevance to social or economic policy. A new

[1] Quoted in Buchez and Roux, *Histoire Parlementaire de la Révolution Française*, XXXI. 102.

line had been drawn in blood between those who were prepared
to make concessions to the ancien régime, to restore order and
end the Revolution and those who were not, and who now
classed the conservative revolutionaries among the enemies of
the nation—and the forces of order had shot and sabred more
men in one day than the Parisian crowds had lynched in the
first two years of the Revolution. In Paris, although not to the
same extent in the provinces, the defence of a largely bourgeois
revolution was already passing into the hands of *sans-culottes*,
while the majority of the bourgeois leaders were now prepared
to offer to the king the concessions they had refused in 1789,
lest they should be pushed towards political democracy and the
social levelling that they expected it to bring. The Champ de
Mars affair both revealed and accelerated this division.

The repression of late July and early August could only
succeed if the constitutional monarchists could come to terms
with the king, isolate the irreconcilable counter-revolutionaries
and put an end to the instability of the past two years. But the
prosecution of those implicated in the events of the 17th served
mainly to discredit the authorities, since the official version of
the day's events was at variance with the facts. It was difficult
for the party of order itself to apply revolutionary methods and
the Assembly rejected proposals to create a special repressive
tribunal. More fundamentally, the conservative revolutionaries
could not risk too open a breach with the *sans-culottes* while the
counter-revolutionary threat remained as serious as ever.
Barnave, Duport and the Lameths therefore made a supreme
effort to come to terms with the king. Louis XVI had been
'suspended' until the constitution was completed. Their plan
was to use the final drafting sessions in order to revise the texts
already voted, in the hope that Louis would realize the futility
of further resistance and would sincerely accept the terms of a
constitution amended in his favour. Barnave and his allies were
prepared to meet the king on many of the points that he had
criticized in the memorandum left behind during his flight, to
restrict the franchise to a wealthy minority, to strengthen the
powers of the monarchy, even to accept the creation of an
Upper House. The *Feuillants* were, in fact, adopting much of the
old programme of the *monarchiens* which they themselves had
helped to defeat in 1789. After two years of revolution and with

religious conflict blazing over much of the country, there was little prospect of their succeeding. The Court, which had nothing to lose by appearing to accept the concessions they offered, urged its partisans to co-operate with the Feuillants. With more sincerity, Malouet concerted his tactics with their leaders. This policy foundered on the opposition of the Right. Molleville, who knew them well, commented, 'It was then the opinion of a great majority of the royalists that the new constitution must necessarily perish through its own defects and that great care should be taken not to reform a single one of them.'[1] On the Left, Robespierre and Pétion, leading the fight against constitutional revision, won unaccustomed support from back-benchers who feared the personal ambition of Barnave and his friends and whose persistent suspicion of the king had been confirmed by his recent flight. The proposals of the *Feuillants* fell between these two stools and they were unable to induce the Assembly to implement more than a fraction of their projects, notably the restriction of the franchise. Even if they had succeeded entirely there is no ground to suppose that they would have appeased the king, the aristocracy and the recalcitrant clergy.

And so the promulgation of the constitution on 13 September 1791 and the amnesty for political prisoners that followed on the 15th, which announced the virtual completion of the work of the Assembly and should have constituted the last acts of the Revolution and the reconquest of national unity, decided nothing. The Parisian crowd demonstrated its feelings by booing the deputies and giving a hero's reception to Robespierre and Pétion. Many of the noble deputies profited from their new freedom to cross the frontier and join the *émigré* army that the prince of Condé was forming in the Rhineland. Provence and Artois wrote to Louis XVI on 10th September that, as monarch, he was not entitled to accept the constitution. Should he do so, they would assume that he had succumbed to intimidation and respect his 'real will' by disregarding his orders—a clear threat to the king that his brothers would not follow him in any policy of compromise.[2] To the deputies the king declared on the 13th, 'I have no longer any doubt as to the will of the people. And so

---

[1] Molleville, *Annals of the French Revolution*, IV. 300.
[2] *Ibid.*, IV. 161–76.

I accept the constitution. I undertake to maintain it at home, to defend it against attack from abroad and to enforce its execution in every way that it puts within my power.' But Marie Antoinette had already written to the Austrian ambassador that the constitution was 'monstrous'. She continued, 'We cannot go on like this. . . . Our only source of help lies with the foreign Powers; at whatever price they must come to our aid'. To her brother, the Emperor, she wrote on 8th September, 'It is for the Emperor to put an end to the disturbances of the French Revolution. Compromise has become impossible. Everything has been overturned by force and force alone can repair the damage'.[1] France was, in fact, more divided than ever and the Revolution was only beginning.

[1] F. Feuillet de Conches, *Louis XVI, Marie Antoinette et Madame Elisabeth, Lettres et Documents Inédits* (Paris, 1864), II. 229–36, 302.

V

<hr>

The Re-shaping of France, 1789–1791

<hr>

Nous avons fait la Révolution pour avoir des jurés.

BOYER-FONFRÈDE

The political record of the Constituent Assembly is not particularly impressive. We have seen it harassed and sometimes paralysed by bitter division. Debates were often rowdy and decisions prompted by the needs of faction. The Right made no attempt to play a constructive rôle as a conservative opposition, while the *Feuillants* found themselves campaigning in 1791 for measures they had defeated in 1789. And yet this same Assembly and its indefatigable committees, when they turned to the reorganization of the structure and institutions of the State, acted with boldness, magnanimity and a surprising amount of agreement. Within two years they transformed the appearance of the country by revolutionary measures that were not merely radical but also lasting.

The pace and survival of reform on this scale implies that the ground had been well prepared before the Assembly met. There had indeed been recurrent attempts at reform throughout the eighteenth century, such as Maupeou's abolition of the parlements and Turgot's fiscal and economic policies. With insignificant exceptions these had foundered on the opposition of vested interests and the immense inertia of the ancien régime. Thanks both to the theoretical writings of the *philosophes* and to more specific works such as Dupaty's advocacy of legal reform, educated men agreed in their rejection of tradition as conferring respect, their conception of a rational order in the State and their appreciation of the need to make French institutions more efficient and more humane. Many of the deputies had themselves published speculative works or plans for the reform of particular institutions. Differences of emphasis, of course, remained, with the Left stressing the equal rights of all and the Right more concerned to preserve order, but in this field even the more acrimonious debates frequently led to conclusions that both sides could accept.

To appreciate the shape taken by the transformation of French society one must constantly bear in mind a duality that underlay the whole process. In intention it consisted of the application of universal and immutable principles for the general good. In practice, while benefiting all classes, it tended to transfer power from the various sections of the aristocracy to the general body of the wealthy and educated, of whom the nobility were only a minority. To ignore the latter aspect would be ingenuous; to disregard the former would be to misunderstand the peculiar nature of the French Revolution. At no time was the expropriation of any social class seriously contemplated. Even the 4th of August decisions were, in more than a merely superficial sense, a renunciation by the privileged. In spite of the occasional punitive decree, such as that abolishing titles of nobility, the Assembly in the main treated the French people as a united family. The ferocious tendencies so common in twentieth-century revolutions did not appear until the complete breakdown of national unity in 1792. Hence the initial emphasis was on humanity: on the more equitable application of less barbarous laws, on equality of opportunity and the abolition of all that was degrading and pauperizing in the ancien régime. This generous impulse, together with the fact that their own livelihood was not seriously threatened, might have enabled the privileged orders to resign themselves to the new society. Had things gone as the Assembly intended, the nobility would have found solid compensation for the loss of its superior status. The compensation paid by the State to holders of offices whose venality was now abolished—which Ferrières set as high as 800 million livres—put a great deal of liquid capital into the hands of the *épée* and the *robe* just as the Church lands were coming on to the market. Had the political situation evolved differently, the result would have been to divide the greater part of the spoils of the Church between the aristocracy and the wealthier members of the middle class and to give both a stake in the Revolution.

The mere fact of compromise restricted what could be done for the poor by limiting the spoils available for re-distribution. Nevertheless the humbler citizens gained a good deal; they, more than the privileged, benefited from relatively impartial and humane justice; some of the burdens on the peasant were abolished without his having to pay any compensation; the town artisan profited from the abolition of the *octrois* and of indirect taxation. But the conciliation of the aristocracy—and, for that matter, of many of the middle class, too—imposed bounds on what could be done for those lower in the social scale. The artisan found himself firmly excluded from political action at either the municipal or the national level, while the peasant remained the economic dependant of the aristocrat who was no longer his seigneur. On the land in particular, it had become apparent by 1791 that there was a contradiction between the hopes held out to all by the Declaration of the Rights of Man and the language of 4th August on the one hand and on the other the acceptance by the Assembly of the sanctity of property, which was interpreted to include all those feudal survivals which had not been specifically abolished.

As early as 29 September 1789 Thouret, in the name of the constitutional committee, submitted to the Assembly a draft scheme for the reorganization of French local government that was to be adopted, with only minor alterations, early in the following year. This project, besides transforming the administrative structure of the country, provided a new framework to which judicial and religious institutions were also adjusted. In local government, as in so much else, the France of 1789 was the heterogeneous product of a conflict of rival forces—tradition, royal absolutism, provincial particularism and the ambition of the parlements. The ensuing 'balance' might have gratified the antiquarian tastes of Montesquieu, but it was a Civil Servant's nightmare. The country was divided into 35 provinces,

33 fiscal *généralités*, each under its intendant, 175 *grands bailliages*, 13 parlements, 38 *gouvernements militaires* and 142 dioceses.[1] There were wide variations from one part of the country to another as regards indirect taxation and internal customs duties. The south, with the inevitable exceptions, observed Roman law, while the north was ruled by a series of medieval 'customs'. For this series of superimposed jig-saw puzzles which it would defy the ingenuity of any cartographer fully to illustrate, the Constituent Assembly substituted a system that was rational, uniform, decentralized and representative. These objectives became the four cardinal points of the compass by which the deputies steered their way through the reform of French institutions as a whole. They were to some extent prompted by tactical considerations: decentralization would deprive the royal Government of the weapons necessary for counter-revolution; the electoral process would replace both the royal agent and the local magnate; a new and uniform division of the territory would break the hold of parlements and provincial Estates. It says a good deal for the insight of the constitutional committee that it should have assessed the situation so clearly and evolved a complete programme of local government within three months of the fall of the Bastille.

France was divided into 83 Departments, each of a roughly similar area judged suitable for an administrative unit. In this way the old provinces were broken up, but the new divisions were far from arbitrary. Each province became one or more Departments, the local deputies in the Assembly were responsible for fixing the new boundaries and a serious attempt was made to ensure that the new Department formed a coherent geographical unit. The Departments naturally varied a good deal in population: the Pyrénées-Orientales had only 114,000, while Lyons raised the population of the Rhône-et-Loire to 579,000. But even this was relatively uniform in comparison with the *bailliages* of the ancien régime which varied from 7,500 to 774,000. Each Department contained a number of Districts, which roughly corresponded in area to the English

[1] See the maps in G. T. Mathews, *The Royal General Farms in Eighteenth Century France*, and *French Government and Society* (ed. Wallace-Hadrill and McManners, 1957).

'hundreds', and the lowest administrative unit was the Commune, a centre of population that could be a hamlet, a provincial market town, or Paris itself. The Department was intended to be the principal unit, to which the District was subordinated, while the 44,000 Communes confined themselves exclusively to village or municipal affairs. Commune, District and Department were each administered by an elected council.

This forced the Assembly to face the problem of the franchise. With little immediate protest from the Left, it was decided that the vote should be restricted to men over 25 who paid in direct taxation the local equivalent of three days' wages. Historians have perhaps been unduly critical of the Constituent's rejection of universal suffrage. It was estimated that roughly four and a half million 'active' citizens were enfranchised and the heads of most families were probably entitled to vote. By comparison with any other country in Europe the provision was generous indeed. The officers of the Commune were chosen directly by all the active citizens and could therefore claim to represent the opinion of a considerable proportion of the local population. The fact that in the Paris elections of October 1790 less than 5 per cent of the electorate took the trouble to vote suggests that the extension of the franchise to all adult males might not have made much difference. More significant than the level of the franchise itself was the fact that elections to the District, the Departmental and the national assemblies were indirect. The active citizens gathered in primary assemblies where one man per hundred was chosen to act as an elector, and it was these electors whose choice filled the higher posts. The qualification for an elector was originally fixed at the payment of direct taxes to the local value of ten days' wages. This was perhaps less restrictive than appears at first sight, for in Lyons at least the value of a day's wage was set at the artificially low figure of 10 sous, which made 4,450 eligible as electors.[1] When the Constitution was revised in the summer of 1791 the *Feuillant* leaders induced the deputies to impose much more severe qualifications that would have excluded all but the very wealthy. But this revision is of primarily theoretical interest, since the elections to the new National Assembly had already taken place and the new conditions were to be swept away with the Constitution itself

[1] J. Jaurès, *Histoire Socialiste*, I. 406.

in the summer of 1792. Of more lasting importance was the fact that the poorer citizens could rarely afford the time to attend election meetings that often lasted over several days in a town that might be some distance from their homes.

The new system represented an extreme reaction from the centralization of the ancien régime, for there was no effective link between the Government in Paris and the elected local bodies. Although the latter were instructed to enforce the law and not to interpret it, a Departmental council with strong local support enjoyed a fair amount of autonomy, while a powerful Commune—notably that of Paris—could largely disregard the will of the Department. There was nothing in this curtailment of the powers of the Central Government that need offend an aristocracy whose main complaint in the years before the Revolution had been against 'ministerial despotism'. More serious, from the viewpoint of the nobility, was the exclusive reliance on the electoral process and the predominant rôle played by the towns, for indirect election tended to favour the urban bourgeoisie at the expense of the countryside. On the whole the nobility does not seem to have taken a leading part in local government, although in some towns such as Bordeaux liberal nobles sat beside merchants, lawyers and shipowners.[1] But if the middle-class townsmen tended to take over the administration of the country this did not imply either a uniform political trend or a victory for radicalism. The political alignment of the town councils varied, with Lyons conservative and even royalist, while Nantes looked more towards the sans-culottes. In general the Departments were in the hands of the wealthy bourgeois, constitutional monarchists alarmed at the trend of events in Paris in the early summer of 1791 and hoping for a rapprochement with the king and the nobility. The Communes were often more radical, and the villages in the hands of the seigneur's enemies, but even these village councillors were for the most part substantial farmers whose natural inclination to uphold the rights of property was tempered only by their determination to evade their feudal obligations.[2]

[1] The British Embassy's report of 19 February 1790 that two-thirds of the recently-elected mayors came from noble families seems improbable. (*Despatches from Paris, 1784–90*, p. 293.)

[2] See, for example, G. Lefebvre, *Les Paysans du Nord pendant la Révolution Française* pp. 374–92.

One important result of the new administrative system was to initiate the whole community into the practice of self-government and to provide a substantial proportion with experience in administration. At least half a million—or roughly one active citizen in eight—must have held some elected local office. Such training was invaluable to men without previous political experience. At the highest level it enabled ambitious bourgeois politicians to establish the local reputation that was eventually to secure their election to the Convention in 1792. Three future members of the Committee of Public Safety, Couthon, Robert Lindet and Jeanbon Saint-André, began their political careers in this way, together with many others who were also to make their mark, such as Levasseur and Le Bas amongst the Montagnards and the Girondins Guadet, Vergniaud and Rebecqui. At a lower level, village and town politics brought forward their own local leaders and this political apprenticeship made possible the highly-organized Revolutionary Government of 1793.

This reorganization of French local government was also lasting. The Departments and Communes are still there, their boundaries and subdivisions corresponding, with minor exceptions, to those drawn up in 1789–90. The whole emphasis of the system was admittedly transformed by the introduction of the Napoleonic prefect, who restored the primacy of the Central Government, but the actual administrative map of France has not been subsequently re-drawn.

Much more ephemeral was the Constitution of 1791, swept away by the insurrection of 10 August 1792 before it could leave any lasting impress on the country.[1] Typical of the preoccupations of the deputies was the system of representation which showed that the concept of a unified democracy was still in the future. Each Department was to have three seats in the Assembly—apart from Paris, which had one—in recognition of its separate entity; 249 more seats were distributed among the Departments in proportion to population and an equal number in proportion to the assessment of the Departments for direct taxation. Since the last two criteria tended to reinforce each other the result combined an element of federalism with an emphasis on the more urban and highly-developed

[1] For text see Thompson, *French Revolution Documents*, pp. 109–47.

areas. Contemporaries were probably less impressed by the details of the Constitution and its omissions than by the majestic edifice as a whole, with the Declaration of the Rights of Man as its solemn preamble, constituting a triumphant proclamation of eighteenth-century faith in men's ability to govern themselves by the light of reason.

Perhaps the greatest glory of the Constituent Assembly was its reform of the legal system which prompted the cautious Seligman to write: 'The history of deliberating assemblies offers few examples of an effort so majestically sustained.'[1] In this field also the Assembly inherited a chaotic situation. Royal and seigneurial courts overlapped and many departments of Government had their own tribunals. There was no uniform system of civil or criminal law. Judicial frontiers were ill defined, confusion endemic and the possibility of appeal from one court to another almost endless. Criminal cases were tried in secret by judges applying mechanical rules as to what constituted legal proof, and punishments were ferocious and degrading. As always in the ancien régime, privilege was the key to exceptional treatment and sometimes conferred virtual immunity from prosecution.[2]

Here the Assembly found itself in relative agreement on principles. There was no serious attempt to defend either the *status quo* as a whole or the vested interests of particular bodies such as the parlements. Here also the remarkable quality of the deputies had a chance to make itself felt, for the Constituent Assembly included the flower of the legal talent of France. Young lawyers with bold schemes for reform, such as Duport, who was 30 in 1789, men of established reputation drawing on a lifetime's experience, like Thouret and Tronchet in their fifties and sixties, men from every quarter of the legal field, from le Pelletier, *président à mortier* of the Paris parlement, to obscure provincial barristers like Robespierre, all had something to offer. Political enmities were set aside, as when Duport and Robespierre fought their great losing battle for the abolition of

---

[1] On this subject see E. Seligman, *La Justice en France pendant la Révolution* (Paris, 1913), and G. Michon, *L'Histoire du Parti Feuillant: Adrien Duport* (Paris, 1924).

[2] See, for example, the chapter *scandales judiciaires* in H. Carré, *La Noblesse de France et l'Opinion Publique au Dix-huitième Siècle*.

the death penalty, and the legal debates tended to bring out the best in them all—it was Robespierre himself who declared that it was better to release a hundred guilty men than to punish one innocent. Duport caught the mood of the Assembly when he said, 'Let us make haste while we are still in our political youth, while the fire of liberty still burns within us and our holy and generous enthusiasm still endures.'

Thus emboldened, the Assembly began by making a clean sweep of the entire judicial labyrinth: parlements, *bailliages*, feudal courts and special tribunals. With them perished the venality of judicial offices. The Declaration of the Rights of Man outlawed the *lettre de cachet* and introduced the principles of *habeas corpus*. The new courts were based on a simple and uniform organization and were meant to discourage litigation rather than to prolong it. Civil cases had to begin before a *bureau de conciliation* which tried to induce the parties to settle their differences out of court. There was to be a justice of the peace in each Canton, or electoral district (each Section in the case of Paris), and a civil court in each District. Appeal was possible from one District court to another—the Assembly feared that a more hierarchical system might set up new parlements—while a central *cour de cassation* could order re-trials on procedural grounds. Criminal justice began with the justice of the peace who referred the more serious cases to the criminal court of the Department, from whose verdict there was no appeal.

True to its faith in the merits of the elective process and the virtues of the common man, the Assembly also decided that all judges and public prosecutors were to be elected and that criminal cases should be tried by a jury, in fact, by two juries, one to decide whether there was a case for putting the accused on trial and the second to pronounce on his guilt. Duport and Robespierre fought hard for the extension of trial by jury to civil cases, but the majority of legal opinion in the Assembly was against them. The deputies' concern for the protection of innocence was paralleled by their humane approach to guilt. Punishment was viewed as corrective rather than vindictive, penalties were reduced, branding abolished, the death sentence reserved for a small number of the most serious crimes and the barbarity of breaking on the wheel replaced by the machine whose warm recommendation by one of the Paris deputies, Dr. Guillotin, was to provide it with its famous name.

The new system of justice met with no serious opposition. The seigneurs appear to have acquiesced in the extinction of their courts and the few parlements that tried to protest against their own abolition, notably Rennes, and with more moderation, Paris, Rouen, Metz and Dijon, found that public indifference or hostility left them completely helpless. How far the new courts implied a change of personnel is a question that admits of no confident answer at present. Practice probably varied a good deal from one Department to another. The six civil courts in Paris were supplied with judges drawn in the main from the more outstanding lawyers of the Assembly, of all shades of political opinion. At Agen seven of the nine judges elected had held posts in the local royal court, while at nearby Nérac all the royal officers were displaced by the clientele of the local deputy. The Paris bar, though officially abolished, reconstituted itself on an informal basis, and in general experience probably counted for as much as revolutionary sympathies. There was an obvious danger of political justice, in a time of major social upheaval, but the new men were little disposed to countenance threats to order or property, even if the immediate victims happened to be their political opponents, and there was certainly nothing approaching a judicial 'Terror' before 1792. According to Seligman, the compensation paid by the State to those who had previously bought judicial offices amounted to no less than 450 million livres. It would be most interesting to know how the beneficiaries disposed of this considerable capital. It seems likely that a good deal of it, especially since it was paid in *assignats*, was used for the purchase of secularized Church property. It may well be that this accelerated the trend for the successful lawyer to become a country gentleman alongside the old territorial nobility.

But questions of this nature should not blind us to the general social consequences of the legal reforms. France now had a judicial system that compared favourably with any in Europe for economy, impartiality and humanity. The seigneur had lost what judicial influence he still retained in 1789 and the process of election ensured that the countryside would not be dominated by a justice of the peace who was also the local squire and greatest employer of labour. The propertied classes might grumble at the meticulous caution of a legal process ill adapted to the maintenance of order in times of social tension, but the new judges and juries took their responsibilities seriously and appear on the whole to have given honest verdicts and reasonable sentences.

One aspect of the reconstruction of France of particular concern to the aristocracy was the future of the armed forces. Of the 9,578 army officers in 1789, 6,633 were noble, together with nearly a thousand in the navy.[1] Now that the Civil Constitution of the Clergy had deprived the aristocracy of its monopoly of the higher posts in the Church, the armed forces offered the only 'honourable' career left open to them—for the prejudice against trade, shared by nobility and commoners alike, could not be terminated by decree of the Assembly. For precisely this same reason the educated bourgeois were especially determined to force this particular Bastille of privilege. In the case of the army, the danger to the aristocracy of being swamped by bourgeois numbers was long-term rather than immediate, for the intruders would presumably have to start at the bottom and the accelerated promotion of *roturier* officers already in the lower ranks would take some time to transform the character of the service as a whole. But the navy was confronted by a rival, in the form of the merchant service, whose captains considered themselves as competent at handling a ship under sail as the proud officers of the *Grand Corps* who had for so long humiliated them. Their objective was to reduce to a minimum the peacetime establishment of the royal navy so that they themselves could take over the quarter-deck and the captain's cabin on the outbreak of war. The nobility were therefore faced by a serious threat to both their careers and to the prestige of the sword if the Assembly should carry its work of levelling into the armed forces.

The army had been considerably improved towards the end

---

[1] On the army see Spenser Wilkinson, *The French Army before Napoleon* (Oxford, 1915), and E. G. Léonard, *L'Armée et ses Problèmes au Dix-huitième Siècle* (Paris, 1958); on the navy, M. Leclère, 'Les Réformes de Castries', *Revue des Questions Historiques*, CXXVIII (1937), and N. Hampson, *La Marine de l'An II* (Paris, 1959), and 'The Comité de Marine of the Constituent Assembly', *The Historical Journal*, II (1959).

of the ancien régime, especially by the Army Council, set up in 1787 with Guibert, the revolutionary tactician, as its secretary. The drill book, finally revised in 1791, remained in force until 1830 and Gribeauval's artillery went unchanged through the Revolutionary and Napoleonic wars. The Council continued the work of Saint Germain, intended to benefit the poorer provincial gentry by the gradual abolition of purchase and the establishment of military training colleges in the provinces. The elimination of superfluous officers brought the total down from 35,000 to below 10,000. France now had the makings of a powerful army, but the Army Council had actually aggravated the main source of weakness, the monopoly of the highest ranks by the *noblesse de cour*. Only the pillars of Versailles society could aspire to the highest posts. Below them lay the frustrated majority of provincials, themselves struggling to keep down the *roturiers* and those who had been promoted from the ranks. The Revolution was therefore welcomed by many of the gentry who hoped that the defeat of the *noblesse de cour* would open the way to their own promotion. Several of the leading generals of 1792-3, such as Kellermann, Wimpfen, Dillon, and Dumouriez himself, belonged to this class, which had already manifested its disloyalty to the Government by its mutinous behaviour in 1787-9.

On the whole the minor nobility in the army had little cause for dissatisfaction with the work of the Assembly. The abolition of purchase probably did something to console them for the opening of the officer corps to commoners. In September 1790 it was decreed that one-quarter of the sub-lieutenants were to be promoted from the ranks and the remainder chosen by a competitive examination—in which the children of military families ought to have been able to hold their own. In January of the following year the number of staff officers was reduced from 216 to 34, but there was no attempt at any general purge of the army, the great majority of whose officers remained noble. The fact that the provincial gentry do appear to have bitterly resented the ending of their officially privileged position in the army and the abolition of noble rank itself, in June 1790, suggests that they were more interested in social status than in the actual benefits it conferred.

As regards the rank and file, the most notable intervention of the Assembly was the abolition of the hated militia which had been drawn almost entirely from the peasantry. Dubois-Crancé's plea for national conscription was rejected and the regular army was still recruited by voluntary enlistment. For the time being the militia was not replaced, but the National Guard provided a semi-military police force which was used to reinforce troops in dealing with civil disturbances and could form a reserve in the event of war.

The situation in the navy was in some ways similar, excellent equipment and training being offset by social divisions between the officers. Since the Court nobility tended to neglect the naval service the conflict within the aristocracy was less marked, but a minority of commoners, mostly prevented from rising above the rank of sub-lieutenant, resented the privileges granted to birth, while both groups despised the merchant navy and hoped to keep the two services apart.

The naval committee of the Constituent Assembly, which originally included five serving or retired naval officers out of a total membership of twelve, was at first paralysed by internal division. When the balance within the committee had been altered in favour of the revolutionaries its proposals for reform provoked bitter conflicts on the floor of the Assembly. It was generally agreed to open the navy to all classes of society, but the Right fought strenuously to prevent the creation of a hybrid service whose officers would pass from merchantmen to ships of the line in time of war. This conflict between the advocates of a purely fighting service and the supporters of a mixed navy amounted, in fact, to a social struggle between the nobility and the seafaring bourgeoisie. In the end the former succeeded in persuading a majority of the Assembly that the virtues of a professional navy outweighed other considerations, and the rules of promotion were drawn up in such a way as to prevent easy transfers from the merchant service. As in the case of the army, the existing officers were retained, with the exception of staff officers unfit for active service. In order to avoid flooding the navy with officers of relatively advanced years, 600 of the 840 sub-lieutenants were retired on two-thirds pay with the incongruous result that the service in 1791 contained an appreciably higher proportion of aristocratic officers than it had done in 1789!

The seamen, who were conscripted for service in wartime only, were granted the dangerous right to elect their own *syndics* or mobilizing officers, in accordance with the principle that free men could only be expected to obey officials they had helped to choose. The same concern to treat the seamen as citizens led to the promulgation of a naval penal code which granted them the privilege of trial by jury. The retention of some cruel and humiliating punishments in the new code provoked a mutiny in the Brest fleet in 1790 which eventually obtained their abolition.

It is therefore quite erroneous to pretend that the Constituent Assembly sacrificed the interests of national defence to the ambitions of an impatient bourgeoisie. The armed forces remained predominantly aristocratic and it would have taken many years before the right of *roturiers* to compete for admission would have seriously affected the social composition of the officer corps. That the change was, in fact, much more rapid was due to the collapse of national unity rather than to the conscious intention of the Assembly. From 1789 onwards discipline in the armed forces tended to break down. Regiments disobeyed their officers and crews mutinied. In the ports the naval authorities frequently found themselves at loggerheads with the new municipalities. The natural reaction of the deputies would have been to intervene on the side of the officers—the debate on the naval penal code showed how remote these educated gentlemen were from the world of the lower deck—but they suspected, with good reason, that the officers were mostly royalists. Motives of self-preservation therefore led them to exonerate their lower-deck supporters. The officers tended to come to the conclusion of the Commander-in-Chief Ashore at Brest, that 'One cannot exercise authority without compromising one's self', and they began to leave the services in considerable numbers, either to retire or to escape to Artois's caricature of a Court at Coblentz, where purchase was restored, the provincial gentry kept in their places and the reforms of the last years of the ancien régime abolished, or to the much more serious army that the veteran Condé was raising at Worms. The more officers emigrated the more the Assembly tended to suspect those that remained. After Varennes a new oath of loyalty was imposed, from which the king's name had disappeared. This was refused by 1,500 army officers, and by the end of 1791, 3,500—more than half of the total of noble officers in 1789—had left.[1] The situation in the navy was much the same: in March 1792 almost half of the lieutenants and captains had officially resigned, while many of those whose names were still on the active list had, in fact, disappeared. The cautious reforms of the Assembly were therefore overtaken by the growing political conflict. The aristocracy was not evicted from the armed forces; most of the noble officers chose to leave a cause which their consciences no longer allowed them to support, and the social transformation of the officer corps was a by-product of the general division of society as a whole.

During the period 1789-91 French society was also affected by a deliberate transfer of wealth. The two most important aspects of this process were the sale of Church property and the execution of the decisions of the 4th of August. An examination of the motives of the deputies and of the results of their actions reinforces the conviction that their objective was compromise rather than social revolution.

The social repercussions of the sale of Church property, particularly land, depended on the conditions of sale. Here the Assembly was in a dilemma. Thouret, Delley d'Agier and the philanthropic duc de La Rochefoucauld all stressed the need to use this opportunity to spread the ownership of land by selling the Church estates in small lots for low prices and on deferred terms. On the other hand, the whole object of the sale was to rescue the State finances from the bankruptcy of the ancien régime, which logically implied getting the highest price possible and enforcing prompt payment. Many deputies were also sceptical of the economic wisdom of splitting large holdings into a number of small plots. The result of these conflicting pressures was a series of compromises and the frequent changes in the conditions for the sale of Church lands offer quite a good guide to the changing moods of the various Assemblies.[2] The first decree of 14 May 1790, offered terms reasonably favourable to the poorer classes: 12 per cent of the purchase price was

[1] Spenser Wilkinson, *op. cit.*, pp. 115–20.
[2] See M. Garaud, *Histoire Générale du Droit Privé Français (de 1789 à 1804); la Révolution et la Propriété Foncière*, pp. 313–26.

to be paid at once and the remainder, with interest at 5 per cent, over a period of 12 years.[1] Municipalities were also to divide the lots as far as practicable—a vague recommendation that left plenty of scope for local interpretation. On the other hand, sales were to be by auction—which meant high prices—and at the administrative centre of the District—which made it difficult for the poorer peasants to attend them.

Garaud has estimated that the property of the Church was worth roughly three milliard livres. The reserve price on land was fixed at twenty-two times the annual rent, by contemporary standards a low estimate, especially since the State redeemed all feudal burdens to which the Church lands were subject. However, the auctions generally realized prices well above the original valuation. The famous vineyard of the Clos Vougeot, for example, was assessed at 395,472 livres, but realized 643,710. An analysis of over half of the sales in the Côte d'Or shows an average sale price 63 per cent above the original estimate, and arable land in the Rhône department is said to have realized three and a half times the reserve price.[2] Prices naturally varied in accordance with the amounts available— Church lands were much more extensive in the north than in the south—the proximity of large towns with a wealthy bour- geois clientele, and other factors, but the sales were well sup- ported all over France, even in areas like the Vendée that were later to become centres of religious civil war. In Paris half of the Church property was sold in 1791, in the district of Stras- bourg one-third, and in the Nord two-thirds had been alienated by 1793. From the viewpoint of the State the return depended not so much on the price paid as on the speed of payment, for the steep decline of the assignat was to allow of the cheap repay- ment of the later instalments in debased currency. Lefebvre's conclusion, based on his exhaustive examination of the records of the Nord, was that the majority of purchasers completed their payment too soon to profit very much from the fall in the assignat —which possibly implies that they possessed substantial capital.[3]

[1] The figures quoted apply to land only; those for buildings were somewhat less favourable to the buyer.
[2] See A. Vialay, *La Vente des Biens Nationaux pendant la Révolution Française* (Paris, 1908), pp. 102–51, and M. Marion, *La Vente des Biens Nationaux pendant la Révolution* (Paris, 1908), *passim.*
[3] Lefebvre, *op. cit.*, p. 461.

Even so, he estimates that the State did not recover more than one-half to one-sixth of the real value of the Church property. In general, therefore, one may say that an exceptional opportunity was offered to those with capital available to buy property, and particularly land, well below its market price.

The social consequences of this vast transfer of property can more conveniently be discussed later, so as to take into account the sale of the *émigré* estates as well as those of the clergy.[1] It is sufficient here to indicate that all classes participated. The nobility were not averse from joining in the expropriation of the Church and, as we have seen, they and the upper middle class often possessed ready capital in the form of compensation for offices. Middle-class purchasers tended to acquire the greatest area of land, though the peasants were the most numerous buyers. By the end of 1791 the sale of Church property had not produced anything resembling a major social revolution. It had, if anything, reinforced existing class distinctions as regards land ownership while at the same time increasing the holdings of individuals at all levels of the social scale.

The poorer peasant farmer, who could not afford to bid for Church lands, was much more concerned with the fate of the feudal burdens affecting the land that he already owned, rented or sharecropped.[2] The Assembly had declared in August 1789 that it 'entirely abolished the feudal régime', and the peasants were only too ready to interpret this bold preamble at its face value. But the lawyers of the Constituent Assembly, and notably Merlin de Douai and Tronchet, who presided over the two sub-committees charged with implementing this aspect of the decrees of 4th August, assumed that established usage implied legal ownership. Merlin, who was responsible for defining the difference between the 'personal' dues abolished without compensation, and those concerning land ownership, which

[1] See below, chap. x.
[2] See P. Sagnac, *La Législation Civile de la Révolution Française* (Paris, 1898), pp. 92–138; P. Sagnac and P. Caron, *Les Comités des Droits Féodaux et de Législation et l'Abolition du Régime Féodal* (Paris, 1907), *passim*; A. Aulard, *La Révolution Française et le Régime Féodal* (Paris, 1919), pp. 152–206; Garaud, *op. cit.*, pp. 168–209.

were preserved, found himself faced with intractable borderline cases where payments in cash or kind could be interpreted as representing the commutation of personal servitudes at some distant period in the past. He tried to cut this Gordian knot by the assumption that dues associated with a past transfer of land represented a legitimate form of property. Since the actual origin of the majority of these dues was unknown, everything turned on the onus of proof—which neither side would normally be able to provide. Merlin induced the Assembly to decide in favour of the seigneur, who was guaranteed in the possession of many of his ancient rights, except in the most improbable event of the peasant being able to prove that these had not been originally associated with a transfer of property. In default of the original charter it was further decreed that proof of forty years' exercise by the seigneur would be regarded as constituting a valid title. In consequence, while all peasants found themselves relieved of some burdens, such as the abuse of hunting rights, and a minority were freed from the relics of personal servitude, the great majority found themselves still liable to the full onus of the heaviest obligations. The Assembly demonstrated in other ways its support for landlords, whether noble or *roturier*. When tithes were abolished in 1790 it was specifically stated that their value could be added to rents. In 1791 mining rights were transferred to the landowner, the State being merely authorized to intervene if he refused to exploit them. The *droit de triage* by which the seigneur could, in certain circumstances, enforce the division of common lands, taking one-third for himself, was admittedly abolished in 1790, but common lands were not to be restored unless partitioned within the previous 30 years and in violation of the original ordinance of 1669.

The main burdens on the peasant were therefore maintained and Tronchet's sub-committee which determined the conditions of their buying out *(rachat)* returned him as dusty an answer as Merlin had done. Not merely was the rate of compensation fixed at twenty times the annual payment in cash or twenty-five times the payment in kind, but all *droits casuels*—the exceptional payments incurred from time to time, for example when land was bought or sold—had to be redeemed at the same time as the *droits fixes*, and in the case of holdings that shared common dues, the redemption of all had to take place at the same time. A concession was made in November 1790, when the separate *rachat* of the *droits casuels* was authorized, but the terms were still too high for the majority of peasants to contemplate. A man who owed one-third of the value of his harvest to the seigneur would have to find the cash equivalent of seven or eight years' entire harvests to redeem the *droits fixes* alone. Anyone with sufficient capital to do so would probably have been better advised to invest in Church lands, free of all feudal burdens. In consequence, *rachats* were comparatively few and the majority of those that took place were effected by nobles and bourgeois. So far as the law was concerned, the majority of peasants were not very much better off than they had been before the Revolution.

In these circumstances there were bound to be some who would profit from the disturbed state of the country by simply refusing to pay. In the Lot-et-Garonne at the end of 1790 a regular peasant army took the field insisting that those nobles who claimed the continued payment of their dues should produce the original titles proving an actual transfer of land.[1] How far this resistance was general and to what extent it was effective are still controversial questions. It is clear that practice varied from one part of the country to another and that nowhere were payments either entirely suspended or completely honoured, but it is not at all obvious on which side the emphasis should be placed. Lefebvre, basing his views to some extent on the Nord, stressed the effectiveness of peasant resistance.[2] In this Department the yield of the tithe fell in 1790, although the 1789 harvest had been appreciably better than that of 1788. Lefebvre maintained that few dues were paid to the seigneurs, that the State did not press its claims in the case of the Church lands that it was administering and that in some villages the peasants illegally divided up the common lands. Aulard, on the contrary, maintained, 'that payment was the rule, non-payment the exception—a frequent, indeed a very frequent exception, but nevertheless an exception'.[3] He stressed the transfer in

---

[1] See J. Viguier, 'Les émeutes populaires dans le Quercy en 1789 et 1790', *Révolution Française*, XXI (1891).
[2] Lefebvre, *op. cit.*, pp. 379–92.
[3] Aulard, *op. cit.*, pp. 191, 210–41.

December 1790 from the local authorities to the State of
responsibility for the collection of dues owing on Church lands
as an indication that their enforcement was seriously intended,
quoted the fact that many examples are known of the *rachat* of
feudal dues belonging to the State and suggested that the
peasants found it less easy to intimidate or bargain with the
representatives of the nation than with the individual seigneur.
The correspondence between the great landowner, Cossé-
Brissac, and his intendant hints that the increasingly conservative attitude of the Assembly in 1791 encouraged the latter to
press more forcefully for the recovery of the dues owing to his
employer. This correspondence serves as a useful reminder that
the question is not merely whether certain dues were paid in
1789–91 or not. Arrears in payment were common under the
ancien régime and seigneurs who thought it prudent to ignore
defaulters while the countryside was in a state of unrest had no
intention of renouncing either their future claims or the back-
payments owing to them. There can be no doubt as to the state
of mind of the peasantry, bitterly disappointed at the evapora-
tion of the hopes raised by the decrees of 4th August, whether
they paid and grumbled or refused and trembled or revolted.
The Assembly was bombarded with reproaches, of which the
following, from the active citizens of the commune of Puivert
(Bouches-du-Rhône) on 20 January 1792 is typical: 'We
thought, after the decree suppressing the feudal régime, that
we were as free in our property as in our persons; two years'
experience has shown us that we are slaves. We have no
seigneur any more—he is at Coblentz; he has left us his agent
and *fermier* who badger and persecute us just as they did before
the Revolution. The *ci-devant* is only our creditor now, but he
has exchanged the rôle of noble for that of an inexorable liti-
gant: unless you come to our help we are ruined.' [1]

The lawyers of the Constituent Assembly, far from destroying the 'feudal' basis of the economic power of the nobility, had
gone far to endow it with the sanctity conferred by an elected
parliament. In so far as there was an antithesis between the
appeasement of the peasantry and the conciliation of the landed
gentry, the Assembly opted for the latter, leaving the mass of
the rural population a potential reservoir of revolutionary energy.

[1] Quoted in Sagnac and Caron, *op. cit.*, pp. 295–6.

Such burdens as had not been lifted—and they formed by far
the greater part—seemed more firmly settled on the shoulders
of the peasantry. It was frequently possible to defy the law, but
not without risk, and the bolder spirits must have wondered
uneasily what the future held in store for them when the
transient disturbances of the Revolution should have given way
to a more settled order.

The everyday life of the country was less affected by the first
years of the Revolution than might have been expected. There
was perhaps a tendency for the aristocracy to leave their exposed
châteaux for the relative security of the towns. Few towns
escaped some sort of disturbance, but this was normally of short
duration and the period was one of insecurity rather than of
continuing disorder. In Paris itself the life of the Court in the
palace-prison of the Tuileries was no more than a shadow of
what it had been at Versailles, but one has only to glance at the
diary of Gouverneur Morris, the United States ambassador, to
see the salons continuing uninterrupted, with the political situation as much a source of new conversational interest as of personal alarm. The aristocracy obviously—too obviously—hoped
that the Revolution was nothing more than a storm to be
weathered. Marie Antoinette expected to awake from her
nightmare when the faithful commons should turn against the
handful of intriguers who had misled them. In the meantime
there remained the theatre and the opera—which Ferrières was
describing to his wife about the time that the king and queen
left for Varennes. In fact, of course, profound and irreversible
changes had already taken place and this was no more than the
Indian Summer of Talleyrand's famous 'douceur de vivre'. But to
contemporaries, who could not foresee the path that the Revolution was so soon to take, the structure of French society did not
seem to have changed very much, except where the Church was
concerned. It was not any social transformation effected by the
Constituent Assembly that split the nation in two, but the fact
that the monarchy and the aristocracy refused to consider as
more than temporary concessions such changes as were made.
Beyond the frontiers Artois and Provence claimed to represent
the real will of the king, while Condé's camp attracted the
growing nucleus of an aristocratic army of liberation. At home
the resistance of a large part of the clergy was inclining a

reluctant but imperious Assembly towards punitive measures that would drive the vacillating king to implore his fellow monarchs to come to his rescue. Both sides were soon to turn to foreign war as a means of resolving the political deadlock and with the outbreak of war the Revolution would be forced into new and strange courses and such national cohesion as remained in 1791 would perish in the conflict.

VI

◇◇

The Turning-Point

◇◇

La guerre révolutionna la Révolution.

M. REINHARD

T H E most obvious contrast between the Legislative Assembly, which began its session on 1 October 1791, and the Constituent Assembly it replaced was that the clergy and nobility no longer enjoyed separate representation. Their numbers dropped to rather more than a score from each group, and those elected had presumably given proof of their attachment to the new order. The makers of the constitution had, by a self-denying ordinance, excluded themselves from the new Assembly, all of whose members were therefore inexperienced in parliamentary affairs. Of the 745 deputies, over two-thirds came from local government or were judges and magistrates in the new courts. The Doubs, for example, drew its entire parliamentary team from the *directoire* of the Department and all but one of the Seine-et-Marne deputies came from local government bodies.[1] Socially, this perhaps indicated a slight swing away from the notabilities of 1789 in favour of younger men who had used the Revolution as a means to a political career and built up a local following. But once again the overwhelming majority were

[1] A. Kuscinski, *Les Députés à l'Assemblée Législative de 1791* (Paris, 1900), *passim.*

132

drawn from the educated middle class, with the lawyers more conspicuous than farmers and merchants.

The mood of the new deputies seemed in favour of conciliation, for 264 at once joined the Feuillant Club and another 70 followed them within a couple of months. The Jacobins began with no more than 136 deputies, including only 5 of the Paris deputation of 24, and the sympathies of those who joined neither club were perhaps more likely to lie with the Right than with the Left. This predominance of moderate deputies was, however, offset by the fact that the most talented members of the Assembly came from its Left wing, notably from those who were to become known as Girondins.[1] The nucleus of this group, as its name implied, came from the Gironde. Vergniaud, Guadet, and Gensonné were Bordeaux lawyers and Ducos was the son of a wealthy business man. These able young men—Vergniaud, at 38, was the oldest, and Ducos was only 26—had come to Paris to exercise on the national stage the capacity for political leadership of which their local successes had convinced them. Associated with them was a man of a very different stamp, Brissot, the editor of the *Patriote Français*. Brissot's varied career, which had included a debtor's gaol in England as well as the Bastille, had at one time brought him into the employment of the duc d'Orléans. He impressed his contemporaries by his activity rather than by proof of firm political convictions. There could be no doubt as to his ambition, but his previous record inspired little confidence in either his disinterestedness or his ability to subordinate his impulsive temperament to the requirements of statesmanship. The third element in the loose agglomeration of the Girondins was centred round the salon of Madame Roland, the ambitious wife of an elderly and self-righteous Civil Servant. Madame Roland, fired with the vision of transforming France into a modern replica of the ancient Rome that filled her impassioned imagination, was debarred by her sex from taking any direct part in politics, but her salon served her as a kind of personal club.

Of varying temperament and activated by different and sometimes conflicting motives, the Girondin leaders never formed a homogeneous group, nor did their followers ever constitute a political party in the modern sense. But in the autumn

[1] See M. J. Sydenham, *The Girondins* (1961), *passim*.

of 1791 they were sufficiently in agreement to induce the Assembly to attack the opponents of the Revolution in the hope of forcing the king to declare himself openly on one side or the other. This onslaught on the *émigré* nobility and the refractory clergy was conceived in such violent terms as to put an end to the fiction of national unity. In the summer of 1791 Madame Roland had written that a civil war would be 'a great school of public virtue. Peace will set us back . . . we can be regenerated through blood alone.'[1] The Girondin deputies in the Legislative Assembly seem on the whole to have shared her conviction that the division of French society was too deep for conciliation and that the safety of the revolutionary cause demanded the violent destruction of its opponents.

On the religious question they were soon made aware that they were confronted not by small and isolated minorities but by dangerous popular movements. The Assembly had been in session for less than a fortnight when, on 10 October 1791, Gensonné and another deputy reported that the 'non-juror' priests in the Vendée and the Deux-Sèvres enjoyed massive local support. When the Department of the Deux-Sèvres ordered all recalcitrant priests to leave the District of Châtillon the 56 Communes in the District offered to pay double taxation if they might keep their priests. Both sides were using the ominously political terms of *patriote* and *aristocrate* to denote religious allegiance. Early in November new disturbances were reported from the Maine-et-Loire, with armed bands reopening churches and terrorizing the local authorities, and there was a serious riot in Caen, also due to religious differences. On 14th November the violent Isnard stressed the need for the Assembly to destroy its enemies if it was not to dishearten its supporters. 'Your policy should aim at forcing the victory of one side. Caution is merely weakness. The bravest are the best and an excess of firmness is the safeguard of success. We must amputate the gangrened limb to save the rest of the body.' On 29th November the Assembly voted repressive measures against the refractory clergy. When these were vetoed by the king the conflict between legislature and executive became obvious and the prospect of any reunification of the nation under the new constitutional monarchy began to recede.

[1] *Lettres de Madame Roland* (ed. Perroud, Paris, 1902), II. 313.

In the meantime the Assembly had been confronted by a second problem, that of the *émigré* nobility assembling in arms across the frontier in preparation for a legitimist crusade of liberation. Here the issues were somewhat different, since all shades of opinion, including the king, were virtually unanimous in condemning this open appeal to civil war.[1] Nevertheless, when the Assembly debated the question of the *émigrés*, the Girondins, by the violence of their attack, gave the impression that they were more concerned to score a political victory than to induce the *émigrés* to return. Brissot insisted on the need for concentrating on the leaders—the king's brothers—which, he asserted, would force the king's Ministers to declare themselves for or against the Revolution. This was perhaps the first manifestation of the tactical plan of the Girondins: by exacerbating revolutionary divisions, to bring down the Ministers and force on the king a Girondin Ministry that would reduce him to a mere figurehead. On 30th October Isnard supported Brissot with his customary passion. Isnard's justification of popular excesses—'the long impunity enjoyed by important criminals is what has turned the people into executioners'—was one that the Girondins had cause to regret in the following year. On 8th November the Assembly passed a ferocious decree stipulating that all *émigrés* who remained assembled after 1st January were to be sentenced to death and their property sequestrated. The king once again ordered the princes and the humbler *émigrés* to return. Once more his brothers refused to obey. Louis XVI, with that readiness to sacrifice the interests of the Crown to pressure from the aristocracy which had imprisoned him in sterile opposition to the Revolution since 1789, then vetoed the decree of the Assembly, thereby giving the erroneous impression that his sympathies were on the side of the *émigrés*.

The two issues of the refractory priests and the *émigrés* were soon to be dwarfed by a third question which was to dominate the subsequent course of the whole Revolution—the outbreak of war. In the mind of Brissot, who can almost be regarded as personally responsible for the war, an attack on the Habsburg Emperor was essentially another means towards hastening the climax of the Revolution and forcing the king to capitulate to the

[1] See, for example, Ferrières, *Correspondance Inédite*, p. 425; Malouet, *Mémoires*, II. 195.

Girondins. A bellicose foreign policy seemed to him the logical complement to the proscription of the *émigrés*, since the latter depended on foreign support for their military preparations. He succeeded in convincing himself that a successful campaign would solve most of the problems of the revolutionaries. Victory would consolidate the assignat and bring back commercial prosperity. He declared in the Jacobin Club on 12th December that France needed war 'to purge her of the vices of despotism. Do you wish at one blow to destroy the aristocracy, the refractory priests, the malcontents: destroy Coblentz. The head of the nation will [then] be forced to reign through the constitution.' The irrepressible Isnard, prophesying a victorious crusade, had already asserted that war would force the Ministers to choose between a policy of which the public approved and the vengeance of the law.

The Court, after some hesitation, took up the gauntlet and Marie Antoinette worked to ensure that the Emperor and the King of Prussia would seize on any French ultimatum to the Elector of Trier as a *casus belli* authorizing the invasion of France and the restoration of royal power by the only force in which the queen had confidence. Even Lafayette and his supporters, although they had no wish to precipitate a final trial of strength between the Court and the revolutionaries, accepted the idea of a limited war in the hope that they would be able to use the armed forces under their command to impose their own settlement on the extremists of both sides.

For Barnave and the Feuillants the war was an unmitigated disaster, since it ended any hopes they might still have entertained of consolidating the precarious constitutional monarchy. But by the end of 1791 they had come to realize that the Court was paying no attention to their advice, while Girondin war propaganda had destroyed what influence they retained over public opinion. The Lameths left Paris for the army, Barnave retired to Dauphiné in January 1792 and the Feuillant Party was left leaderless and impotent. The strongest opposition to the war came not from them but from an unexpected quarter. As the Court's acceptance of war became more obvious, some of the members of the Jacobin Club became suspicious of a policy that enjoyed the queen's support. Gradually this attitude hardened into a conviction that the war policy was a trap designed by the Court.

Those who shared this suspicion, notably Robespierre, Billaud-Varenne, Couthon, Desmoulins, and Danton, all prominent members of the Jacobin Club, were, however, unable to make much of an impression on their fellow members. Apart from the difficulty of resisting the growing tide of public opinion, urged on by the Girondin Press, the Montagnards, as this opposition group was later to be called, were in a difficult situation, since they assumed that war would in any case be declared by the Emperor and the King of Prussia. Their destructive analysis of Girondin policy, in which Robespierre excelled, lost much of its effect when they themselves could offer not peace but merely the prospect of a defensive war fought on French soil. In these circumstances the partisans of war were able to brush aside all opposition and on 20 April 1792 Louis XVI, with the almost unanimous support of the Assembly, declared war on the Emperor, who was soon joined by his Prussian ally.

Royalists and revolutionaries therefore combined to launch, as an instrument of domestic policy, a war that was to last, almost without interruption, for twenty-three years. From the outset the war simplified all issues and eliminated all nuances. Henceforth the struggle lay between those who, with whatever reservations, wished for the restoration of royal authority at the price of the defeat of France, and those whose attachment to the Revolution led them to make whatever concessions might be the price of military victory. The war therefore imposed new divisions that tore families, friends and colleagues apart, besides adding a new depth of bitterness and hatred to a conflict in which each side regarded the other as traitors.

The division amongst the conservatives can be illustrated by the example of Ferrières and Malouet, both constitutional monarchists and moderates by temperament as well as conviction. Malouet, who had condemned the attack on the constitution from the Right, now affirmed that the king had a right to call on the support of his Austrian ally.[1] Ferrières took the opposite view, 'I will never agree to introduce a foreign army into France. If there were a civil war between the two parties, that would be different; but I could never consider an invasion, flooding my country with Germans, Hungarians, Spaniards,

[1] Malouet, op. cit., II. 227.

without being seized by a feeling of horror for men who could contemplate such a crime, and if I had to choose, it would be against them, and not against my country and my fellow citizens.'[1] And so the commoner fled to England in August 1792, while the marquis passed the Terror keeping the minutes of the municipal assembly in the Commune where his château still stood. The war was the watershed of the Revolution and many who had stood close together in 1791 found themselves estranged by a barrier of hatred and proscription within the next few years.

More unexpected was the violent division on the Left, which was to prove scarcely less enduring. Girondins and Montagnards were revolutionaries of similar temperament, social origin and political conviction. What separated them in the winter of 1791–2 was essentially a question of political, almost of military tactics. But each side convinced itself that the other was an agent of counter-revolution and so were engendered the hatreds that were to lead most of the leaders to the scaffold. For these men, too, this was the parting of the ways, and it was the war that determined their subsequent political attitudes. The Jacobin Club was paralysed by the violence of their dissensions. The tone of debates fell to a new level of personal abuse, with the Montagnard, Chabot, alleging that the wife of his opponent, Condorcet, had been seduced by the War Minister, Narbonne. The Girondins replied in kind and for a time the revolutionary forces seemed to have been reduced to a deadlock. When Girondin nominees took over three of the Ministries in March 1792 and the Girondins called for loyal support for generals such as Lafayette, in whom they themselves had little confidence, Marat replied by urging the troops to assassinate their leaders.

The future was to reveal another consequence of the war, as yet unsuspected, that was to leave a profound impression on the Revolution. The French forces, crippled by the indiscipline of the troops and the desertion of many of their officers, were in no condition to repel an invasion. The defence of France therefore rested on popular levies who would make up in numbers and enthusiasm for what they lacked in training and discipline. The Government weakened by the decentralization of the constitution and revolutionary upheavals, was in no position to obtain the necessary numbers by a policy of ruthless conscription

[1] Ferrières, *op. cit.*, p. 429.

and would have to rely, in part at least, on volunteers. The latter were unlikely to be forthcoming in sufficient numbers from the peasantry or the middle class. The defence of the Revolution during the critical first phase of the war would therefore rest largely in the hands of the urban working population, the *sans-culottes*. As early as June 1791, during the Varennes crisis, when it had been necessary to allow 'passive' citizens, i.e. those not entitled to the vote, to enroll as auxiliaries in order to swell the number of National Guards volunteering for service with the regular army, the Parisian District of Saint-Étienne-du-Mont had provided four auxiliaries for every bourgeois guardsman.[1] In September 1792, when the Section *Bon Conseil* was enrolling volunteers for the defence of Paris against the Prussians, nearly two-thirds of the 300 men raised were artisans and most of the remainder shopkeepers and minor office-workers, while the middle classes were represented by two surgeons' apprentices and two architects.[2]

The *sans-culottes*, who were henceforth to occupy a central position in the Revolution, are not easily defined. The word had political as well as economic connotations and could be assumed, as a revolutionary *titre de noblesse*, by men like the wealthy brewer, Santerre. On the whole, however, the general feeling was that the *sans-culottes* were poor. Pétion, defining the term in April 1793, said, 'It means the have-nots (*les hommes qui n'ont pas*) as distinct from the haves.' The *sans-culotte*, unlike the gentleman, had had no classical education. His speeches were often rhetorical and he liked to throw in such classical allusions as had come to him at second hand, but his education was of a rudimentary character. He usually worked with his hands as an artisan, kept a shop, or was employed in some minor clerical post. The *sans-culottes* formed the mass of the population of all the great cities of France, between the wealthy bourgeoisie and the small proletariat whose struggle for physical survival left it little time or energy to spare for politics.[3] The *sans-culottes*

[1] Jaurès, *Histoire Socialiste*, II. 1159.

[2] C. L. Chassin and L. Hennet, *Les Volontaires Nationaux pendant la Révolution* (Paris, 1899), I. 390–413.

[3] On the Parisian sans-culottes see F. Braesch, *La Commune du 10 Août* (Paris, 1911), pp. 4–25; A. Soboul, *Les Sans-culottes Parisiens en l'An II* (Paris, 1958), pp. 407–681; and G. Rudé, *The Crowd in the French Revolution*, pp. 12–20. Much information on the provincial sans-culottes is to be found in R. Cobb, *Les Armées Révolutionnaires* (2 vol., Paris, 1961–3).

did not form an economic class. Shopkeepers, especially those selling food, were suspicious of economic controls and insistent on the protection of property. Master-craftsmen might have more radical views on both these subjects but were more conservative on the question of wages and strike action by their journeymen. This social and economic diversity was at first a source of strength to the *sans-culottes* since it enabled the more politically educated, such as the master-craftsman who could afford to buy the newspapers of Marat or Hébert, to influence the men in his workshop and sometimes to carry them with him to a meeting of his Section or to a political demonstration. One of the most surprising aspects of the Revolution is the speed with which political news and slogans filtered down in this way to a large audience, many of whom were probably illiterate.[1]

The *sans-culottes* brought to their politics the attitudes and experience of their own environment. They were straightforward men, accustomed to rough living and brutal treatment by authority, used to planning on a short-term basis, and advocates of simple solutions. It appeared natural to them that those denounced as enemies of the Revolution should be promptly exterminated. If many nobles were counter-revolutionaries, it would be as well to exclude the aristocracy as a whole from army commissions. If the good *sans-culotte* brought up a large family of young patriots, then the constitutional clergy should set an example by themselves marrying. At once credulous and suspicious, they tended to see everything in black and white, to accept the verdicts of the revolutionary tribunal as the voice of impartial justice and to believe any rumour against a man who had fallen from popular favour. The *sans-culottes* also differed from bourgeois politicians in that they could not afford to view price fluctuations with the detachment of an Adam Smith. Faced with a sudden rise in prices, they demanded a scapegoat and a prompt remedy, and arguments of economic orthodoxy carried little weight against their own privations and the suffering of their families.[2]

The political force of the *sans-culottes* was considerable, but

---

[1] For a discussion of this subject see Rudé, *op. cit.*, pp. 210–32.

[2] See R. Cobb, 'The revolutionary mentality in France, 1793–94', *History*, XLII (1957), 181, and 'Quelques aspects de la mentalité révolutionnaire', *Revue d'Histoire Moderne et Contemporaine*, VI (1959), 81.

their range was limited by the fact that the greater part of their time was devoted to earning their living. Hitherto they had provided little more than a chorus to the revolutionary actors, intervening only on rare occasions, as in July 1789 and at the Champ de Mars. The enfranchisement of the passive citizens in August 1792 was to throw open to them the Sections of Paris and other important towns—local assemblies, meeting in the evening, where they could intervene on their own ground, in the presence of men of their own kind, when the working day was over, and by their resolutions bring pressure to bear on the municipality, and, in the case of Paris, on the Assembly in their midst.

Whatever they might choose to say for the benefit of the galleries, none of the bourgeois politicians, with the partial exception of Marat, was anxious to be forced into dependence on such redoubtable allies. But the declaration of war raised the question of whether the politicians would be able to defend the Revolution without relying on the *sans-culottes*. If they could not, what concessions would be necessary to enlist *sans-culotte* support under bourgeois leadership, and would the humbler partners be content with such a subordinate rôle, or would they claim the right—which Rousseauist democrats would find it hard to deny them—to dictate the policies whose execution depended primarily on their own exertions?

Already, during the winter and early spring serious disturbances in many parts of northern France had given a foretaste of what peasant and *sans-culotte* demands were going to involve. Petitions to the Assembly requested that it be declared illegal to sell grain except on the open market and that public granaries be built to store the surplus product of good harvests for release in bad times. One deputy, Forfait, of le Havre, proposed the creation of a central food commission with power to supervise the internal grain trade. There was a widespread agrarian revolt in the countryside around Paris and in the rich corn-growing plain of the Beauce. Groups of up to 8,000 peasants and rural artisans invaded the town markets, imposed their own prices on everything offered for sale and announced their intention of reducing rents. Farther south, in the Lot, some of the common lands were divided by the peasants on their own initiative. The townsmen in the area of the agrarian revolt tended to remain aloof, if they were not actually hostile to the movement, but the towns had their own problems. When the price of sugar suddenly doubled in Paris, probably as a result of speculation by the wholesalers, the Sections demanded that the Assembly should pass a law against hoarding. To the *sans-culottes* those who tried to profit from the national emergency were as much enemies of the people as declared counter-revolutionaries. Indeed, they were only too ready to assume that the wealthy merchants who were trying to play the market were, in fact, hoping to starve them into surrender or provoke them into an attack on the revolutionary order.

From this suspicion it was only one step to the assertion that the war and the revolution had put the whole country under a state of siege and that private property must yield to the common interest. The social and economic theories of the *sans-culottes* sprang directly from their personal experience, and were not to evolve far beyond the form they took in 1792. Dolivier, a parish priest at Etampes, where the mayor had been murdered during the recent agrarian revolt, came to Paris with a petition in defence of his parishioners.[1] This petition stated bluntly that 'the nation alone is the real owner of its land'. The natural right of the poor to earn a livelihood conflicted with the legal right of the owners of property—i.e. food—to dispose of it as they wished. This conflict, Dolivier explained, was due to a 'great error' which it was still too dangerous to mention, but which he clearly insinuated was the maintenance of absolute property rights. In a personal note attached to the petition, Dolivier defended the imposition of price controls on wheat and asserted that since the owners of property depended on the protection of society, property itself was a social institution rather than a matter of natural right. Jaurès saw in Dolivier's petition 'the great socialist light . . . already making its presence known across the distant plains, lighting the far horizon with a scarcely visible, perhaps deceptive glow.' [2] More prosaically, Mathiez commented that Dolivier was doing no more than claiming on behalf of the nation the economic sovereignty that the monarchs of the ancien régime had been accustomed to assert for

---

[1] See A. Mathiez, *La Vie Chère et le Mouvement Social sous la Terreur*, pp. 71–76.
[2] Jaurès, *op. cit.*, II. 1099.

themselves, and was, in fact, demanding no more than State control of the grain trade in times of scarcity.[1] Nevertheless, Dolivier quoted Rousseau in his support and his principle that the enjoyment of property rights was subordinate to the interest of society as a whole was capable of endless developments, none of them congenial to a middle class which looked to the Revolution to free property from the restraints of the ancien régime.

The reaction of the revolutionary politicians to the wave of peasant and *sans-culotte* agitation indicated both their realization of the need for popular support and their preoccupation with political objectives. In an open letter to Buzot, Pétion, the mayor of Paris, wrote on 6 February 1792 that the bourgeoisie was drawing away from the people and, afraid that the Revolution was degenerating into a war of the 'have-nots' against the 'haves', was trying to come to terms with the aristocracy. It was typical of Pétion that he should have been content to assert the need for re-forming the 'popular front' of 1789 without any analysis of what this would entail. Robespierre, dealing with the Dolivier petition in his newspaper, did at least admit the existence of a social problem, but he failed to reproduce the more revolutionary parts of the petition, and after dismissing the Aunt Sallies of equal distribution and collective ownership of property as absurdities, he hastened to switch the debate to more congenial moral grounds with the comforting reflection that 'riches which entail so much corruption are more harmful to those who possess them than to those deprived of them'. This was unlikely to impress the *sans-culottes*, who would have preferred to make the experiment for themselves. The Montagnards seemed unable to realize that such remarks, and their scornful slogan at the time of the sugar shortage that revolutionaries were not interested in 'bonbons', could only infuriate those who were less preoccupied with 'riches' than with not going hungry.

The majority of the Assembly was more concerned to safeguard property than to conciliate the peasants. Couthon's proposal on 29th February that in contested cases of feudal obligations the onus of proof should be on the seigneur, met with no success. The suggestion of the *comité féodal* on 11th April that seigneurs should be required to provide proof of their right to *droits casuels* encountered strong opposition and was carried only

[1] Mathiez, *op. cit.*, p. 74.

by astute parliamentary manoeuvring on 16th June. Danton's proposal in the Jacobin Club that the incidence of taxation should be altered to transfer some of the burden from the poor, met with no response in the Assembly. Where property and taxation were concerned, the deputies were still defending conservative positions that had been outflanked by the collapse of the forces of compromise on the political and religious fronts.

In the provinces the counter-revolutionaries prepared to profit from the allied invasion; their opponents took the law into their own hands and anarchy threatened. Marseilles struck a blow for the Revolution by sending a column of National Guards to occupy royalist Arles. This defeat of the counter-revolutionaries in the lower Rhône valley set off a wave of château-burning in the Gard. But a little farther north a royalist insurrection broke out in the Ardèche, where the comte de Saillans, in the name of the *émigré* princes, ordered the arrest of local councillors, magistrates and members of revolutionary clubs. Another rising in Brittany was dispersed by the National Guards of Quimper. It was not surprising if the revolutionaries assumed that these were merely the first sparks of a conflagration timed to coincide with the allied invasion. In the summer, particularly after the proclamation of a state of emergency (*la patrie en danger*) on 11th July, local authorities increasingly took the initiative in disarming suspects and disregarded the royal veto on a second Bill against the refractory clergy. Over half of the Departments ordered the arrest of such priests, a few were murdered and it was clear that events were moving towards a crisis.

The Girondins, who had been the prime agents in setting in motion this chain of events, were determined to use the crisis in order to seat the Revolution, as personified by themselves, in positions of command. In March they brought down the Ministry by the impeachment of the Foreign Minister, Delessart, and under the dubious leadership of the adventurer Dumouriez, obtained the ministries of the Interior and Finance for their own nominees, Roland and Clavière. The king, however, was far from disarmed. In June he vetoed two Bills, one against the refractory clergy and the other for the formation of a camp near Paris of 20,000 National Guards from the provinces. When Roland replied with a threatening letter repeating the Girondin *leitmotif* that the king must choose between the Revolution and its enemies, Louis XVI on 12th June dismissed the Girondin ministers. The Girondins then patched up a truce with their Montagnard opponents and the united Jacobin Club began to harry the royal Government. On 20th June an armed demonstration invaded the Tuileries and seemed about to lynch the royal family. The king, whose passive courage was at its best on such an occasion, put on the red cap of liberty—an emblem recently introduced by the Girondins as the symbol of revolutionary patriotism—and drank to the health of the nation, but refused to withdraw his two vetoes. The crowd eventually retired and the indignity to which the royal family had been exposed led to a movement of sympathy in their favour. The fiasco of 20th June won a little time for the Court, but could not avert a more decisive trial of strength which was now only a matter of weeks.

The actual timing of the crisis was largely determined by the military situation. About 28th July news began to reach Paris of the manifesto published at the request of Marie Antoinette by the Prussian Commander-in-Chief, the Duke of Brunswick. This manifesto declared the Parisian population responsible for the safety of the royal family and announced that National Guards who resisted the approaching Prussian army would be treated as *francs-tireurs*. As a weapon of intimidation it was a complete failure, but the warning that the allies did not intend to treat their opponents according to the laws of war was not lost upon the revolutionaries, who replied with attempts to incite a 'class war' of 'people' against nobility within the enemy's ranks. From the outset it was clear that the conventions of eighteenth-century warfare were likely to go by the board. Moreover, the threat to the whole revolutionary order prevented that consolidation of conservative propertied interests which had dominated Paris a year before. In so far as the wealthy had invested in the spoils of the Church they tended to prefer the hazards of the Revolution to the risk of expropriation by the victorious *émigrés*, and for that, too, the war was responsible.

Evading the royal veto on an armed camp, the Assembly had invited National Guards from the provinces, on their way to the front, to come to Paris, ostensibly for the 14th of July celebrations. These *fédérés* tended to have more radical views than the deputies who had invited them, and by mid-July they were petitioning the Assembly to dethrone the king. The *fédérés* were reluctant to leave Paris before a decisive blow had been struck, and the arrival on 25th July of 300 from Brest and five days later of 500 Marseillais, the victors over the counter-revolution at Arles, who made the streets of Paris echo with the song to which they gave their name, provided the revolutionaries with a formidable force of shock troops.

In Paris itself the Court felt, not without some cause, that it had a reasonable prospect of averting or repelling the threatening attack and holding out until the arrival of the Prussians. By bribery on an unprecedented scale it hoped to buy the neutrality of the *sans-culotte* leaders whom it regarded as mere rabble-rousers. It was also encouraged by the Girondins, who committed a tactical mistake that was to have momentous consequences. About the middle of July, Vergniaud, Brissot, and Guadet tried to repeat their manoeuvre of March and force the king to accept a Girondin Ministry. Once negotiations with the Court were opened, the Girondins tried to suspend 'agitation that serves no purpose'.[1] Brissot, who had justified the war as a means of bringing the Revolution to a climax, now maintained that a military crisis was no time to overthrow the monarchy or change the constitution. They therefore worked, in the Assembly and in Paris, to avert an armed uprising. The Montagnards, who suffered from no such secret inhibitions, were nevertheless hesitant, either because they feared that an insurrection would fail or because they had no desire to transfer power to an Assembly which they regarded as scarcely more trustworthy than the Government.

The initiative therefore lay with the Parisian *sans-culottes* in the 48 Sections into which the city was divided.[2] Some of these Sections had welcomed the *fédérés* and offered them hospitality. From 25th July onwards they were in permanent session and about the same time two of the more radical of them, *Théâtre Français* (which included the Cordelier Club) and *Croix Rouge*,

---

[1] Lasource in the Jacobin Club, 29 July 1792.
[2] For a survey of the political attitudes of the Sections see Braesch, *op. cit.*, pp. 162–72.

began admitting 'passive' citizens. Sections and *fédérés* had each their central committee and it was these bodies that appear to have organized the coming insurrection. On 31st July *Mauconseil* at a crowded meeting with about 600 present, voted that it no longer recognized the king and intended to march on the Assembly on the following Sunday, 5th August. The radical Section *Quinze-Vingts*, of the Faubourg Saint-Antoine, on 3rd August invited the other 47 Sections to join it in an armed march on the Assembly on the 5th. Pétion, who, as mayor, was mainly concerned to avoid committing himself in advance to what might turn out to be the losing side, induced the *Quinze-Vingts* to give the Assembly until 11 p.m. on 9th August to dethrone the king. Court and Sections prepared for battle. The garrison of Swiss Guards at the Tuileries was reinforced and strengthened by several hundred volunteers from the gentry. The Assembly, which found itself in the uneasy position of umpire, by a vote of 406 to 224 on 8th August acquitted Lafayette, who had returned from the front in July to threaten the deputies, and closed its session on 9th August without taking any decision on the fate of the king. At once the *fédérés* and the National Guards mobilized, while deputies from the Sections occupied the *Hôtel de Ville*, expelled the councillors and installed themselves as the Insurrectionary Commune. On the morning of 10th August the insurgent forces marched on the Tuileries, whence the royal family fled to the protection of the Assembly. After a moment when it appeared that the Swiss Guards might fraternize with the revolutionaries, fighting broke out and the insurgents, massed in the courtyard, suffered heavy casualties. They were not to forget what they assumed to have been an ambush and henceforth the Swiss were the objects of violent hatred on the part of the *sans-culottes*. When, after considerable fighting, the revolutionaries were winning the upper hand, the king ordered his forces to cease fire, with the result that many of them were massacred by the insurgents. The capture of the Tuileries had been a very different affair from the taking of the Bastille in 1789. *Fédérés* and National Guards had lost 376 killed and wounded, while the casualties on the royal side were estimated at about 800. By the afternoon the palace had fallen, but the future of the monarchy was still undecided, the *sans-culottes* felt that their work

had merely begun and that their dead were still unavenged.[1]
With the fall of the Tuileries the face of Parisian society
underwent an abrupt change. So long as the constitutional
monarchy had remained in being the social life of the salons had
continued. Now the United States Ambassador, Gouverneur
Morris, found his foreign colleagues withdrawn by their
Governments and his aristocratic French acquaintances lying
low. With the city gates closed, men like Malouet went into
hiding and the prisons filled with what was left of the liberal
nobility.[2] Agents of the Commune requisitioned for the army
such carriage-horses as still appeared in the streets. For the
Parisian nobility it was 10 August 1792 rather than 14 July
1789 that marked the end of the ancien régime.

The August insurrection greatly increased *sans-culotte* influence in Paris. Whereas the old Commune had been predominantly middle class, the new one contained twice as many artisans
as lawyers—and the latter were often obscure men, very different
from the brilliant barristers of 1789. Moreover, the Commune
itself was little more than 'a sort of federal parliament in a
federal republic of 48 states'.[3] It had only a tenuous control over
the Sections, which began practising the direct democracy of
Rousseau. 'Passive' citizens were admitted to meetings, justices
of the peace and police officers dismissed and the *assemblée
générale* of the Section became, in some cases, a 'people's court',
while a new *comité de surveillance* hunted down counter-
revolutionaries.

The impact of events on the Assembly was almost as striking.
Over half of its members fled and on the evening of 10th August
only 284 deputies were in their seats. Relieved of a conservative
majority, hostile ministers and a royal veto, the Girondins tried
to reap the harvest that others had sown. Their own nominees
took over all the ministries with the exception of Justice, which
went to Danton. They had the king suspended and voted the
immediate election of a sovereign Convention, to be chosen by
universal male suffrage, that would decide on the future
organization of the State. The Girondins were now free to

---

[1] Almost all the casualties on the revolutionary side were *sans-culottes*; see
Rudé, *op. cit.*, pp. 105–6.
[2] For Malouet's account of his own escape, see *Mémoires*, II. 237–48.
[3] Braesch, *op. cit.*, pp. 236–71, 294–9, 282.

implement their own radical programme. On 18th August the deportation of all refractory priests was ordered. A number of measures in favour of the peasantry culminated in the decree of 25th August, perhaps the most important in the whole chain of feudal legislation. All dues owed to seigneurs were abolished without compensation unless the beneficiaries could produce their original titles. The social motive of the legislators was made quite clear by their exclusion of 'individuals who were neither seigneurs nor owners of fiefs'. The intention of the Assembly was perhaps to strike at the aristocracy rather than to liberate the peasantry, but the one implied the other. Communities such as the city of Bordeaux could sometimes produce their charters, but the great majority of seigneurs were less fortunate. The main demands of the peasantry had now been met in full. Punitive legislation against the *émigrés* allowed the Assembly to go even farther. *Émigré* property had been put under State control in April and its alienation voted on 27th July, but effective action was impossible so long as the king remained on his throne. On 14th August François de Neufchâteau observed that 'the sale of *émigré* property offers a means of binding the country people to the Revolution' and induced the Assembly to vote terms of sale primarily directed to this end. The detailed Bill presented by Goujon on 30th August provided that the *émigré*'s parents were to have the usufruct, and his children the ownership of a proportion of his property that was not to exceed one-quarter. The remainder was to be divided into lots of not more than four acres and alienated to tenants who offered a perpetual rent in preference to those who wished to buy outright. When this Bill was given a final reading on 2nd September an unknown deputy, perhaps profiting from the fact that the Assembly's attention was distracted by events in Paris, introduced significant changes: purchasers were to have priority over prospective tenants and the maximum of four acres was replaced by the vague provision that local authorities were to ensure that *émigré* property was 'divided as usefully as possible into small lots'. Even thus diluted, however, the new law threw a vast amount of property on to the market and the peasants were to obtain a substantial proportion of the spoils.[1]

[1] On the sale of *émigré* property see below, chap. x.

Marat had told the poor in his newspaper that they would never obtain any benefit from the Revolution except as the sequel to an outbreak of violence. It was, in fact, the repudiation of the fiction of national unity personified by the constitutional monarchy that made possible such concessions to the peasantry at the expense of their seigneurs. But the Girondins were not to be allowed to reap all the political profit from these operations. At a time when they were helping to implement social legislation of such magnitude they must have found it particularly galling to be attacked by the Commune as conservatives and crypto-royalists.

To some extent the Commune's hostility was the inevitable result of the Girondin attempt to forestall the insurrection of 10th August. Of more importance was the fact that it reflected a conflict of political temperament that was to last as long as the active rôle of the *sans-culottes* in the Revolution. The Commune demanded immediate and decisive action: the dethronement of the king and the punishment by a special tribunal of those who had fought on his side. The Assembly, moved both by constitutional principle and by *bienséance*, declared itself unable to do more than suspend Louis, and wished to house the royal family provisionally in the Tuileries. The special court, reluctantly created on 17th August, after Robespierre, in the name of the Commune, had threatened the deputies that 'the people are resting but they are not asleep', proved so merciful as to convince the *sans-culottes* that they had been cheated. Petitions for the execution of those who exchanged assignats for specie and for the punishment of financial speculators and hoarders of metallic currency reflected the *sans-culotte* assumption that there was a prompt political remedy for every economic problem. The Assembly's refusal to comply was the automatic reaction of gentlemen who had read the works of the liberal economists.

The conflict was, in the main, one of ministerial caution against the anarchic forces of popular enthusiasm; a question of manner, almost of manners, rather than of principle. The rump of the Assembly had no objection to the adoption of the equalitarian—and Roman—'citizen' in the place of the 'monsieur' that was all that remained of the old hierarchy of forms of address. The deputies had no pity for the 'non-juror' clergy and little patience with the *constitutionnels*, but the *sans-culottes* and their spokesmen took up anti-clericalism with a vigour that threatened the survival of any Christian Church at all. Manuel had the *rue Sainte-Anne* renamed *rue Helvétius* and the Section Montreuil declared its support for the marriage of one of its priests. To the uneducated *sectionnaires* clerical marriage was no more than the assertion of an obvious human right and a demonstration of the alliance between a reformed Church and a revolutionary State. They could not understand that such an assumption of total popular sovereignty deprived the constitutional bishops of any control over matters spiritual and was bound to alienate many Catholics who put their religion before their genuine revolutionary sympathies.

The Assembly, which even in eclipse retained some *amour propre*, resented the hectoring tone and the almost open threats of the frequent deputations from the Commune. Men who were subsequently to become eminent Montagnards, such as Cambon, Choudieu, and Thuriot, joined in the protest against a Commune which 'disorganizes everything, is always in the way . . . wants to overturn everything'.[1] Truncated and discredited as it was, some tatters of national sovereignty still dignified the Assembly. Towards the end of August it began to react against dictation from Paris and the Commune was thrown on the defensive.[2] This conflict of authority, which tended for the moment to preoccupy and paralyse both authorities, coincided disastrously with a sudden sharp deterioration in the military situation.

As if to remind the revolutionaries that the insurrection of 10th August had, in fact, decided nothing, the Prussian army crossed the French frontier on the 16th. A week later the powerful fortress of Longwy fell so quickly that Vergniaud declared it to have been handed over to the enemy. By the end of the month the Prussians were at Verdun, the last fortress barring the road to Paris, and in the capital there was a well-justified belief that Verdun, too, would offer no more than a token resistance. The war, which had appeared to bring the triumph of the Revolution, now seemed likely to lead it to disaster. The Commune and the Council of Ministers under the

---

[1] Choudieu, 30 August 1792.
[2] Braesch, *op. cit.*, pp. 431–5.

leadership of Danton began feverishly preparing a last-ditch defence of Paris. On 29th August household searches for arms and suspects were carried out throughout the city, bringing popular apprehension to a new level of excitement. Had the revolutionaries been able to read Fersen's letter of the same day—'Barnave and Charles Lameth are arrested and I hope they will be executed; no one has merited it more than they'—they would have been confirmed in their suspicions of the treatment they might expect from royalists who had so little pity for their own discarded allies.[1] While the prisons filled with suspects the main preoccupation of the Commune was to obtain an army of volunteers for the defence of Paris—no easy matter, since previous appeals after Varennes and in June 1792 had drawn off most of the likely candidates. The municipal authorities dramatized the situation in order to work on the popular imagination. On 2nd September the alarm gun was fired and drums beat the citizens to their Sections. The walls of Paris were plastered with recruiting posters whose opening sentence, 'To arms, citizens, the enemy is at our gates!' was taken literally by many readers. In the Assembly, Danton concluded the most famous of all his speeches: *'De l'audace, encore de l'audace, toujours de l'audace, et la France est sauvée!'* Once more the *sans-culottes* responded and in the next three weeks, 20,000 marched from Paris for the defence of the Revolution.

Meanwhile the city streets echoed with the sinister rumour of a plot by the imprisoned counter-revolutionaries to escape at the head of a murderous band of common-law prisoners, profit from the absence of the *sans-culotte* warriors and seize Paris until the Prussians should arrive. The obvious conclusion was drawn by the placards of Marat calling for the massacre of these enemies of the Revolution. Some of the Sections, notably *Poissonnière*, *Luxembourg* and perhaps *Arcis*, also advocated a prison massacre on 2nd September, while more moderate Sections contented themselves with proposals for the conscription of tepid revolutionaries and financiers and the imposition of special taxation on the rich.[2] It seems likely that the Commune's *comité de surveillance*, reorganized on the 2nd to

---

[1] Jaurès, *op. cit.*, III. 47.

[2] Braesch, *op. cit.*, pp. 480 *et seq.*; P. Caron, *Les Massacres de Septembre* (Paris, 1935), *passim*.

include Marat, had prepared for a prison massacre and perhaps set it in motion.

On the afternoon and evening of 2nd September *sans-culotte* bands began investing the prisons and butchering their occupants. The Commune, unable or unwilling to intervene, contented itself with organizing rudimentary 'courts' which saved many lives. The attempts of the Assembly to stop the massacres by the despatch of popular deputies to reason with the crowds were brushed aside. The *septembriseurs* who carried out this dreadful work were not criminals or sadists but ordinary *sans-culottes*, convinced that they were saving the Revolution, in no way ashamed of their work, for which they expected, and received, payment. Simple, violent men, they were as delighted to embrace the prisoners who were acquitted as they were resolute in hacking to pieces those whom they regarded as guilty. The horrible business continued for several days until, when growing public revulsion and firm action by some of the Parisian leaders finally put a stop to it, between 1,100 and 1,400 prisoners had been murdered, including many priests. The attempt of Robespierre and Billaud-Varenne, both members of the Commune, to obtain the arrest of the Girondin leaders, at a time when this was tantamount to a death sentence, met with no success, and the warrant issued by the *comité de surveillance* for the arrest of Roland, Minister of the Interior, was annulled by his colleague, Danton.

The September massacres probably seemed to many *sans-culottes*, even in retrospect, a legitimate form of self-defence. Few educated men shared this opinion. Nevertheless the massacres contributed to divide the revolutionary leaders as well as to envenom the relations between the Girondins and the Parisian *sans-culottes*. Montagnards such as Levasseur de la Sarthe regarded the slaughter in the prisons as an 'abominable incident in a sublime drama'. Paris had saved France by her *'élan populaire*, insurrection, anarchy', which no true revolutionary could regret, however much he deplored some of its consequences. To have stopped the massacres, assuming this to have been possible, would have involved the same mobilization of the forces of order that had triumphed at the Champ de Mars. In the process the spontaneous movement of national defence would have collapsed and 'Paris would have witnessed the triumphant entry of foreign bayonets and the restoration of the régime of 1788'.[1] Such men regarded the massacres as an aberration to be discreetly ignored. But what was realism to the Montagnards appeared mere logic-chopping to the Girondins. It was too much to expect that those whose lives had been endangered by Robespierre, Billaud and Marat should either forgive or forget. For them, the Parisian *sans-culottes* were henceforth identified with murder and anarchy. They returned endlessly to the subject of the massacres and their attacks on the Commune and appeals for the support of the forces of order and property perpetuated the division amongst the revolutionaries that had begun with the declaration of war.

From the ending of the massacres to the first session of the Convention on 21st September uneasy peace reigned in Paris while French and Prussian armies manoeuvred in the Argonne. As yet the conquests of the revolutionaries remained provisional. The invasion had not been halted and the king had not even been deposed. The French victory of Valmy and the proclamation of the republic were soon to dispose of both of these questions—but merely to raise new and more intractable problems. Now that the revolutionaries had declared war on Court, *émigré* nobility and refractory clergy it remained to be seen whether they could assemble enough support to make representative government practicable. The bitter enmity between Girondins and Montagnards and the demonstration of *sans-culotte* violence suggested that new divisions and new crises lay ahead.

[1] R. Levasseur, *Mémoires* (Paris, 1829), I. 44–47.

VII

~~~~~~

The Division of the Republicans

~~~~~~

*Ce sont eux (les Girondins) qui nous ont forcés de nous jeter dans le
sansculotisme qui les a dévorés, qui nous dévorera tous, qui se
dévorera lui-même.*

Attributed to DANTON by GARAT

THE National Convention was a sovereign body, elected to
draft a new constitution and to govern France in the meantime.
A democratic electorate was free to return any deputies it liked,
with the result that 189 members of the Left of the Legislative
Assembly were re-elected, together with 96 from the Constituent Assembly. The social composition of the Convention
was similar to that of its predecessors, the great majority of the
deputies being drawn from the urban middle class, with the
lawyers predominating. There were 48 clergymen and quite a
number of ex-nobles, including seven marquises and one prince
of the blood, Orléans, who had re-named himself Philippe
Égalité. At the other end of the social scale were two working
men, an armourer from Saint-Étienne and a wool-carder from
Reims, together with half a dozen others whose rank in society
was scarcely more elevated. On the whole, a democratic electorate had returned the same sort of men that the active citizens
had chosen in 1791. Not more than one million of the five
million eligible went to the poll, which in some cases was lower
than it had been in the previous year. The widening of the
suffrage seems, therefore, to have had very little effect.

The local government elections held in the autumn of 1792 showed a similar trend. Even the municipalities, where election was direct, were filled by men of bourgeois origin. With comparatively few exceptions, the *sans-culottes* were unsuccessful in elections, despite universal suffrage. Unable to win power for themselves, they were later to become the agents by which a despotic central government controlled their recalcitrant fellow townsmen. The case of Paris was, however, somewhat peculiar. The parliamentary elections, held under the shadow of the September massacres, returned 24 radicals who were to form the nucleus of the Montagnards in the Convention. The *conseil général* of the Commune was similarly radical in politics, besides being of much humbler social origin. But the election of a mayor revealed the strength of moderate opinion even in Paris. In October the Girondin candidate, Pétion, routed all his Montagnard opponents. When he refused to serve, the former royal Minister, d'Ormesson, defeated two Montagnard candidates, both of whom, rather curiously, were ex-nobles. D'Ormesson declined the dangerous honour and his successor, Chambon, who was suspected of royalism, nevertheless obtained half the votes of the revolutionary Section, *Quinze-Vingts*. It was not until Chambon resigned in his turn that the Montagnards were able to secure the election of their candidate, Pache, in February 1793.

But even if the electorate had a weakness for gentlemen, the political climate was revolutionary enough. Everywhere the symbols of monarchy disappeared: in the streets of Paris, where the Place Royale became the Place des Vosges, in the fleet, where the *Républicain* replaced the *Royal Louis*, and the transformation of the *Souverain* into the *Peuple Souverain* taught political theory to the seamen. Soon *Monsieur* had become a term of abuse, implying lack of republicanism. It was not long since Ministers had been addressed as *Monseigneur*; now they became 'Citizen Minister'. The emphasis was on social fraternity and the rejection of anything suggestive of class distinction. The revolutionary use of the second person singular (*tutoiement*) became universal and many deputies discarded the powdered hair and fastidious dress of the ancien régime for the untidy informality of the *sans-culotte*. The use of 'revolutionary' names had begun before the fall of the monarchy. As early as March 1792 an unfortunate girl had been christened 'Pétion-Nationale-

Pique'. Few serious politicians followed the example of 'Ana-
charsis' Clootz and 'Anaxagoras' Chaumette, and those who did
change their names appear to have been men of a particularly
flamboyant temperament, those with a 'moderate' past to live
down, and unfortunates like the naval architect, *né* Leroi, who
called himself Abauzir!

When the Convention met the military situation was under-
going an extraordinary transformation that seemed to confirm
the Girondin prophecies of easy victory. After Valmy the
Prussians withdrew to the frontier and in November French
troops occupied the left bank of the Rhine. The Austrians, who
had been besieging Lille in October were defeated by Dumouriez at Jemappes on 6th November and evacuated the Austrian
Netherlands. Nice was occupied and Savoy proclaimed its union
with France. These successes made it safe to quarrel at home.

The Assembly began harmoniously enough, with the abolition of the monarchy, but within a few days the Girondins
launched a bitter attack on their Montagnard opponents. On
24th September Kersaint called for 'scaffolds for the assassins
and those who provoke assassination', and the conflict continued almost without interruption until the expulsion of the
Girondin leaders from the Convention on 2 June 1793. The
Girondins could at first rely on the votes of a majority of the
deputies, many of whom were alarmed as well as scandalized
by the September massacres. But their insistence on mono-
polizing all positions of authority and their shrill attacks on the
Montagnard leaders soon irritated men who regarded party as
faction. One by one able deputies such as Couthon, Cambon,
Carnot, Lindet and Barère began to gravitate towards the
Montagnards, while the majority—the Plain, as it was called—
held itself aloof from both sides. Girondins and Montagnards
were in almost complete agreement on matters of policy. Both
were sincere in their attachment to the Revolution and to the
Republic, in their hatred of privilege, their anti-clericalism and
advocacy of an economic policy that combined liberalism with
social welfare.[1] Both dreamed of building a new France more

---

[1] Even the conservative Roland wished to sell *émigré* property in very small
lots. M. Marion, *La Vente des Biens Nationaux pendant la Révolution*, p. 124. On
the absence of any conflict of principle between Girondins and Montagnards see
M. J. Harrison, 'The Conflict of Ideas between the Gironde and the Montagne as
reflected in the Press' (unpublished M.A. thesis, Manchester, 1960), *passim*.

prosperous, more enlightened and more humane than any of its neighbours. What divided them was political ambition, and above all the suspicions engendered earlier in the year. The Girondins were convinced that Robespierre and his associates aspired to a bloody dictatorship, while the Montagnards believed their opponents to be ready for any compromise with conservative, and even with royalist forces, that would guarantee their remaining in power. The bitter enmity between the two groups soon reduced the Convention to a state of vociferous paralysis. Debate after debate degenerated into a verbal brawl from which no decisions emerged. The political deadlock, which had repercussions all over France, eventually drove men on each side to accept dangerous allies, royalists in the case of the Girondins, *sans-culottes* in that of the Montagnards.

During the summer there had been disturbances in various parts of France, generally caused by the shortage or high price of grain. Serious grain riots in the Aude brought out an insurgent force of six thousand in August. The authorities of the Haute-Garonne imposed controls on the grain trade, while at Tours in September popular pressure led to the imposition of a controlled price on bread, which reduced the price of the one-pound loaf from four sous to two. The District of Chaumont in the Haute-Marne used both troops and National Guards to enforce its requisitions of corn. It is against this background that we must set the activities of the commissioners sent out by the Council of Ministers and the Paris Commune at the end of August and the beginning of September.[1] These agents were primarily concerned with organizing national defence, but some of them took a wide view of their mandate and tried to stimulate the zeal of the *sans-culottes* by offering hints of revolutionary social legislation to come. Momoro in particular, a member of the Paris Commune, included in his personal draft of a new Declaration of the Rights of Man: 'The nation guarantees industrial property only.' A mere temporary guarantee was all that he offered to 'what is falsely described as territorial property, until such time as laws on this subject shall be drafted'. More significant than such theorizing by a few isolated ex-

[1] See P. Caron, *La Première Terreur. I. Les Missions du Conseil Exécutif Provisoire et de la Commune de Paris* (Paris, 1950), *passim.*

tremists, and the temporary improvisation of local authorities, was the fact that the Government and the Assembly took the first steps along the road to economic controls. On 4th September the Ministers authorized their agents to requisition food and transport for the army at prices fixed by the local authorities. On the 9th the Assembly authorized municipalities to resort to requisition in order to keep civilian markets supplied—permission which many of them had already anticipated—and a week later Vergniaud himself proposed and the Assembly decreed a census of all grain stocks, to facilitate requisitioning. In September, therefore, all shades of revolutionary opinion seemed to be inclined towards the control of the grain trade.

During the early months of the Convention the unrest in the provinces intensified but the deputies reverted to economic liberalism, perhaps because of the improvement in the military situation. The result was to reopen the gap between the revolutionary bourgeoisie on the one hand and the peasants and *sansculottes* on the other. The first trouble came from Lyons, where the shrinking of the luxury market led to the unemployment of thirty thousand silk workers at a time when bread cost five sous the pound—almost double the price in Paris. The Jacobin Club in Lyons called for the erection of a guillotine to intimidate financial speculators and food hoarders. The municipality refused, but an angry crowd set up the guillotine on the night of 25th–26th August. A month later a more serious insurrection, in which women played a leading part, forced the municipal authorities to reduce by decree the price of bread, meat, butter and eggs, and to agree to the special taxation of the rich in order to provide subsidies to bring down the price of necessities.

In November a serious peasant revolt developed in the Île de France and the Beauce. The harvest had been, on the whole, satisfactory, and in any case it was far too early for a serious shortage to arise. What presumably happened was that heavy requisitioning for an army now numbering over half a million had greatly reduced supplies, while continuous inflation was forcing up prices. Labourers and rural artisans derived no compensating benefit from the anti-seigneurial legislation of August unless they owned some land. Wages on the big farms in the Beauce were probably lagging behind prices, and so the agitation took the form of a demand for price controls. Markets were plundered at Versailles, Étampes, and Rambouillet, and in late November and early December a considerable rural insurrection swept through Chartres, Blois, Vendôme, Nogent-le-Rotrou, le Mans, Tours and other towns in the area, almost everywhere succeeding in imposing a reduction in the price of bread. Three representatives sent by the Convention to restore order had to agree to the imposition of price controls and were lucky to escape with their lives. They reported that a leading part in the insurrection was taken by members of the clergy, and the crowd that threatened them reproached the Convention with its alleged hostility to religion. This was another reminder that the religious division did not always correspond to political and social alignments. Much of the 'extremist' thought on social issues was provided by members of the clergy like Dolivier and Jacques Roux,[1] and many peasants of the Left as well as the Right had probably more confidence in the local *curé* than in the revolutionary gentlemen from the towns.

The Convention had both to deal with the peasant revolt and to answer repeated petitions from local authorities for the imposition of price controls. The Departments of Indre-et-Loire and Seine-et-Oise—both troubled areas—called for the fixing of a maximum price for grain. The majority of the Paris Sections also demanded the control of the price of all necessities.[2] The deputies, however, drew back from the emergency controls authorized in September and retreated towards economic liberalism. A first debate, on 3rd November, led merely to the vote of twelve million livres to increase corn imports—a policy that could have no immediate effect. On the 19th the Assembly heard a letter from Roland condemning controls as likely to lead to violence and civil war. 'Government . . . consists primarily in anticipating and preventing the undesirable in a negative way. . . . Perhaps the only action that the Assembly can allow itself to take in the matter of food supplies is to pronounce that it should take no action.' Roland maintained that the agitation was directed from Paris and was linked with the counter-revolutionary intrigues of the aristocracy. Saint-Just, at barely twenty-five the youngest member of the Assembly and a Montagnard, replied with a penetrating analysis of the

[1] See below, pp. 163–64.
[2] F. Braesch, *La Commune du 10 Août*, pp. 823–64.

economic situation. He blamed most of the trouble on inflation, but since the Revolution depended on military victory and the war could only be financed by issuing more assignats, a deflationary policy such as he advocated was quite unrealistic. On the issue of controls he agreed entirely with Roland, even on matters of terminology: 'People demand a law on food supplies. Positive legislation on such a subject is never wise.' Robespierre was prepared to go a little further and to maintain requisitioning powers in order to keep markets supplied, while isolated Montagnards such as Lequinio demanded the imposition of a limit to the amount of land that an individual farmer could rent. But when it came to dealing with the peasant revolt, Girondins like Pétion and Buzot and Montagnards such as Danton, Robespierre, Lacroix, Legendre and Jeanbon Saint-André were agreed in demanding repression. Eventually, on 8th December, Creuzet-Latouche won the support of the Assembly for a motion that decreed the death penalty for those who exported corn or interfered with its free circulation within France, and abrogated the requisitioning laws of September. The Convention therefore adopted an attitude of strict economic liberalism, except on the matter of export. The abolition of the special tribunal of 17th August, at about the same time, indicated that the Girondins intended to rule by orthodox means and without any of the exceptional powers that had been judged necessary for the safety of the Revolution in August and September.[1]

The social crisis of the autumn emphasized the similar views of the two main groups in the Convention. No spokesman for either side was prepared to accept the demand from the Parisian *sans-culottes* and from one or two Departments for the imposition of price controls. Both tried to make political capital out of the disturbances, Roland by blaming Paris and the forces of anarchy, Danton and Robespierre by the curious argument that the trial of the king—which the Girondins were trying to postpone—should precede the repression of the peasant revolt. The politicians might believe that the argument had been settled by the voting of Creuzet-Latouche's motion and the despatch of troops to the Beauce, but the local authorities continued to

---

[1] It is perhaps significant that the sale of *émigré* property was suspended on 11th November, ostensibly because local authorities were interpreting the law of 2nd September in different ways.

petition for price controls or, more simply, to disregard the law of 8th December, and the Parisian *sans-culottes*, after the temporary diversion caused by the king's trial, were soon to return to the assault.

It was primarily their bungling of the trial of Louis XVI that lost the Girondins the initiative in the Convention and made them suspect to ardent revolutionaries in Paris and the provinces. On this issue, as on most others, they were badly divided.[1] But virtually all regarded the king as a traitor to the Revolution and most of those who opposed his execution did so on grounds of expediency rather than of justice. Since they were not powerful or united enough to avert the trial, they would have been well advised to let events take their course. Instead they raised disingenuous objections and incurred plausible though unjustified suspicions of royalism without being able to save Louis XVI. The outcome of the trial was wholly unfavourable to the Girondins. Their first major defeat in the Convention convinced ambitious careerists like Fouché that they had best transfer their conditional loyalty elsewhere. The *sans-culotte* leaders in the Paris Sections, already irritated by repeated Girondin denunciations of Paris as the home of anarchy, now took the offensive against the deputies who had tried to save the king. The Montagnards, with the exception of Danton and his friends, had pursued Louis with a rigour beyond *sans-culotte* reproach, but if they assumed that this would guarantee them the unconditional support of the Parisian *sans-culottes* they were soon to be disappointed.

As always, the immediate interests of the *sans-culottes* were economic rather than political. The continuing inflation was leading to sharp increases in the price of some commodities— the cost of soap, for example, doubled in the space of a few months. Nevertheless, the popular agitation in Paris in the first quarter of 1793 cannot be presented simply as a desperate struggle against declining living standards. Bread was sold at a controlled price of three sous the pound, a low figure, although an increase of 50 per cent above the 1791 price. The city bakers were subsidized at a cost to the municipality of about 120,000 livres per day. The surrounding rural areas tried to take advantage of the low price of subsidized Parisian flour and to supply

[1] M. J. Sydenham, *The Girondins*, Appendix C.

themselves on the city markets, but in spite of this additional drain on municipal stocks, and the occasional panic that led to a run on the bakeries, there was no acute shortage during this period. Although not very much is known of the evolution of wages during the winter of 1792–3, employers are unlikely to have offered much effective resistance to pressure for increases, in view of the political situation in Paris. On the whole it seems likely that wages had been rising while the cost of bread remained relatively low. There was, admittedly, a steep increase in the price of what contemporaries called 'secondary' necessities, such as firewood, soap, candles and sugar. Soap was the essential raw material of the laundry-women, and women in general were perhaps more directly affected than their men folk by the rising prices, besides being less well placed to 'negotiate' wage increases by more or less intimidatory means.

The agitation in Paris was therefore not wholly spontaneous and owed something to conscious direction from above. This made it more rather than less dangerous to the Convention, since the movement could not be appeased by some temporary concession, but demanded the implementation of a relatively long-term economic policy. There seems little doubt that behind the *sans-culotte militants* stood Varlet, a young and radical bourgeois, and the abbé, Jacques Roux.[1] Roux, whose early life is obscure, had settled in the populous and predominantly *sans-culotte* Section, *Gravilliers*, which had become a bastion of radicalism. He himself represented his Section at the Commune. His influence was considerable and extended well beyond the *Gravilliers*, but his supporters (known as the *enragés*), had no political organization. Roux was a commander-in-chief who relied on the enthusiasm or anger of the moment to provide him with an army. His seat on the *conseil général* of the Commune was disputed and his control over his Section challenged by the radical Montagnard deputy, Léonard Bourdon. Roux was therefore vulnerable, but for the time being he was the only man to offer a social programme to the taste of the *sans-culottes*, while the deadlock in the Convention forced

[1] A. Mathiez, *La Vie Chère et le Mouvement Social sous la Terreur*, pp. 121–35; M. Dommanget, *Jacques Roux, le Curé Rouge* (Paris, 1948), *passim*; W. Markov, 'Les Jacquesroutins', *Annales Historiques de la Révolution Française*, XXXIII (1960), 163.

the Montagnards to treat him with caution, if not with respect.

At this time there were two main planks to the abbé's platform: the imposition of a controlled price of corn throughout the Republic, and the establishment of the assignat as the sole legal tender. It is not at all clear why the Parisian *sans-culottes* should have been prepared to campaign, as they did, for price controls on bread grains alone, since their own bread was already heavily subsidized. Possibly they argued that the extension of similar controls to the whole country would reduce the pressure on their own markets, or perhaps they saw in the *maximum des grains* the first step towards the imposition of controlled prices on all necessities. This would certainly seem to have been the intention of Roux. The exclusive use of the assignat was perhaps of more immediate concern to the *sans-culottes*. Those who could not follow the economic argument behind the attempt to counteract inflation by demonetizing specie probably felt a sentimental attachment to the currency of the Revolution and were certainly incensed against the money-changers whose activities emphasized, if they did not accentuate the declining value of the assignat. On both financial and economic issues Roux was flying in the face of almost the entire Convention, although Cambon, the spokesman of the finance committee, agreed with him on the question of the assignats. Montagnards and Girondins had rejected price controls towards the end of 1792 and both were agreed on combating inflation by reducing the number of assignats in circulation. But Roux was supported by economics as well as by the pressure of his *sans-culotte* following. Since the Convention had not the power to enforce a substantial increase in taxation—which might have provoked violent resistance and made converts for the counter-revolution—the only alternative to drastic inflation was to protect the assignat by freeing it from competition with gold and silver, and by the imposition of rigorous economic controls. The deputies' liberalism probably helped them to see, more clearly than Roux, the infinite difficulties in the way of enforcing such a policy with the crude bureaucratic means at their disposal, but the future was to confirm the abbé's belief that the alternative to such an attempt was runaway inflation that would press most heavily on the urban *sans-culottes*.

On 13 January 1793 the 48 Sections petitioned the Assembly

for the *cours forcé* of the assignat. Meeting with no success, they returned to the attack on 3rd February, this time supported by the *Défenseurs des 84 Départements*, the *fédérés* still remaining in Paris, over whom Roux seems to have exercised considerable influence. When the Convention once more turned a deaf ear to these proposals, Roux, or whoever was guiding the Sections, changed his objective. On 12th February a new petition demanded the imposition of price controls on corn. The petitioners demonstrated their political impartiality by attacking the views which both Saint-Just and the Girondin, Barbaroux, had put forward during the November debates on the grain riots. The former was particularly roughly handled in a denunciation of 'fine speakers who eat well every day. . . . Amongst these is the citizen Saint-Just.' Both sides in the Convention united in anger against the demands of the petitioners and the aggressive language in which they had been expressed. Marat took the lead in declaring them to be subversive. The Girondin, Lehardy, compared those responsible to vermin. Buzot and Carra denounced them as royalists, Barère and Marat demanded their arrest. Isolated Montagnards, such as Choudieu and Thuriot, pleaded that the petitioners were merely misguided, and the Convention did not, in fact, take any punitive action, but the gulf between the Sectional leaders and the entire Assembly had been made brutally obvious.

This antagonism sharpened during the ensuing fortnight. When the Jacobins refused accommodation to women from the *Unité* Section who wished to discuss the eternal problem of food supplies, they had the unusual experience of being denounced by their own public galleries as food-hoarders. On 24th February the laundry-women who petitioned the Convention to decree the death penalty for hoarding and speculation were snubbed by its Montagnard president, Dubois-Crancé. A second deputation of women, demanding the *cours forcé* of the assignat, reminded the president that the recent Bill to raise 300,000 new recruits for the army might require *sans-culotte* support. Dubois-Crancé promptly adopted a different tone and assured the women that the appropriate committees had the matter in hand. They then withdrew with the disquieting threat, 'They adjourn us till Tuesday, but we adjourn ourselves till Monday. When our children ask us for milk we don't put them off until the day after tomorrow.' On the following day—Monday—a concerted movement, in which women played a leading part, invested many of the grocers' shops, reduced the price of the contents and proceeded to dispose of them. The mayor, Pache, convened the *conseil général* of the Commune and denounced the rioters as counter-revolutionaries, ordering the National Guard to disperse the crowds. But as news arrived of more shops being emptied, the public galleries applauded and denounced as food-hoarders any who complained. Roux, accused of defending the riots, would not repudiate them in the Commune, and he was probably not the only member of the *conseil général* to approve of them. The National Guards, themselves drawn largely from the *sans-culottes*, were reluctant to act, and order was not finally restored until the 27th.

The Convention naturally reacted violently. Marat was in a particularly awkward position. Foreseeing trouble, he had written an article in his *Publiciste Parisien* which appeared on the morning of the 25th, advocating 'the pillage of a few shops and the hanging of hoarders at their own shop-doors' as the most satisfactory way of dealing with shortages and high prices. This was no more than a typical Marat *boutade*, intended to sweeten for *sans-culotte* consumption an essentially moderate programme—the trial before a special court of a few notorious hoarders, and an appeal to wealthy philanthropists to import necessities and sell them at cost in order to force down prices. The pillage of the grocers had already started before Marat's paper appeared on sale. Superficially, however, he appeared to be responsible, and it was perhaps this vulnerable position that led him to take the offensive and denounce the riots as a Girondin plot. Collot supported him and Dubois-Crancé affirmed that the Parisians were being led astray by *émigrés* disguised as *sans-culottes*. Robespierre embroidered on this theme and in a revealing passage asserted that the movement must have been counter-revolutionary, since some of the crowd had even denounced the Montagnards. He went on to lecture the *sans-culottes* on the need to act only for worthy—i.e. political—causes, and not for 'paltry merchandise'. On the 26th the Girondins counter-attacked. Salles discomfited the Montagnards by reading out Marat's article—which met with some applause from the galleries. Bancal proposed that Marat be provisionally expelled from the Assembly and given a medical examination to test his sanity, and the debate degenerated into the usual inconclusive faction fight. The Convention's treatment of the incident illustrates very clearly both the universal rejection of price controls and the extremes of suspicion and abuse that nullified all debate.

On the 27th the Paris Commune gave ground to the *sans-culottes*, to the extent of petitioning the Convention to pass a law against hoarding and to provide a programme of public works. Chaumette, the spokesman for the Commune, although he seems to have had genuine sympathy for the *sans-culottes*, was far from accepting Roux's programme. Nothing was said about price controls and the Commune accepted the 'orthodox' financial policy of reducing the number of assignats in circulation. The only support that Roux had so far won outside the Sections came from the influential newspaper, *Révolutions de Paris*, which now began to advocate general price controls.

At this point a sudden deterioration in the military situation relegated social and economic problems into the background, while at the same time strengthening the bargaining power of the *sans-culottes*, the most reliable defenders of the Revolution. Towards the end of 1792 the Convention's policy of 'revolutionizing' the Austrian Netherlands and its incautious offer of help to all peoples striving to recover their liberty, alarmed neutral, and especially British opinion. The opening to trade of the Scheldt, closed by the Treaty of Utrecht in 1713, threatened British economic interests and seemed to confirm the French intention to remain in Belgium. On 2 February 1793 the Convention, regarding a breach as inevitable, declared war on England and Holland, and on 7th March, on Spain as well. To the enmity of the two main territorial Powers of central Europe France had now added that of the three maritime nations. A British squadron in the Straits of Dover made it difficult for France to import Baltic grain. A French naval armament programme considerably more ambitious than that of Britain added notably to the cost of the war and to inflationary pressure.[1] Furthermore, the sea-borne mobility of Britain and Spain enabled them to come to the support of counter-revolutionary

[1] N. Hampson, *La Marine de l'An II*, chap. ii, vii.

movements in coastal areas, while the French now had to defend a new frontier along the Pyrenees.

In the meantime the campaigning season had opened badly. The defeat of Miranda, protecting Dumouriez's right flank, forced the commander-in-chief to abandon the invasion of Holland and fall back on the Austrian Netherlands. Parisian opinion at once took alarm and everyone's thoughts turned to the invasion of the previous August. Danton, resuming his old rôle, appealed for the immediate despatch of volunteers to the front and, more ominously, for the release of imprisoned debtors. Girondins and Montagnards for a short time almost overcame their mutual suspicions in a common attempt to save the Republic—and to discourage the *sans-culottes* from murderous initiatives in the same direction. The result was a number of emergency measures aimed at reinforcing the power of the Central Government and destroying the counter-revolutionaries within France. On 9th March it was decided to despatch 82 deputies throughout the country to stimulate recruiting. Next day a revolutionary tribunal was created to judge political offenders and forestall popular 'justice'. The need appeared all the more urgent since Varlet and a few fellow hotheads tried to launch an insurrection in Paris. The movement won the sympathy of the Cordelier Club and one or two Sections, but foundered on the hostility of the Commune and the Jacobins and accomplished nothing more than the destruction of a few Girondin printing presses.

The news of the insurrection in the Vendée led to further emergency legislation.[1] On 19th March the death penalty was decreed against all rebels captured under arms—a measure responsible for more bloodshed than the revolutionary tribunal itself. Two days later it was voted to establish *comités de surveillance* in all Communes and in the Sections of the major towns. Originally intended merely to keep an eye on foreigners, these rapidly became a political police authority controlling the *certificats de civisme* on which public employment depended. On the 23rd, Departments were authorized to deport any clergyman denounced by six citizens from his own Canton and on the same day a ferocious Bill regulated the situation of the *émigrés*. Those who returned to France were to be put to death; any

[1] See below, pp. 170–71.

property inherited by *émigrés* during the ensuing fifty years was to be confiscated by the State; no sale or mortgage of property to which they were the heirs-presumptive was allowed, and all gifts, legacies and dowries which they had made since 1 July 1789 were annulled. The Convention was no doubt anxious to confiscate property that intending *émigrés* had sold or pretended to sell before their flight, but this retrospective legislation, upsetting the economic basis on which marriages had been contracted and invalidating inheritances, threatened the property rights of many aristocratic and bourgeois families. On 6th April a Committee of Public Safety of nine members was elected by the Convention to supervise the executive. Three days later the Assembly voted to send deputies, armed with very wide powers, to act as political commissars attached to each army in the field. Some Girondins supported each of these measures, which produced little immediate change, for the revolutionary tribunal handled few cases and treated these leniently, while the Committee of Public Safety was slow to assert itself. Nevertheless the majority of the Girondins could scarcely approve of this avalanche of emergency legislation which put paid to all their hopes of stabilizing the Revolution. They were further compromised in the public eye by their past praise of Dumouriez, whom they had tried to present as their man during the heroic days of Valmy and Jemappes.

Dumouriez now blamed the failure of his attack on Holland on the mismanagement of the Convention. Defeated at Neerwinden on 18th March he opened negotiations for a truce that would allow him to march on Paris. When his army refused to follow him Dumouriez himself went over to the enemy on 5th April, taking with him Égalité's son, the future Louis Philippe. The worst had been avoided, but for some days Paris could not be sure that the army had remained loyal and it was, in any case, defeated and leaderless. At the same time Custine was driven from the Rhineland, leaving 25,000 men besieged at Mainz, while the 'noble Duke of York' with his immortal 'ten thousand men' landed in the Netherlands to reinforce the Austrians, who were soon besieging Valenciennes. France was again faced with invasion, betrayed by a new Lafayette, and this time the enemy disposed of a long campaigning season in which to destroy the Republic.

While Dumouriez was falling back through the Austrian Netherlands a major civil war had broken out in the Vendée.[1] On 11th March the tocsin sounded in 600 villages, calling the peasants to arms. The attempt to raise troops, 3,520 from the Vendée and 5,920 from the Deux-Sèvres, in accordance with the decree of 7th February, for the mobilization of 300,000 men, provided the occasion for the revolt. If the peasants were forced to march, it would be against the Republic. Although the initial objectives were local, the avowed aim of the movement soon came to be the restoration of the old order.[2] A council meeting at Châtillon-sur-Sèvre annulled the sale of Church lands in the area and decreed that the question of tithes would be settled at the Restoration. From the outset the civil war was fought with great ferocity, even by twentieth-century standards. Torture, collective reprisals, pillage, devastation and the murder of prisoners were introduced by the rebels and to some extent at least copied by their opponents. The massacre of republicans began at Machecoul in the first days of the insurrection and soon over 500 had been murdered in the little town alone.

The Vendéan armies were reluctant to advance outside their own territory and never offered a direct threat to the capital, but on their own ground, where the thick hedges of the small fields and the sunken roads were defended by men who knew every inch of the country, these peasant armies that could transform themselves overnight into civilians and re-form again as quickly, defied the hasty levies of National Guards that were thrown against them. The rebels quickly established control of an area about sixty miles square which gave them plenty of room for manoeuvre. An offensive eastwards in early May captured Thouars and spread panic along the Loire. More serious was a thrust southwards a little later, when an army of 30,000–40,000 stormed Fontenay, taking 4,000 republican prisoners, and threatened the important naval base of Rochefort. It seemed inevitable that, even if Rochefort were held, the tiny port of les Sables d'Olonne, on the very fringe of rebel territory, must fall to the royalists and offer them communication with England and

[1] See L. Dubreuil, *Histoire des Insurrections de l'Ouest* (Paris, 1929); E. Gabory, *La Révolution et la Vendée* (Paris, 1925–8), P. Bois, *Les Paysans de l'Ouest* (Paris, 1960), and the various collections of documents edited by C. L. Chassin.

[2] On the origins of the revolt see C. Tilly, 'Some Problems in the History of the Vendée', *American Historical Review*, LXVII (1961).

a safe beach-head for British troops. It was against this sombre background of defeat and treason, invasion and civil war, that the Revolution moved towards a new crisis.

All over France April and May were disturbed months. There were innumerable minor outbreaks, especially in the countryside, where the peasants protected their recalcitrant clergy and refused to provide recruits.[1] In Brittany these movements were often serious enough to require the despatch of punitive columns of troops and National Guards and this diversion of manpower considerably delayed the mobilization of the fleet. But the most serious incidents, apart from the Vendée, occurred in the towns. All of the main cities of France, Paris, Lyons, Marseilles, Bordeaux, and Nantes, were shaken by divisions amongst the revolutionaries which, in the case of the first three, led to municipal revolutions. These movements still remain somewhat obscure, for in many cases essentially local issues were given a misleading national colouring in terms of 'Girondin' and 'Montagnard'.[2] The insurrection of 10 August 1792 had displaced the constitutional monarchists, often the leading figures in local society, from municipal politics. They and the royalists had tended to boycott the autumn polls, leaving the field open to the republicans. The divisions amongst the latter are harder to explain. At Lyons, for example, Roland and Chalier had fought on the same side during the early years of the Revolution. By August 1792 the partisans of each divided the city between them. Perhaps the advent to power of the republicans revealed divisions which had been latent in opposition, and personal rivalries may have played an important part. Certainly the events of August and September seemed to divide those who were prepared to condone, if not to advocate violence from those determined to maintain order and to protect the lives and property even of counter-revolutionaries. Each side was driven to look for allies and in the process the moderates

---

[1] See, for example, M. Giraud, *Levées d'Hommes et Acheteurs de Biens Nationaux dans la Sarthe en 1793* (Le Mans, 1920), *passim*.

[2] H. Wallon, *La Révolution du 31 mai et le Fédéralisme en 1793* (Paris, 1886), covers the whole field, but too superficially to solve many problems. On Lyons, see E. Herriot, *Lyon n'est plus* (Paris, 1937–40), and C. Riffaterre, *Le Mouvement Anti-Parisien et Anti-Jacobin à Lyon* (4 vol., Lyons–Paris, 1912). M. Dayet, *Un Révolutionnaire Franc-Comtois, Pierre-Joseph Briot* (Paris, 1960), shows the interaction of national and local politics in the case of a relatively quiet town, Besançon.

were drawn towards the royalists and the extremists made common cause with the leaders of the *sans-culottes*. The balance of forces varied from one town to another. Municipal politics in Toulon had been violent ever since 1789 and moderate republicanism made little appeal there. In Bordeaux, the Girondin fief *par excellence*, it was the extremists who found themselves isolated. Lyons and Marseilles were more equally divided, while municipal politics in Nantes were dominated from March onwards by a universal concern to defend the city against the Vendéan rebels. In one important respect Paris was different from all the others. The fact that the Convention sat in the capital meant that Parisian municipal politics were under continual parliamentary scrutiny. It was perhaps this awareness of national responsibility, at a time when the Girondin Press was denouncing Paris as the home of anarchy, that held the Parisian Jacobins to a much more moderate course than their sister-clubs in the provinces. One result of this was that, in Paris, the Montagnards cut themselves off from the *sans-culottes*. In some of the provincial cities the relationship between the two was much closer, and there the Jacobins were more influenced both by the *sans-culotte* programme of ensuring the livelihood of the poor at the expense of the rich and by *sans-culotte* methods of violence.

In Lyons, and probably elsewhere, the division of the revolutionaries seems to have encouraged moderates and open counter-revolutionaries to return to the political field. In February 1793 the moderate republican mayor, Nivière-Chol, defeated his Jacobin opponent and secured his own re-election by a vote of 8,097 in a total poll of 10,746. In the elections for mayor in November 1791 the total poll had amounted to only 3,573. Admittedly, since then passive citizens had been enfranchised, but we have seen that this did not appreciably increase the national poll in the elections to the Convention. There would be no obvious reason for the Lyons *sans-culottes* to display an exceptional interest in defeating the candidate of the Jacobin Club and the most likely explanation of the high poll in favour of Nivière-Chol is the sudden rallying to his support of voters who shared his concern for order, but not necessarily his republicanism.

The tense municipal politics of Lyons and Marseilles were

brought to a climax by the military crisis of the spring of 1793. The new levy of troops imposed an unpopular burden on towns that had already provided substantial contingents—nearly 3,000 had gone from the Rhône-et-Loire in 1792 and many of these must have come from Lyons. The representatives on mission despatched from the Assembly to stimulate recruiting had been mostly chosen from the Montagnards, and these deputies used their authority to support their allies in the provinces. In March, Rovère, Basire, and Legendre were able to unseat the moderates in Lyons and hand over the city to the partisans of Chalier and the local Jacobin Club. In Marseilles the Montagnards appear to have been divided amongst themselves, and when the two representatives in the city, Boisset and Moïse Bayle, dismissed the mayor and his *procureur* and began organizing a 'revolutionary army' for use against political enemies in the Midi, the local Girondins were able to profit from the disunity of their opponents, seize power and expel the two deputies. Their victory was achieved by means of the Sections, the ward organizations of the city which formed its electoral units. As we have seen in the case of Paris, the Sections were admirable instruments of *sans-culotte* activity, since they met in the evening at places within easy reach of all their members. The fact that municipal revolutions were generally the work of the Sections therefore implies that the moderates who seized power had at least a measure of popular support. This would seem to have been the case in the Hautes- and Basses-Pyrénées and in the Landes. Barbaroux may have been pleading his own cause when he claimed that, in Marseilles, 'the poorer classes themselves joined the property-owners', but Goodwin has shown something of the kind happening at Caen in May, and the counterrevolution at Toulon in July seems to have had the active support of the dockyard workers.[1] It is therefore clear that the divisions within the towns of France in the spring of 1793 are not to be explained in purely economic terms.

[1] A. Richard, *Le Gouvernement Révolutionnaire dans les Basses-Pyrénées* (Paris, 1923), pp. 23–25; J. Jaurès, *Histoire Socialiste*, IV. 1289; Barbaroux, *Mémoires* (ed. Alfred-Chabaud, Paris, 1936), p. 213; A. Goodwin, 'The Federalist Movement in Caen during the French Revolution', *Bulletin of John Rylands Library*, XLII (1960), p. 313; N. Hampson, 'Les Ouvriers des Arsenaux de la Marine pendant la Révolution Française', *Revue d'Histoire Économique et Sociale*. XXXIX (1961); R. Cobb, *Les Armées Révolutionnaires*, I. 49.

Nevertheless, the struggle was not without an element of class conflict. Montagnard deputies were inclined to preach 'the war of the poor against the rich' and conscription was sometimes accompanied by a special levy on the wealthy to equip the new recruits. On 19th April the Department of the Hérault, ordered to raise yet another contingent, for the defence of the Spanish frontier, decided on a new method of sweetening the unpalatable pill. A local committee of public safety, selected from local government bodies by the representatives on mission, with the advice of the local Clubs, was to select recruits individually and pay for their equipment and the maintenance of their families by a forced loan imposed on the rich, whose personal assessment would also be determined by the same committee. Rather surprisingly, the Convention approved this measure on the 27th and ordered its general application. The Hérault flattered itself that it would free keen but indigent revolutionaries to take up arms, while simultaneously reducing the mass of assignats in circulation. In practice, the new measures provoked almost universal discontent. The wealthy, unless they happened to have suitable political connections, feared ruthless expropriation, while the most ardent *sans-culottes* were not necessarily those most anxious to leave for the front. The result was to encourage a coalition between the wealthy and the counter-revolutionary without arousing any counter-balancing enthusiasm amongst the *sans-culottes*.

In Lyons the victorious extremists had shaken off the restraint of the representatives on mission and were demanding a local revolutionary tribunal and the creation of a local revolutionary army maintained at the expense of the rich. On 14th May the local authorities, in the presence of Dubois-Crancé, Albitte, Nioche, and Gauthier, decided to create a committee of public safety that would raise a force of 6,400 and a levy of six million livres; only the holders of *certificats de civisme* would be allowed to vote in future elections and the Girondin Press was to be excluded from the Department. Chalier attempted to impose on the National Guard an oath of loyalty which called for the extermination of 'tyrants, aristocrats, feuillants, moderates, egoists, hoarders, usurers, speculators and all the useless individuals of the sacerdotal caste'. The convocation of the Sections to elect *comités de surveillance* on 28th May offered his opponents

174

an opportunity to rally their forces, and on the following day violent fighting broke out. The municipality was overthrown and replaced by a council consisting of the president and secretary of each Section. Chalier and his leading supporters were thrown into prison. Whatever the *arrière-pensées* of the men behind this movement, it seems clear that the insurrection itself had a good deal of popular support. By the end of May, therefore, Lyons, Marseilles, Bordeaux and Caen were in anti-Montagnard hands.

Paris could not be expected to remain aloof from these conflicts, but there the balance of forces was somewhat different and the eventual Montagnard victory in the capital outweighed all the reverses elsewhere. By this time the more imaginative Girondin and Montagnard deputies had convinced themselves that their opponents were engaged in the most hair-raising plots. The Girondin, Salles, 'proved' to Garat, who had replaced Roland at the Interior, that for the past five years Égalité had been at the head of the Montagnards, with Lafayette as his accomplice. The Cordelier Club 'negotiated with Europe and had emissaries in every Court'. The aim of the Montagnards was to put the Duke of York on the throne. He would then be murdered by Égalité, who would in turn be murdered by Marat, Danton and Robespierre. Danton would then murder his two associates and claim the throne for himself![1] Desmoulins' *Histoire des Brissotins*, officially sponsored by the Jacobin Club, did not soar to quite such imaginative heights, but nevertheless 'proved' that the Girondins, agents of Pitt, Égalité and Prussia, had been in British pay since 1789, as well as being the instruments of Dumouriez.[2] It was clear that the two sides could not co-exist much longer in the same Assembly.

The Montagnards believed that only the elimination of the Girondin leaders, who would cling to power so long as they remained in the Assembly, could enable the Convention to lead the Revolution to safety. But the *enragés*, who were in enthusiastic agreement on this point at least, would be only too likely to massacre the Girondin deputies if given the chance. The Montagnards were opposed in principle to the violation of

---

[1] Quoted in Jaurès, *op. cit.*, IV, 1163–6.
[2] The *Histoire des Brissotins* is reprinted in Buchez and Roux, *Histoire Parlementaire de la Révolution Française* (Paris, 1834–8), XXVI. 266–310.

parliamentary immunity and they realized that a violent purge of the Convention would provoke the provinces to civil war. As a way out of this dilemma they decided on an appeal to the Departments to disown their Girondin deputies. The 'appeal' itself was drafted by the Jacobins, on 4th April, in such violent terms as to provoke the Girondins to impeach Marat, who presided. When it was presented to the Assembly by a deputation from the Sections, Girondin extremists jumped at the pretext for consulting the electorate, and it was not without difficulty that the more responsible members of both sides secured the abandonment of the ill-advised proposal. Robespierre still clung to the idea of keeping within the law, and urged restraint on the Jacobins, to the surprised indignation of the public galleries.[1] Since the Plain would not sacrifice the Girondins to the Montagnards, Robespierre's policy proved completely impracticable.

The Girondins induced the Convention to send Marat before the revolutionary tribunal—which promptly acquitted him. In the meantime the *enragés* were profiting from the national emergency to secure the adoption of their economic programme. On 11th April the support of Cambon won for them the *cours forcé* of the assignat. A week later the Paris Department itself petitioned for the *maximum des grains*, and this time there were no demands for the arrest of the petitioners. The Assembly discussed the issue in comparative calm, from 27th April to 2nd May and eventually voted that each Department should take the average price of grain over the past few months as a maximum, to be reduced monthly until September. The *enragés* had therefore secured both of their immediate aims. These initial successes encouraged them to further efforts, their immediate aim being the elimination of the Girondin leadership from the Convention, a shift to a political objective that may have owed something to Montagnard influence and may even have represented a *quid pro quo* for the economic concessions.

At this point the attempt to raise a levy of 12,000 men for the Vendée enabled the Girondins to conduct the kind of counter-attack in the Sections which had already overthrown the Montagnards in Marseilles and was later to defeat them in

[1] See the reports to the Minister of the Interior of 11th and 18th May, by Terrasson and Dutard, reprinted in A. Schmidt, *Tableaux de la Révolution Française* (Leipzig, 1867), II. 209, 244.

Lyons and Toulon. On 1st May the Commune adopted the Hérault method of recruitment and Chaumette later made it clear that the intention was to spare the artisans and to conscript office workers. Several Sections showed themselves reluctant to adopt the Hérault system and all who hoped to escape conscription or punitive taxation had a powerful incentive to attend their Sections in the hope of winning control of the bodies that would nominate the reluctant soldiers of the Revolution. The Girondins, at the risk of seeming to oppose recruitment, tried to profit from this movement in order to reverse the balance of power in Paris. For the whole of May, and especially during the first fortnight, many Sections became battlegrounds— although the weapons used were no more murderous than chairs. Each side urged on its supporters and the struggle assumed something of the nature of a class conflict. The Montagnard journalist, Audouin, called upon 'locksmiths, carpenters, quarrymen, masons, cabinet-makers, in a word, all of you artisans and *sans-culotte* working men' to flock to the Sections. Hébert, deputy *procureur* of the Commune, in his inimitable style as the *Père Duchesne*, acknowledged the effectiveness of the Girondin offensive in terms that defy translation : '*Des visages inconnus, des faces à gifles de marguilliers, des banquiers, des marchands de sucre, des bandes de fourriquets aux culottes serrées, des godelureaux frisés et parfumés, ont inondé toutes les Sections.* These villains have had the audacity to seize the registers, to appoint themselves presidents and secretaries. Several *comités révolutionnaires* have been dismissed by these brigands and in a word the counter-revolution has triumphed in several Sections.' [1] The Girondins themselves helped to stress the element of class hostility. At the end of April Pétion, in a 'letter to the Parisians' that contrasted significantly with his 'letter to Buzot' of 6 February 1792, repeated his old argument that the Revolution was turning into a war of the 'haves' and the 'have-nots', but this time his sympathies were clearly with the former. The Montagnards and *enragés* fought back, the *sans-culottes* of one Section illegally swelling the voting and

[1] Audouin, *Journal Universel*, 7 May 1793, and Hébert, *Le père Duchesne* No. 234, both quoted in Harrison, *loc. cit.*, p. 257. For a remarkable eyewitness account of Paris at the time, see the reports of Dutard in A. Schmidt, *op. cit.*, I and II.

chair-wielding strength of their neighbours, and by the end of May they had recovered control over most of the Sections, although their hold was still precarious.

While the Sectional battle was still in full fury the Girondins launched a new offensive in the Convention. On 15th May Guadet demanded the summons of the reserve deputies (*suppléants*) to Bourges, in case of an attack on the Convention, and the replacement of the Paris Commune by the presidents of the Sections. Barère induced the Assembly to take the less drastic course of nominating a committee of twelve to investigate the behaviour of the Commune. This committee, on 24th–26th May, arrested Hébert, Varlet and four other suspects. Events now marched swiftly to a climax. *Enragé* elements in the Sections were preparing an insurrection. The Jacobins and the Commune, convinced that it was imperative to silence the Girondins, now decided not to oppose a movement that filled them with more misgiving than confidence. Robespierre's last word at the Jacobin Club, on 29th May, 'I am incapable of prescribing to the people the means of its salvation', was not the most memorable of revolutionary slogans.

The insurrection of 31st May–2nd June, the third Parisian revolt and the last one to succeed, was strikingly different from its predecessors of 14th July and 10th August in that it was directed not against troops but against the principle of the inviolability of the Assembly, and conducted by leaders whose main concern was to prevent it from getting out of hand. The 10th of August served as a pattern. Twenty-eight Sections—a bare majority—answered the appeal of a committee of six to choose representatives who would speak in the name of the sovereign people of Paris. This committee—the names of five of its members are unknown—was probably representative of the *enragés* rather than the Montagnards, but Dufourny, a member of the Jacobin Club, was one of its members. The representatives of the Sections then elected an executive committee of nine, including Varlet, and composed mainly of obscure *sans-culottes*. The Nine ordered the tocsin to be rung in the early morning of 31st May, but Pache prevented the firing of the alarm gun until the afternoon. The Nine appointed Hanriot to command the National Guard and suspended the Commune, but immediately reinstated it. This touching proof of confidence in the municipality was to allow the latter to exercise a powerful moderating influence over the course of the insurrection. The Sections were ordered to arrest suspects, but were slow to respond. The Girondin element was still powerful in several of them and *Beaurepaire* even declared that it had taken Roland under its protection. The Convention did not seem sure how to interpret the events of the morning. Couthon said that it was an insult to the people of Paris to maintain that they were in a state of insurrection and Vergniaud had no difficulty in persuading the Assembly to vote that the Sections had deserved well of the country. The Convention also voted to disband its Committee of Twelve and to pay forty sous a day to *sans-culotte* National Guards who were standing to arms. Robespierre's demand for the arrest of the Girondin leaders was ignored and the deputies suspended the session without taking any further action. At the Commune, Chaumette lost his temper when faced with repeated demands for a march on the Convention.

That night the Montagnards could congratulate themselves on having prevented a violent attack on the Assembly, but the negligible results of the day's work led to recriminations that threatened to break up the revolutionary front. Robespierre and Marat were absent from the Jacobins, where Billaud-Varenne attacked Marat and Chabot criticized Danton. Varlet, who had apparently hoped to have Pache arrested, denounced the half-heartedness of the Commune, which had been only too successful in restraining the *enragés*. The 1st of June proved equally disappointing. No effective action was taken until the evening, when the Department of Paris petitioned the Assembly for the arrest of the Girondin leaders. Only a hundred or so Montagnards had gathered at the Convention when the tocsin began to ring and they contented themselves with referring the petition to the Committee of Public Safety.

The 2nd of June was a Sunday and there was not much prospect of continuing the popular agitation longer, since most of the *sans-culottes* could obtain considerably more than the forty sous voted them by the Convention, if they returned to work. By now the Commune, perhaps convinced that it could control events and avert bloodshed, had determined to secure the expulsion of the Girondins from the Convention. The Assembly's session began with the courageous deputy Lanjuinais, far from any thought of compromise, denouncing the insurrection, demanding the disbanding of all insurrectionary bodies and calling for the outlawry of any who formed new ones. Then arrived the Commune's threatening demand for the trial of the Girondin leaders: 'We have come, for the last time, to demand justice against the guilty. . . .' This was referred to the Committee of Public Safety with a request for an immediate report. Barère, for the Committee, announced shortly afterwards that there was no ground for prosecuting the Girondins, but that they were invited to suspend themselves for a limited period. Isnard, Lanthenas, and Fauchet took advantage of the offer, and the first two survived the Terror unharmed. Lanjuinais and Barbaroux refused, and they spoke for the remainder, most of whom were absent. The debate continued, while the Convention was surrounded by picked battalions of National Guards who served both to protect the deputies from any mob violence and also to subject them to the threat of military intervention. The Montagnards were divided between their desire to have done with the Girondins and their indignation at the pressure to which the Assembly was subjected. On the motion of Barère they left the Chamber, but an impenetrable ring of National Guards left them no alternative but to return. Eventually, at the suggestion of Couthon, they voted to put 29 leading Girondins under house-arrest, without preferring any charge against them.

The 31st of May soon came to be regarded as one of the great *journées* of the Revolution. It shared with 14th July and 10th August the honour of having a ship of the line named after it. But the results of the three-day crisis left all the participants dissatisfied. Danton's hopes of a last-minute compromise with the Girondins had been shattered. Although the Montagnards had succeeded in averting bloodshed the outrage to the Assembly might well set the provinces on fire. At the same time, their restraint had prevented any decisive action, for a vote of the Convention would be sufficient to restore the Girondins to their seats—if they had not already escaped to begin a new civil war. But at least the Montagnards now had a chance to govern the country and to infuse new energy into national defence. The *enragés* had much less to show for three days' work

THE DIVISION OF THE REPUBLICANS

in which they had assumed both the initiative and the risks. What exactly they had hoped to achieve is by no means clear, but their objectives were presumably not limited to the political victory of the Montagnards. As it was, the Convention failed to honour the promise it made on 2nd June to create a Parisian revolutionary army, and petitions for general price controls (*maximum général*), a purge of all noble officers, the arrest of suspects and the arming of the *sans-culottes* all went unheeded. The *enragés* must have felt that they had pulled the Jacobins' chestnuts out of the fire for them.[1] They were as far as ever from controlling the Convention, or even the Commune, and their demands were still unlikely to receive much attention unless supported by a new threat of force.

[1] See D. Guérin, *La Lutte des Classes sous la Première République* (Paris, 1946), I, chap. ii.

VIII

<hr>

The Precarious Victory of the Sans-culottes

<hr>

Il a toujours regardé les lois sur le maximum, l'agiotage et les accaparements, comme des lois de terreurs dont l'exécution ne pouvait guère être procurée que par elle.

(Interrogation of the Besançon revolutionary, P. J. BRIOT)

DURING the six weeks that followed the inconclusive *journées* of 31st May–2nd June life continued very much as before. In the Convention, Ducos and Boyer-Fonfrède courageously kept up the fight in the name of their arrested Girondin colleagues. On 6th June seventy-five deputies signed a protest against the purge of the Assembly. With a good deal of sympathy from the Centre, or *Marais*, the remaining Girondins campaigned for the recall of the arrested deputies and debates were at times as noisily inconclusive as in previous months. The Committee of Public Safety, preoccupied with justifying the recent *journées* to the nation as a whole, and genuinely anxious for compromise, was more suspicious of the Commune than of the defeated Girondins. Barère's report on the recent insurrection, read on 6th June and mainly directed against the Commune, concluded with a demand for the dismissal of Hanriot and all *comités révolutionnaires*, and for an end to the Commune's censorship of newspapers and letters. Even Saint-Just, as uncompromising a Montagnard as any, when he presented to the Assembly on 8th July the proposals of the Committee for dealing with the

182

Girondins, appealed for unity and reconciliation: 'Proscribe those who have fled from us to take up arms . . . not for what they have said but for what they have done. Judge the rest and pardon the majority. Mistakes must not be confused with crimes and you have no wish to be severe. The time has come at last when the people may hope for happiness, when liberty is no longer a matter of party faction. No, you have not come here to disturb the land but to comfort it after the long misery of its enslavement. Let us restore domestic peace. . . .' Montagnards such as Chabot and Billaud-Varenne who demanded a combination of violence and social levelling—the arrest of suspects, progressive taxation of the rich and the creation of a well-paid *sans-culotte* militia—were isolated and without much influence. The majority hoped that the new constitution, drafted in great haste and voted on 24th June, would reunite the various revolutionary factions and win back all but the most irreconcilable Girondins.

The Paris Commune, while more insistent on the punishment of the Girondin leaders, was equally opposed to violence and eager to clear itself of the charge of aspiring to dictatorship. When the *enragé*, Leclerc, called for a policy of violence, Hébert joined in the universal outcry against him. The insurrectional committee that had directed—or tried to direct—the *journées* was disbanded, the majority of its members being absorbed into the revolutionary 'establishment' as a new Committee of Public Safety of the Paris Department, in which capacity they had no significant influence on the subsequent course of the Revolution.[1] The Paris Sections were as divided as they had been in May, with a score or so advocating more radical policies and about as many in opposition.[2] Three Sections went so far as to open negotiations with the Girondin faction in Normandy, whose forces were marching on Paris. The divided state of Parisian opinion was clearly revealed on 18th June when elections were held for the post of Commanding Officer of the National Guard. On the first poll Raffet, of the very conservative *Butte des Moulins* Section, came slightly

[1] See H. Calvet, *Un Instrument de la Terreur à Paris: le Comité de Salut Public ou de Surveillance du Département de Paris* (Paris, 1941).
[2] A. Soboul, *Les Sans-culottes Parisiens en l'An II*, pp. 36–89; R. Cobb, *Les Armées Révolutionnaires*, I. 40–47.

ahead of Hanriot, and it was not without some difficulty that the Montagnards secured the election of the latter at the second ballot. The Sections were once again agitated by a new levy of men for the Vendée and the attempt to arrest suspects encouraged each to protect its own citizens against the rest.

It was in the provinces that the purge of the Convention produced the sharpest reaction. While the frontier Departments and those close to the Vendée accepted the *fait accompli*, most of the remainder denounced the Parisians' usurpation of the right to interfere with a national assembly. The Departmental authorities called for volunteers for a march on Paris. Superficially, the situation of the Montagnards was hopeless, with the revolt of most of the provinces superimposed on foreign invasion and civil war. But the rapid drafting of the new constitution appeared to confirm their claim that they were sincere democrats who had been prevented by Girondin intrigue from governing the country effectively. When popular hostility to the recruitment of men for the armies on the frontiers was so marked it was virtually impossible to raise new forces for a civil war and the 'federalist revolt' proved to be a fire of straw. Encouraged by the conciliatory attitude of the Montagnards, the rebel authorities retracted their proclamations and made their peace. With the exception of Toulon, where the deputies of the Sections overthrew the Montagnard municipality in July, the only persistent opposition came from areas which had already declared against Paris before hearing of the insurrection of 31st May: Lyons, Marseilles, Bordeaux, and Caen. In this respect, too, no decisive results had been achieved by the *journées*.

The objectives of Montagnard policy were those defined by Saint-Just: to restore the unity of the revolutionaries by reconciling opponents and to win support by what Robespierre described as 'popular laws', without making any concessions to the *enragé* programme of economic controls enforced by violence and intimidation. On 6th June the sale of *émigré* property was resumed. In villages which owned no common land heads of families owning less than one *arpent* (very roughly, an acre) were to receive an *arpent* on a perpetual lease.[1] Despite this

---

[1] On 13th September this was amended to offer such heads of families, instead of an actual grant of land, an interest-free loan of 500 livres, repayable over 20 years, which could be used for the purchase of *émigré* land.

gesture towards the poor, the instruction that local authorities were to split up *émigré* holdings 'so far as may be possible without damaging each farm or estate' was somewhat less radical than the previous law of 2 September 1792.

On 10th June the division of common land was ordered if one-third of the members of a village requested it, the common to be divided equally amongst all inhabitants, irrespective of age and sex, whether they previously owned any land or not.[1] Although sometimes greeted with enthusiasm, this right to divide up the common was by no means universally enforced, the poorer peasants often preferring a share in communal grazing rights to the exclusive ownership of a fraction that might be too small to be of much value. Of more practical importance was the law of 17th July which completed the destruction of 'feudalism'. The new law, besides ordering the destruction of all feudal title deeds, stipulated that all feudal dues and claims, 'even those preserved by the law of 25th August' (1792) were to be abolished without compensation. Obligations of a non-feudal character, relating purely to the ownership of land were specifically retained. The intention of the Assembly seems clear enough: to uphold property rights in general, while abolishing feudal liabilities even when documentary proof survived that they had originally been incurred in connection with a transfer of land. In practice, however, it was impossible to draw any sharp distinction between feudal and non-feudal contracts, since many commoners, when making leases in the years before the Revolution, had added to the rent a nominal *cens* that entitled them to *droits casuels* or introduced a few scraps of feudal terminology into the conveyances. Called upon to interpret the law of 17th July, the Convention, on 25 February 1794, decreed the abolition of all obligations where the contract was 'originally sullied by the slightest mark of feudalism'. The result was therefore to expropriate many *roturiers* who paid dearly for the snobbery or business acumen of themselves or their ancestors. The law, thus interpreted, led to considerable protest and litigation, but the radical ruling of February 1794 survived all subsequent assaults and remained the law of the land.[2] It is

---

[1] See G. Bourgin, *Le Partage des Biens Communaux* (Paris, 1908).

[2] M. Garaud, *Histoire Générale du Droit Privé Français: la Révolution et la Propriété Foncière*, pp. 227–39.

impossible to assess with any accuracy the social repercussions of this legislation, but Aulard described it as 'a revolution within the Revolution' and Sagnac condemned it as 'the most unjust expropriation of the Revolution'.[1]

The Montagnards at the same time provided France with her first democratic constitution. The detailed provisions of the Constitution of 1793 are of mainly theoretical interest, since it never came into operation, but at least the principle of universal manhood suffrage had been proclaimed and was henceforth to become a part of the French radical tradition.[2] The discussion of the revised Declaration of the Rights of Man gave rise to much speculation about the relationship between private property and the claims of society. The deputy Harmand declared that the man who was hungry and in need required more than *une égalité mentale* and denied the existence of any absolute right to private property. Robespierre defined property in conditional terms as the right to dispose of that portion of one's goods which is guaranteed by law. The final version adopted by the Convention was much more conservative, the right to property being defined in terms as absolute as those of 1789— perhaps with a view to reassuring provincial opinion against the repeated Girondin assertions that the Montagnards were social and economic levellers. Robespierre's advocacy of progressive taxation similarly found no place in the final text. On the other hand, the responsibility of society to provide work for the able-bodied and subsistence for all, and to make education universally available, was officially placed on record. On 13th July Robespierre read to the Convention a draft scheme for a national educational system which had been prepared by Le Pelletier, a Montagnard deputy murdered by a royalist at the time of the king's execution. Le Pelletier's text may be quoted as an example of 'advanced' Montagnard ideas in the first half of 1793: 'The revolutions of the past three years have done everything for the other classes of citizens and practically nothing for what is perhaps the most important, the proletarian citizens whose only property is their labour. Feudalism is destroyed, but not

---

[1] A. Aulard, *La Révolution Française et le Régime Féodal*, p. 252; P. Sagnac, *La Législation Civile de la Révolution Française*, p. 148.

[2] For the text of the constitution see J. M. Thompson, *French Revolution Documents*, pp. 238–52.

for their benefit, for they own none of the liberated fields. . . .
Civil equality is restored, but they have neither education nor
instruction.' But the Le Pelletier Education Bill, like the constitution itself, was to remain an aspiration. The 'proletarian
citizens' might be impressed by the solicitude of those who
governed in their name, but they also demanded more tangible
results.

The first serious Parisian challenge since 2nd June came, in
fact, when representatives of the Commune were congratulating
the Convention on the voting of the constitution. Jacques Roux,
who was a member of the deputation, tried to present an address
of his own. Headed off by Robespierre, who had the session
adjourned, he returned to the attack on 25th June, bitterly
criticizing the deputies' attempt to preserve national unity by a
policy of moderation. 'Have you outlawed speculation? No.
Have you decreed the death penalty for hoarding? No. Have
you defined the limits to the freedom of trade? No. Have you
banned the exchange of assignats for specie? No. . . . Deputies
of the *Montagne*, why have you not climbed from the third to
the ninth floor of the houses of this revolutionary city? You
would have been moved by the tears and sighs of an immense
population without food and clothing, brought to such distress
and misery by speculation and hoarding, because the laws have
been cruel to the poor, because they have been made only by the
rich and for the rich. . . . You must not be afraid of the hatred
of the rich—in other words, of the wicked. You must not be
afraid to sacrifice political principles to the salvation of the
people, which is the supreme law. Admit then that, out of
timidity, you accept the discredit of the paper currency, you
prepare the way for bankruptcy by tolerating abuses and
crimes that would have made despotism blush in the last days
of its barbaric power.' Whether or not Roux was directly involved, the renewed outbreak of *taxation populaire* that started
on the following day, when soap was seized and sold at a price
fixed by the laundresses themselves, must have convinced the
deputies that they could not hope to keep control over the *sans-
culottes* while the *enragé* leader was still at large. On 30th June
the Montagnards set about his destruction. A deputation of
twelve leading politicians including Robespierre, Billaud-
Varenne, Collot d'Herbois, Hébert, and Thuriot, went from

the Jacobin Club and induced the Cordeliers to expel him. On 4th July Marat published a savage attack on him, and his local rival, the deputy Léonard Bourdon, persuaded the *Gravilliers* Section to disown him. Robespierre kept up the pressure during the summer, denouncing him to the Jacobin Club as an enemy agent on 5th August and three days later persuading the Convention to order an enquiry into his conduct. Roux was to win back the *Gravilliers* later in the month, but never to recover his former influence. Henceforth the *enragés* were on the defensive.

While refusing any concessions to the threat from the streets, the Montagnards were also winning some successes in the provinces. The 'federalist revolt' over most of France collapsed almost as quickly as it had arisen. Even the insurrection in Normandy came to nothing after the rout at Pacy-sur-Eure of the column marching on Paris. For a time it looked as though the Montagnards might succeed in isolating the Girondin leaders who had fled from Paris to organize local resistance, and win the confidence of the nation as a whole, which alone could preserve them from dependence on the *sans-culottes*.

The immediate issue turned on the course of the war. The balance of power in the Committee of Public Safety was transformed in July by the elimination of Danton and the advocates of a compromise peace and their replacement by more radical Montagnards, including Robespierre himself. The new committee would be judged by its success in winning the war, but it would inevitably be some months before the energy of the Government could be transferred to the armies and munition factories. Until the Committee could repel the invaders and destroy the insurrection in the Vendée it would have to bear the responsibility for its predecessor's omissions and mistakes, and perhaps make substantial concessions to popular feeling until it should be strong enough to guarantee the frontiers and impose order at home.

All through June things had been going badly in the Vendée. An eastward thrust in the middle of the month had given the rebels temporary possession of Angers, Saumur, and Chinon, and spread panic as far as Tours. The withdrawal of this raiding force was followed on 28th–29th June by a desperate battle for Nantes. The capture of the great trading port would have constituted a major rebel triumph and might conceivably have allowed the royalists to obtain British reinforcements and thereby transformed the whole nature of the insurrection. The peasant army penetrated the suburbs, but was eventually thrown back after much bitter fighting. The defeat before Nantes, however, had little immediate effect on the situation of the rebel forces. On 5th July they destroyed Westermann's army before Châtillon and the republican record remained on the whole one of failure. The continuing bloody defeats infuriated public opinion, which attributed them to the incompetence or treason of the republican commanders and demanded that the Government should dismiss the ineffective and punish the disloyal.

July and August were bad months on the frontiers, too. Within three weeks Mainz, the besieged relic of the conquests of the previous autumn, capitulated to the Prussians and the Austrians seized the frontier fortresses of Condé and Valenciennes and invaded northern France. Spanish troops crossed the Pyrenees and began advancing on Perpignan. The Piedmontese took advantage of the diversion of republican forces to Lyons in order to invade France from the East. In Corsica Paoli's revolt, soon to have British naval support, was to expel the French from the whole island. British troops opened the siege of Dunkirk in August and in October the Allies invaded Alsace. The military situation could scarcely have been more desperate.

The problems of the republican Government were complicated by the success of the royalists in winning at least partial control of the last centres of the provincial revolt, Lyons and Marseilles, and thereby making an armed conflict with Paris inevitable. The comte de Précy was put in charge of the defence of Lyons on 8th July and the rebel authorities in the second city in France began executing their defeated opponents, Chalier going to the guillotine on the 16th. Both sides prepared for battle. On 12th July the Convention ordered troops to be sent against Lyons and the siege of the great city began on 8th August. The disaffection of Lyons greatly hampered military communications with the south-east and perhaps encouraged Marseilles to take up arms against the Montagnards. The Marseilles forces advancing on Lyons were thrown back and republican troops entered the Mediterranean port on 25th August, just in time to prevent it from capitulating to Hood's fleet, cruising offshore. At Toulon they were too late. The

municipal counter-revolution of July for a time temporized with
the Montagnard Government in Paris. Faced with the advance
of republican troops, the Toulonnais on 27th August handed
over the town, the arsenal and the fleet to Hood and proclaimed
Louis XVII as king.[1] Thus at one blow there passed into enemy
hands, without a shot being fired, 26 of the Republic's 65 ships
of the line and 16 of its 61 frigates, a disaster worse than
Trafalgar, since there was no guarantee that the undamaged
French fleet would not reinforce the allied navies.[2] There could
hardly have been a more convincing demonstration of the extremists' thesis that the Republic had more to fear from the
treason of its old commanders than from the possible incompetence of rapidly-promoted *patriotes*. The fact that few of the
captains who surrendered their ships were of noble birth merely
seemed to confirm the opinion of one of the observers of the
Minister of the Interior that the 'patriots of 1789' had now
joined forces with the nobility against the Revolution.

In addition to the long series of military reverses there were
other incidents well calculated to excite the fury of the revolutionaries and to convince them that their opponents had abandoned all the restraints of civilized behaviour. The heroic folly
of Charlotte Corday, when she murdered the *sans-culotte* idol,
Marat, on 13th July, was perhaps the most striking example.
She had been in touch with Girondin rebels in Normandy and
they were very understandably, though erroneously, believed
to have used her as their agent. Marat's murder was a blunder
as well as a crime, for, as Levasseur pointed out, he had served
the Montagnards as a kind of safety-valve. His violence won
him the confidence of the *sans-culottes* without giving him any
serious influence in the Convention, and his fundamentally
moderate policies preserved his popular clientele from the
seductions of more radical politicians such as Roux and Hébert.[3]
The British declaration that grain would be considered contra-
band inaugurated a form of economic warfare to which the
eighteenth century was not accustomed. The seizure of the
papers of an English spy allowed Barère to inform the Conven-

[1] See Z. Pons, *Mémoires pour servir à l'Histoire de la Ville de Toulon* (Paris, 1825).

[2] For the consequences to the French navy, see N. Hampson, *La Marine de l'AnII*, pp. 219–26.

[3] R. Levasseur, *Mémoires* (Paris, 1829), I. 307–8.

tion on 1st August of a British plot to sabotage the French war effort, burn crops and discredit the assignat by keeping goods off the market. A surprising number of fires in military and naval arsenals seemed to confirm the existence of such a network and led the Convention to declare Pitt 'the enemy of the human race'.

The general result of this long succession of treason, defeat, assassination and espionage was to discredit the Montagnard policy of revolutionary unity by conciliation and to reinforce the argument of the extremists that the leaders of 1789, the officers of the army and navy, the wealthy and educated men who had often led the provincial revolts, the middle class in general, were weary of the Revolution and would accept any terms from the enemy. The defence of France therefore rested on the resolution of a small minority of educated Montagnards supported, they hoped, by the majority of the urban *sans-culottes* and perhaps by the poorer peasants. The advocates of this thesis tended to think in the black-and-white moral terms dear to Robespierre: the enemies of the Revolution were egoists who put the enjoyment of wealth and property before the regeneration of France. Deaf to the appeal of patriotism, they must be intimidated and coerced into supporting a movement from which they had profited more than most. In this way national defence became fused with the social advancement of the *sans-culottes*, the only reliable revolutionary force left, whose lives and livelihood must be preserved by force against the activities of the speculators, food-hoarders, corrupt war contractors and ambitious generals who would betray the Revolution for their personal advantage. Victory, the satisfaction of the *sans-culottes*, and the Terror seemed three aspects of the same goal.

To some extent all the Montagnard leaders were influenced by this kind of reasoning. All became more aware of the need to seek *sans-culotte* support and more prepared to employ violent methods against their adversaries. On 1st August the Convention voted to try Marie Antoinette, to devastate the Vendée and evacuate its women and children, and to arrest all enemy aliens not resident in France on 14 July 1789. Within this general climate of opinion each reacted in accordance with his own temperament. Danton stressed the need to strengthen the Central Government and proposed that the Committee of Public

Safety be given the title of Provisional Government, with control over the Ministers. Robespierre was more concerned with the repression of counter-revolutionaries. On 11th August, in a speech of extreme violence, he attributed all French reverses to domestic treason, at the front, in the Press, in the revolutionary tribunal, in the streets—where popular demonstrators were 'paid to mislead the people'—in the Committee of Public Safety itself. Hébert thought more in terms of his own personal advancement. After the murder of Marat and the eclipse of Jacques Roux, he aspired to become the leader of the Parisian *sans-culottes*. His newspaper, the *Père Duchesne*, written in an inimitable style which combined brilliantly violence, coarse humour, shrewd common sense and feeling for a popular audience, gave him the ear of the *sans-culottes*, while his position on the Commune brought him close to the centres of political power. Hébert now began to strike out for himself, parting company with the Montagnards, attacking Danton and looking to popular support for the means of putting pressure on the Convention.

The Montagnards, in view of the desperate situation, accepted the need to make further concessions to the *sans-culottes*, but they were determined to retain control of the revolutionary movement. The Parisians, however, showed signs of taking the law into their own hands. Infuriated by the accumulation of defeat and treason, they were further exasperated by a shortage of bread that became particularly acute in August. Once more the queues began to form at dawn outside the bakers' shops— and to blame the shortage on a 'famine plot'. Bread was scarce and the prices of all other commodities had been rising rapidly during the past months.[1] The unrest in the Sections, alarmed by rumours of an impending breakdown in the bread supply, was similar to that which had kept Paris on edge from February to May and the question was whether the Convention would be able to avert another *journée*, which this time might overthrow the Montagnards themselves.

In the hope of evading the imposition of general price controls, the Assembly decreed the death penalty for the hoarding of necessities, on 27th July, setting up *commissaires aux accapare-*

---

[1] See G. Rudé, *The Crowd in the French Revolution*, for some examples.

192

ments in each Section to implement the new law.[1] On 9th August the creation of public granaries was voted, but whereas Léonard Bourdon had proposed that a central food administration should fill these by the requisition of all the grain left from the 1792 harvest·and two-thirds of that of the present year, the Convention was content to grant a credit of one hundred million livres to the Committee of Public Safety with which it might purchase grain. In other words, the amended project was a palliative, unlikely to have much effect in the long run and quite inoperative until the new harvest should be threshed.[2] On 15th August representatives on mission were authorized to requisition grain to supply Paris, a measure extended on the 29th to include all Departments short of grain. Departments were authorized to impose price controls on all kinds of fuel on 19th August and on the following day oats were added to the basic foodstuffs subject to controls. A measure of a primarily military nature, although it was to have important economic consequences, was the voting of the *levée en masse* on 23rd August. This attempt at a general mobilization of the entire active population for one mighty campaign to end the war represented a compromise between popular extremism and the views of the authorities on what was militarily practicable. The only men mobilized for the army were bachelors and widowers without children, of the 18–25 age-group—many of whom were already in the army. The remainder, men and women, could be requisitioned at will by agents of the Government for all kinds of work connected with the war effort. The law of 23rd August also provided for the creation of the national armaments factories that would be needed to equip the 400,000–500,000 new recruits. To feed this swollen army, all taxes in arrears and two-thirds of those due by farmers for the current year were to be delivered in kind. The representatives of provincial France who had come to Paris to celebrate the acceptance of the new constitution, in a great festival on 10th August, were ordered to supervise the application of the *levée en masse* on their return home, so that the patriotic fervour of Paris might be spread throughout the whole country.

[1] See H. Calvet, *L'Accaparement à Paris sous la Terreur* (Paris, 1933), for an account of the rather ineffective operation of this law.
[2] On this subject, see A. Mathiez, *La Vie Chère et le Mouvement Social sous la Terreur*, pp. 292–314, 370–85.

On 3rd September was voted the final draft of a Bill for a forced loan on the rich, a measure that had been in the air for the past six months. Calculated on income during 1791, as declared by the taxpayer, personal allowances exempted the great majority of the population. The remainder were taxed according to a sharply-rising sliding scale, all taxable income in excess of 9,000 livres being appropriated by the State. This draconian measure appears to have proved a good deal less effective than was expected, perhaps because it implied a degree of bureaucratic organization beyond the scope of eighteenth-century France. The loan, which was estimated as likely to yield one milliard livres, actually produced rather less than 200 million.[1]

However gratified the Parisian *sans-culottes* may have been by the prospect of a 'people's war', they still suspected the Convention of half-heartedness, reluctance to accept economic controls and indulgence towards the enemies of the Revolution. The advocates of general price controls had been unsuccessful in the Assembly, the trial of Marie Antoinette and the Girondin leaders seemed no nearer and demands for the elimination of all noble officers from the army were disregarded. The Jacobins themselves took up the popular cry for the trial of the queen and the Girondins, the creation of a *sans-culotte* revolutionary army with its own tribunal and guillotine, and the purge of noble officers.[2] Rumours of the entry of the British fleet into Toulon made a popular demonstration virtually certain. Nevertheless, when the *Hôtel de Ville* was besieged on 4th September by a mass of working men calling for higher wages and an improvement in the supply of bread, this seems to have been a spontaneous economic protest rather than a political mobilization of *sans-culotte* forces. All the politicians were taken by surprise. Chaumette dashed to the Convention to denounce the demonstrators as counter-revolutionaries trying to interfere with the *levée en masse*. Robespierre, at the Jacobin Club, asserted that the mayor was surrounded 'not by the people but by a handful of intriguers'. Such arguments might impress middle-class Montagnards, but when Chaumette returned to

---

[1] For a local example of the use made of the forced loan, see M. Albert, *Le Fédéralisme dans la Haute-Garonne* (Paris, 1932), p. 189.

[2] The 'revolutionary armies' were an armed *sans-culotte* militia intended for use in the interior to overawe counter-revolutionaries and, more specifically, to extract hidden supplies of grain from recalcitrant farmers.

the crowd with nothing better than a promise that the Convention had approved in principle the introduction of general price controls, he had to face the reality of hungry and exasperated men clamouring for bread. He seems to have decided on the spot to swim with the tide. Springing on to a table, he declared 'This is open war between the rich and the poor!' and demanded the immediate creation of a revolutionary army. Hébert joined in to propose a mass march on the Convention on the following day to enforce the creation of this revolutionary army.

On 5th September the Convention, always more ready to accept political repression than economic controls, had already voted to accelerate the work of the revolutionary tribunal when Chaumette arrived with the crowd which had marched from the *Hôtel de Ville*. His request for the immediate voting of a revolutionary army produced a violent debate. Billaud-Varenne and Léonard Bourdon proposed more extreme measures, while Jeanbon Saint-André of the Committee of Public Safety and Basire stressed the need to avoid precipitate action. Danton, in a successful diversion, induced the Assembly to vote the payment of forty sous to indigent *sans-culottes* for attendance at each meeting of their Sections. These meetings were to be reduced to two each week. Danton also secured the vote of a credit of 100 million livres for the manufacture of arms. Billaud-Varenne then persuaded the Assembly to agree to the payment of members of the *comités révolutionnaires* of the Paris Sections and provincial Communes. The Convention went on to order the immediate arrest of all suspects and at the end of the session the Committee of Public Safety promised to introduce a motion for the creation of a revolutionary army. Although nothing was done to establish the price controls dear to the *sans-culottes*, the extreme violence of many of the speakers indicated that *sans-culotte mores* had penetrated the Convention itself. Chaumette set the tone with his 'No more quarter, no more mercy for traitors. . . . The day of justice and wrath has arrived!' A Jacobin deputation demanded that Terror be the order of the day. The humanitarian Jaurès, horrified by the change that had come over the Assembly, was moved to write of this debate, 'Revolutions are the barbaric aspect of progress. However noble, however fertile, however necessary a revolution may be, it still belongs to the inferior and semi-bestial stage of human history.'[1] Nevertheless, when Drouet, the man who had arrested the royal family at Varennes, in the excitement of the moment cried 'Let us be brigands for the welfare of the people!' and proposed a general massacre of suspects if the Revolution seemed in danger, he was shouted down and the Convention made it clear that repression, however terrible, was to be legally controlled and not a matter of anarchic vengeance.

The *journée* of 5th September was as important for its implications as for its immediate fruits. The addition of the extremist deputies, Billaud-Varenne and Collot d'Herbois, to the Committee of Public Safety on the following day inclined the Government towards more violent measures. The Committee's delaying tactics on the 5th had been unsuccessful and it realized that further attempts to resist popular pressure in the near future would be ineffective. Accordingly, the Committee and the Convention resigned themselves to the generalization of controls. On 11th September a national maximum price was decreed for all bread grains, flour and forage, and on the 29th the threat of renewed pressure from the streets induced the Assembly to vote the *maximum général*, for so long the objective of the *sans-culottes*. A national price was fixed for tobacco, salt and soap. The price of all other 'necessities' was to be fixed by the Districts at one-third above the prices obtaining in 1790. Wages were similarly to be locally controlled, at 50 per cent above 1790 levels—a provision which presumably took the *sans-culottes* by surprise. The Convention accepted general economic controls with obvious reluctance, but the Committee of Public Safety made a genuine effort to make them work. Henceforth much of the economy was to be regulated by controls and their attendant requisitions. The grain trade virtually disappeared with the incentive to seek higher prices on more distant markets. Towns and whole Departments came to rely for their supplies of corn on requisitions by representatives on mission, until a central Food Commission was created to supervise the distribution of food throughout the entire country. Eventually many municipalities took over the grain trade themselves, supplying the bakers with their flour and selling to the townspeople the ration tickets that could then be exchanged for

[1] J. Jaurès, *Histoire Socialiste*, IV. 1671.

bread. [1] While the food trade was becoming increasingly subject to controls the enormously expanded war industries came to rely almost entirely on requisitions for their supplies of raw materials and labour. [2] The State became, directly or indirectly, the controlling force behind most of the economic activity of the nation. In the economic as well as in the political field coercion took the place of consent, and in view of the rudimentary bureaucratic methods at the disposal of the controllers of 1793, such coercion could only take the form of intimidation by the dramatic punishment of those offenders who were caught. The Jacobin, Brichet, summed up the views of the more violent of his colleagues when he suggested that the revolutionary army, on arriving in a village, should enquire if the principal farmer were wealthy. 'In the affirmative, you can guillotine him—he's bound to be a food-hoarder.'

The crisis of September 1793 marked a decisive turning-point in the Revolution. Henceforth the illusion of national unity was replaced by the ruthless extermination of enemies and the intimidation of the unreliable. The Law of Suspects of 17th September defined—if the term be permissible for such vague and all-embracing classification—the categories of men who were to be held in prison for the duration of the war. [3] Old enemies were despatched by the revolutionary tribunal: Marie Antoinette on 16th October, Barnave on the 29th, twenty-one Girondin leaders on 1st November, the duc d'Orléans on the 7th, Madame Roland on the following day, Bailly on the 11th, Madame Dubarry on 8th December. Some deputies, including Amar of the Committee of General Security, would have included in this proscription the 75 deputies who had protested against the *journée* of 2nd June, but the intervention of Robespierre kept them safely in prison and out of the hands of the public prosecutor, Fouquier-Tinville. The Committee of Public Safety's instructions to representatives on mission reflected the changed mood. For example, Prieur de la Marne wrote to le Carpentier on 7th September, 'Surround yourself with true *sans-culottes* and you will be able to distinguish the conspirators and

[1] See, for example, C. Porée, *Les Subsistances dans l'Yonne* (Auxerre-Paris, 1903), pp. liii–lvi.
[2] See L. Lévy-Schneider, *Le Conventionnel Jeanbon Saint-André* (Paris, 1901), pp. 768–9, for a description of the situation at Brest.
[3] For the text, see Thompson, *op. cit.*, pp. 258–60.

treacherous leaders from those who have merely fallen into a temporary error. Above all, beware of the deceitful civilities of the local government bodies.' The Committee wrote to the representatives with the Army of the Rhine, on 6th October, 'Watch the generals. Make no allowances for them. When the armies are endangered it is almost always because of their treason.' When Lyons capitulated on 9th October the Convention ordered its destruction and the Committee sent Collot d'Herbois to replace Robespierre's friend Couthon, on the ground that Couthon was showing too much indulgence to the defeated rebels. Saint-Just—the man who, in July, had advocated clemency towards the Girondins—defined the principles of the Terror in his speech of 10th October: 'You have no more grounds for restraint against the enemies of the new order, and liberty must prevail at any price. . . . You must punish not merely traitors but the indifferent as well; you must punish whoever is passive in the Republic. . . . These maxims (peace and justice) hold good as between friends of liberty, but between the people and its enemies there is only the sword in common. We must rule by iron those who cannot be ruled by justice. . . .'

This atmosphere of patriotic exaltation, suspicion and violence left a permanent mark on the religious situation also.[1] The revolutionaries, like all their contemporaries, found it difficult to imagine a disestablished Church. Church and State were automatically allies or enemies in a relationship which excluded neutrality. The constitutional clergy had therefore been closely associated with the course of the Revolution. Popular victories were celebrated with a *Te Deum* and new laws expounded from parish pulpits, while the lay authorities were represented at Church festivals. So automatic was the identification of Church and State that in some parts of France failure to attend church was a punishable offence—the assumption being that the absentee was a supporter of the 'non-juror' clergy.[2] Since the overthrow of the monarchy, however, the revolutionaries had become increasingly exasperated with their relig-

[1] See A. Aulard, *Le Culte de la Raison* (Paris, 1904), and A. Mathiez, *La Révolution et l'Eglise* (Paris, 1910).
[2] P. Caron, *Rapports des Agents du Ministre de l'Intérieur dans les Départements*, II. 423.

ious partners. This may have been partly due to political factors such as the reluctance of some of the clergy to accept the execution of the king, but there were more fundamental reasons why the *patriotes* were turning against the Church. The Revolution itself was taking on some of the attributes of a religious cult. With its sacred oaths, altars of the fatherland, sacred trees of liberty, etc., it was gradually assuming the form of a civic religion similar to that advocated by Rousseau in the last chapter of *Du Contrat Social*.[1] As the citizen came to dwarf both the individual and the parishioner, the claims of the Church to represent a standard of values outside civil society were more and more resented. The value of religion was as yet unquestioned, but a distinction was drawn between religion and the clergy and the latter were increasingly judged by the standards of lay society. As an agent of the Minister of the Interior wrote on 7th August, 'I wish all priests were married . . . priests are as useless as religion is useful.' The revolutionaries were offended by clerical celibacy as a threat to morals, an insult to 'Nature' and a repudiation of the citizen's duty to bring up a patriotic family. Since marriage had become a civil contract there was nothing—in the eyes of the State—to prevent a clergyman from complying with his patriotic duty. On 19 July 1793 the case of a bishop who prevented one of his *curés* from marrying aroused the anger of the Convention. Delacroix denounced such action as '*blasphemy* against the sovereignty of the people' and the Assembly eventually voted that bishops who interfered in this way were to be deported and replaced. Some of the parish clergy had already married before the summer of 1793, particularly where the local bishop was favourable, as in the Dordogne, and the sermon of Torné, bishop of the Cher, on 18th August, gave a powerful stimulus to the movement. There were indications of a tendency on the part of the laity to turn away from orthodox Catholicism in favour of a cult of the Revolution itself. In the Loir-et-Cher the renaming of localities with religious names had started in September 1792. Street names were changed in Compiègne in August 1793, in Blois in September and Beauvais in October. The Paris Section, *Croix Rouge*, similarly changed its name to the more revolutionary

---

[1] See J. Gallerand, *Les Cultes sous la Terreur en Loir-et-Cher* (Blois, 1928), introduction to Part III.

Bonnet Rouge. New-born citizens were being given 'un-Christian' names in parts of France and this practice was apparently common in Beauvais in early 1793.[1] On 23rd July the Convention voted to leave only one church bell in each parish, the rest to be melted down for gun-metal, an early illustration of the association of national defence with the attack on the Church. On 28th July the Cordeliers voted to suspend the heart of Marat from their roof and an excitable member of the Club apostrophized the grim relic: 'Precious remains of a god! Shall we be traitors to your shades. . . .' The great festival with which the Convention celebrated the acceptance of the constitution on 10 August 1793 looked to Rome for its inspiration, but to the Rome of antiquity. Christianity was ignored and in so far as the ritual had any significance its inspiration was primarily pantheist.[2]

In September two factors in particular inflated this widespread anti-clericalism into a positive campaign for the dechristianization of France. The first of these was the adoption of a republican calendar, proposed by Romme on 20th September and finally voted by the Convention on 7th October. The new republican era began with the abolition of the monarchy on 22 September 1792. The year was divided into twelve months of thirty days each, with five supplementary 'sans-culottides' at the end. The months, at first known merely as 'First', 'Second' etc., were given names by Fabre d'Eglantine on 24th November, illustrating the seasons to which they applied: *ventôse, floréal, thermidor*, etc. The division of the day on a decimal basis was approved but never implemented. The new calendar symbolized several aspects of revolutionary thought: the substitution of 'reason' for tradition, the cult of an idealized Nature and the breach with Christianity. The Christian festivals disappeared overnight, and Sundays with them, as the week gave place to the *décade*.[3] The enforcement of the *décadi* as a day of

[1] M. Dommanget, *La Déchristianisation à Beauvais et dans l'Oise, 1790–1801* (Besançon, 1918), p. 6.

[2] See Buchez and Roux, *Histoire Parlementaire de la Révolution Française*, XXVIII. 435 *et seq.*, for a good description of the ceremony.

[3] The argument of D. Guérin, *La Lutte des Classes sous la Première République* (Paris, 1946), I. 294, that the ten-day week was designed to increase the 'exploitation' of the working class would be more convincing if he quoted evidence to show that the men concerned, who were paid on a daily basis, preferred leisure to a higher income.

rest and of Sunday as a working day, together with the elimination of religious holidays, was bound to bring the State into conflict with the Church, while the adoption of the new calendar marked a big step towards the elimination of Christianity from everyday life.

The second move in the assault on the Christian religion began on 21st September, when Chaumette, on a visit to his native town of Nevers, encountered the local representative on mission, Fouché. Which of the two 'converted' the other is still open to conjecture, but Fouché, who had been in the area for two months already, had hitherto given no signs of revolutionary extremism beyond naming his daughter, born most appropriately on 10 August 1793, *Nièvre*. After his contact with Chaumette, Fouché at once embarked on a radical policy combining elements of social levelling, national defence and dechristianization.[1] On the 22nd he unveiled a bust of Brutus, 'god of the festival', in the church of Saint-Cyr at Nevers, and from the pulpit attacked 'religious sophistry'. On the 25th he denounced ecclesiastical celibacy, ordering all priests to marry, adopt a child or support an elderly person. At Moulins he declared the object of his mission to be to 'substitute for superstitious and hypocritical cults . . . that of the Republic and Morality'. Ecclesiastical vestments were burned, religious images destroyed and the Bishop of the Allier, followed by thirty of his clergy, persuaded to resign their functions. Back in Nevers in early October he issued a series of decrees intended to guarantee the livelihood of the local *sans-culottes* and to ensure the supply of bread to the market, at the expense of employers and landowners. The churches of the Nièvre and Allier were stripped of their ornaments, vestments and sacred vessels, which were despatched to the national treasury. On 9th October he banned all religious services outside churches and ordered the burial of all citizens in a common cemetery whose gates were to bear the inscription, 'Death is an eternal sleep'. Fouché's initiative revealed most of the characteristics that the dechristianization campaign was to take: the attack on 'superstition', the spoliation of the churches, the pressure on the clergy to resign and to marry; but the Christian religion, although humiliated, was not proscribed, and for the time being the

[1] L. Madelin, *Fouché* (Paris, 1900), I, chap. iv.

churches remained open, though there were few priests left to officiate.

On 26th September Chaumette, describing his encounter with Fouché, urged the Paris Commune to follow the example of the Nièvre, but met with no immediate response. On 23rd October Hébert succeeded in obtaining the destruction of all religious monuments outside churches. Dumont, representative on mission in the Oise, who was following a similar course, appeared in the Convention on 4th November with the spoils of the churches in his Department. Two days later Barère, in the name of the Committee of Public Safety, induced the Convention to authorize Communes to suppress such religious ceremonies as they chose to dispense with. The following day, 7th November, marked the first great triumph of the dechristianizers, when Gobel, Archbishop of Paris, came before the Convention and resigned his functions, followed by several deputies, including some bishops and one Protestant pastor. On the 10th a Festival of Reason was celebrated in Notre Dame, henceforth given over to the new cult, in the presence of the Convention. Five days later Communes were given the power to dispose of Church plate, and the campaign in Paris itself reached its peak on 23rd November when the Commune, under pressure from the Sections, ordered the closing of all churches in the city.

It was the apparent success of the dechristianization campaign in Paris that spread the movement throughout France. The sudden launching of this attack gives some plausibility to the argument advanced by certain historians that the whole movement was a political manoeuvre organized by Hébert and his friends with the demagogic intention of whipping up *sans-culotte* support for themselves. But whatever the responsibility of Hébert and Chaumette and their allies Proli, Clootz and Pereira, politicians who had no sympathy for the Commune, such as Fabre d'Eglantine and Thuriot, supported the campaign. Dumont had begun dechristianization in the Oise without waiting for the Commune. Opinion all over France had been moving in the same direction and the movement would never have spread with such extraordinary rapidity if it had not corresponded to the feelings of many revolutionaries in all parts of the country.

In default of any general account of the dechristianization

movement as a whole, the evidence of regional surveys is fragmentary and incomplete, but nevertheless adequate to suggest the extent of its influence.[1] The changing of the names of towns, villages and their streets and squares became so common as to confuse the Central Government.[2] In Beauvais alone, 65 such changes were recorded. More significant, as reflecting public opinion rather than the views of the municipal authorities, was the bestowal of first names which were not those of saints. Identification is not always easy, since the cautious could satisfy both sides with names such as *Jean-Jacques* or *Marguerite*, but it is clear that the practice, though far from uniform, was widespread. During the height of the movement 178 of the 376 names given at Beauvais were 'revolutionary'. In the Loir-et-Cher such names were common in parts of the countryside. In one or two villages they exceeded two-thirds of the total, although there were none at all in 232 of the Department's 311 Communes. In the town of Saint-Pol, in the Pas-de-Calais, non-Christian names were given to over 40 per cent of the children born during the year II.[3]

The spoliation of churches was widespread and the records of the Convention provide ample evidence of the tribute sent in by zealous representatives on mission and local authorities. The resignation of priests was common, but open to different interpretations. A minority abjured their faith and left the Church for ever. Many more simply resigned, as Gobel had done, and awaited better times. Some of these, however, did not find their way back into the Church, and in any case their resignations must have had a considerable effect on their congregations. Those who abandoned the ministry included many bishops, all the clergy in one District in the Dordogne and the majority of those in the Pas-de-Calais.[4] Faced with the threat of imprisonment,

[1] See in particular Gallerand, *op. cit.*; Dommanget, *op. cit.*; E. Campagnac, *Les Débuts de la Déchristianisation dans le Cher* (Paris, 1912); Cobb, *op. cit.*, vol. II, and Caron, *op. cit.*; and for Paris: A. Soboul, *Les Sans-culottes Parisiens en l'An II*, and P. Caron, *Paris pendant la Terreur* (Paris, 1910–58).

[2] See Figuères, *Les Noms Révolutionnaires des Communes de France* (Paris, 1901).

[3] G. Sangnier, *La Terreur dans le District de Saint-Pol* (Blangermont, 1938), II. 186.

[4] H. Labroue, *La Mission du Conventionnel Lakanal dans la Dordogne en l'An II* (Paris, 1912), p. 145; L. Jacob, *Joseph le Bon, la Terreur a la Frontière* (Paris, 1934), II. 85.

the majority of the clergy in the Loir-et-Cher appear to have followed suit, as did some hundreds in the Oise. If these figures are in any way typical of the situation elsewhere, there can have been few of the clergy officiating in France in the spring of 1794.

The marriage of a priest was a surer indication than his resignation of a decisive breach with orthodox Catholicism, and for this reason married clergy sometimes found favour with the dechristianizers—in the Loir-et-Cher, for example, they were exempt from the obligation to live under surveillance at Vendôme. Not unnaturally, the number of marriages was considerably less than that of resignations, but it was still appreciable. At Beauvais about fifteen priests, including the bishop, married, and by 1803, 50 of the 480 priests in the Oise had done so. In the Loir-et-Cher 64 parish clergy and 13 others married, as did the bishop of the Cher and many of his parish clergy. While the great majority of clerical marriages were concluded during the period of dechristianization, a few had preceded it and quite a number occurred later, when they could not be attributed to fear of persecution. The evidence therefore seems to suggest that the movement made many converts amongst the clergy themselves.

Cathedrals and parish churches were converted into Temples of Reason in most if not all the main towns of France and in rural parishes up and down the country. Burlesque processions mocked the rites of the Church. As picturesque a demonstration as any of the link between dechristianization and defence, in the mind of the *sans-culottes*, was the scene at Moulins on 27th November, when 130 of the local revolutionary army marched past the Club, before leaving for Lyons. 'The two sappers were wearing the mitres of the former bishop of the Allier and his vermeil crozier served the drum-major as a staff.'[1] Such churches as were not taken over by the revolutionary cult were closed. There was said to be not one left open in the Allier, the Pas-de-Calais and the Somme, and not many in the Loir-et-Cher. The local representative on mission ordered the closing of all churches in the Hautes and Basses-Pyrénées, and the arrest of all the clergy in the Landes and Lot-et-Garonne.[2] It would be

[1] P. Caron, *Rapports des Agents du Ministre de l'Intérieur dans les Départements* I. 463.

[2] A. Richard, *Le Gouvernement Révolutionnaire dans les Basses-Pyrénées* (Paris, 1923), pp. 168, 211.

rash to conclude that these Departments were typical of the whole country, but their evidence and the absence of information to the contrary suggests that the dechristianization movement had achieved a wide if temporary measure of success by the spring of 1794.[1]

Dechristianization was not a purely negative movement, but its positive aspect, the cult of Reason, was a matter of feeling rather than of theology and its doctrine varied from place to place. For some, Reason was the 'watchmaker God' of the eighteenth-century *philosophes*. Others put the emphasis on Nature, in a manner reminiscent of Rousseau. Almost everywhere Reason, personified perhaps by some local beauty (generally of good family and irreproachable morals, whatever the royalists might allege), implied a form of deism, and open professions of atheism were very rare. At the end of November the Blois Club might proclaim 'Religion is nothing but a mass of stupidities and absurdity . . . . A true republican cannot be superstitious; he bends the knee before no idols; he worships liberty alone; he knows no other cult than that of loving his country and its laws. The cross has become, in the eyes of the humanist thinker, a counter-revolutionary emblem.' Less than a fortnight later the Central Committee of the Department urged good republicans to 'Worship the Supreme Being, pay homage to Reason, practise the religion of good works and respect the laws; that is the essential morality of the gospels and the doctrine of the *sans-culotte* Jesus its author.' [2] Attempts to transform the content of Catholicism while retaining something of its form—for example, by the invocation of the revolutionary 'martyrs', Le Pelletier, Marat and Chalier—seems to have been uncommon, except as a mere rhetorical flourish.[3]

A religion so vague and abstract had little to catch the imagination of a largely illiterate population and the homilies of local politicians were a poor substitute for the confessional and

---

[1] Dechristianization appears, however, to have been less widespread in the Haute-Garonne than in some neighbouring Departments. Albert, *op. cit.*, pp. 269–75.

[2] Gallerand, *op. cit.*, pp. 377–83.

[3] For some examples, see A. Soboul, 'Sentiment religieux et Cultes populaires pendant la Révolution, Saintes patriotes et Martyrs de la Liberté', *Annales Historiques de la Révolution Française*, XXIX (1957), p. 193.

the *curé*. Before the dechristianization movement was launched there is evidence to suggest that, at least in parts of France, popular attachment to Catholicism, and even to the non-juror clergy, was still strong. Even where church-going was perhaps more a matter of habit than conviction, hostility was often expressed towards clergy who married or resigned. In the Eure there was opposition to the dismantling of church bells. The dechristianizers could not hope to obtain the sudden 'conversion' of the entire population, and the abolition of Sunday worship and the celebration of religious festivals provoked widespread resistance. The new 'emancipation' was sometimes only skin-deep. When a sudden hailstorm threatened the crops at Coulanges-la-Vineuse in the Yonne, the frightened peasants dispersed the local Club, reopened the church and spent the night ringing the church bells, singing hymns and imploring divine mercy.[1] But what is significant is not so much the survival of religious belief as the acceptance of dechristianization by so many revolutionary leaders at the local level. The breach between the Church and the Revolution had now become almost complete. There were very few who, like Grégoire, continued to support the Revolution while remaining dignitaries of the Church. It is true that some revolutionaries opposed dechristianization, but this was often on grounds of tactics rather than of principle. A new source of division had been introduced into French society and had penetrated down to the everyday lives of the peasants in their remote villages.

It was during this period of emergency measures and local innovation, when the Central Government had been driven to accept a policy of political, economic and religious intimidation, without having the means to impose central control, that the *sans-culottes* reached the apogee of their power. Genuine sympathy as well as political expediency inclined the Montagnards to measures of exception in their favour and individual representatives on mission had fewer inhibitions than the Convention about financing public relief by special taxes on the rich, raising *sans-culotte* revolutionary armies and installing the *sans-culottes* in the seats of local power. Moreover, the weakness of the Government, paralysed by the Girondin-Montagnard rivalry

[1] Porée, *op. cit.*, p. lxviii.

until June and then anxiously seeking popular support against the 'federalists', together with the labour shortage caused by the unprecedented mobilization, allowed the *sans-culottes* to protect their own economic interests. Experience was to show that they were better able to look after their welfare than a Montagnard Committee of Public Safety, however well disposed towards them.[1]

Before the passing of the *maximum des salaires* in September 1793 the scarcity of labour had led to a rapid increase in wages. Harvesters' pay in the Dieppe area had nearly doubled since 1789 and day-labour in the Departments of the Centre had more than doubled. In regions where bread was scarce and expensive the increase had been even more marked: for example, from 20–25 sous to 100–110 for agricultural labourers in the Puy-de-Dôme, where bread cost as much as 15 sous the pound. At Bordeaux, where bread was also very dear, skilled carpenters were earning 80–100 sous in June 1793. The agents of the Minister of the Interior stressed that unskilled day-labourers had tended to profit most from the shortage of labour. In the District of Saint-Pol wage increases varied considerably, but farm-labourers seem to have done better than anyone else, with a rise of 150 per cent.[2] Only in industries producing for the luxury market, such as silk at Lyons and Nîmes and tapestry at Aubusson—out of fashion before the Revolution because of the growing taste for wood-panelling and wallpaper—was unemployment serious and labour cheap. Reports from regions as widely separated as the Seine valley and the south-west stressed that wages had in general increased at least as rapidly as prices. In so far as the first *maximum*, of May 1793, was actually enforced, the labourer, who spent well over half his earnings on bread, found his purchasing power correspondingly increased. At Saint-Pol, for example, most prices had tripled by June 1793, but that of rye had increased by only 80 per cent and wheat by no more than 20 per cent.

The price and wage controls of September 1793, if strictly applied, would have circumscribed the gains of the *sans-culottes*. Prices being fixed at 33 per cent above those of 1790 and wages

[1] See N. Hampson, 'Les Ouvriers des Arsenaux de la Marine au cours de la Révolution Française', *Revue d'Histoire Économique et Sociale*, XXXIX (1961).
[2] Sangnier, *op. cit.*, I. 226.

at 50 per cent, the new wage rates were in most places considerably lower than those previously obtaining, while the *sans-culotte*, whose purchases of commodities other than bread were very limited, would not gain much from the *maximum général*. The Parisian *sans-culottes* who had been so vociferous in demanding these controls had presumably not expected that they would apply to wages as well as to prices. If they failed to protest, this was probably because they had no intention of observing the *maximum* on wages, which was apparently not promulgated in Paris until July 1794.[1] This would also seem to have been the case at Moulins, where the *comité de surveillance* recently nominated by Fouché fixed the prices of food and merchandise on 13th October, but does not seem to have controlled wages.[2] In the ports, however, the *maximum des salaires* seems to have been applied everywhere. Except at Nantes and Calais, wages were reduced; at Bayonne by as much as one-third, from 90 sous to 60. Since evasion of the *maximum des prix* was widespread, especially in 1794, the enforcement of wage controls might very well reduce the standard of living of the *sans-culottes*. But such reasoning may not bear much relationship to the realities of life, so far as the working people were concerned. What mattered most was bread, and, irrespective of national policy, this was often subsidized by the municipality, or the navy in the case of the ports, and available in limited quantities, but at a very low price. In the country districts price controls were no doubt frequently evaded, but a rural Commune in *sans-culotte* hands was unlikely to insist very strongly on the application of official wage rates when the harvest had to be gathered quickly and labour was scarce.

The *sans-culottes* were often helped in other ways. For example, exceptional local expenditure—for the provision of schools, the repair of bridges and construction of an armaments factory in the Dordogne; the reduction of the price of bread in the District of Bergues in the Nord; the cost of local administration at Moulins—was often financed by special taxes imposed on the rich alone. Moreover, the Revolution had created a huge

---

[1] G. Rudé and A. Soboul, 'Le Maximum des Salaires Parisiens et le 9 thermidor', *Annales Historiques de la Révolution Française*, XXVI (1954), p. 1.

[2] P. Caron, *Rapports des Agents du Ministre de l'Intérieur dans les Départements*, I. 443–4.

bureaucracy which offered opportunities of full-time or part-time employment to the *sans-culottes*. Since 5 September 1793 members of the *comités révolutionnaires* had been paid three livres a day (increased to five livres on 8th November), and Cambon, admittedly speaking after the collapse of the Terror and from the viewpoint of the Exchequer, estimated that there had been over half a million beneficiaries, who had cost the Treasury nearly 600 million livres in the previous year. The Parisian revolutionary army provided employment for 7,200 and local revolutionary armies enrolled about 30,000 more, some of whom found unauthorized means of augmenting their pay.[1] At the War Office, Bouchotte and his Secretary-General, Vincent, pursued a systematic policy of 'democratizing' the army and its administration. *Sans-culottes* were given preference in appointments and the War Office became a stronghold of the popular movement.

The *sans-culottes* achieved more than an improvement in their standard of living and access to occupations which had previously been closed to them. In the provinces in particular they frequently came to exercise a good deal of power. Representatives on mission, exasperated by the lethargy of their Departments, the silent hostility of local notables who had often declared for the Girondins, and the widespread evasion of revolutionary controls, drastically purged the local authorities, substituting men recommended by the local Clubs and often looking to the *sans-culottes* for the energy that they found lacking amongst the educated. Although policy varied with the individual deputy and with local conditions, there were many who agreed with the agent of the Minister of the Interior who wrote on 24th September, 'I think the majority of the municipalities need to be changed so as to exclude big landowners and farmers who keep the other citizens in a state of dependence so that they don't dare to say a word.' These tactics were applied with a will during the autumn of 1793. At Nantes the bourgeois town council gave way to a municipality that included many *sans-culottes* and no wealthy merchants.[2] In the *pays de Caux*, in the Dieppe area, the municipalities, especially in the country districts, were controlled by day-labourers and town-meetings were boycotted

[1] See Cobb, *op. cit.*, *passim*.
[2] G. Martin, *Carrier et sa Mission à Nantes*, p. 133.

by the yeomen farmers. At Rodez, Taillefer set up a *sans-culotte* commission to purge the local administration. It must not be thought that the term *'sans-culotte'* referred merely to the political opinions of the men who now took charge of local government. There is plenty of evidence to show that the new men were, in fact, often drawn from the poorer classes of society.[1] At Bourg the majority of the municipal council was illiterate and the same was true of most of the rural Communes in the Moulins area. At Pont Audemer, in Normandy, a justice of the peace could read only with difficulty, and in the Eure two of the six members of the provisional committee in charge of the whole Department could barely sign their names. Representatives on mission, often covering two or more Departments, could exercise only a rough-and-ready control over the local authorities and frequently delegated wide powers to their local agents. In the Cher, for example, Laplanche authorized individual members of the Bourges Club to purge the staff of the civil and military administration and to impose revolutionary taxes on the rich. In many cases, therefore, the *sans-culottes* found themselves in control of local government, subject only to the intermittent supervision of an overworked deputy.

Although the *sans-culottes* who were raised to this sudden eminence were often far from suspecting it, their power, both economic and administrative, rested on a singularly precarious basis. Their economic gains had been made by their own efforts while the Government was temporarily paralysed. Although well disposed towards them, the Committee of Public Safety was primarily concerned with the war effort and the prevention of inflation. The *sans-culottes*, in their patriotic fervour, helped to create the beginnings of a wartime dictatorship, but they themselves had most to gain from an *anarchic* Terror. When the revolutionary Government was strong enough to free itself from their influence it would subordinate their own interests to its conception of national policy, and treat any resistance as counter-revolutionary. There was no serious attempt at a fundamental transformation of the economic structure of society. The enjoyment of the fruits of private property was severely circumscribed and various forms of collectivism were provisionally enforced, but the existence of property itself was

[1] For the special case of Paris, see A. Soboul, *op. cit.*, pp. 433–51.

virtually unchallenged and the array of controls and restrictions was considered merely as the temporary expedient of a siege economy. Isolated theorists were groping towards a conception of the social ownership of the means of production, but the most radical of them, Babeuf, was in gaol, and the death penalty was still in force against any advocates of an 'agrarian law' for the redistribution of land. The controlled economy of the year II therefore involved no permanent changes in the economic structure of France and there was a general expectation amongst the Montagnards that peace would bring a return to the economic liberalism in which almost all of them believed.

The political conquests of the *sans-culottes* were no more secure. The mere fact that local councillors and justices of the peace could be almost or quite illiterate speaks for itself. The 'natural' administrators of the country were the wealthy landowners and merchants who could only be excluded from power by the intervention of the Central Government or its agents. The *sans-culottes* themselves were aware of their own limitations. At Evreux, 'the majority of the *patriotes* admit that they are too ignorant and that the former lawyers knew a lot more than they do'. At Rennes, 'with three or four exceptions, all the people of ability in this town are counter-revolutionaries'. In the Allier and the pays de Caux the illiterate municipalities were dependent on the help of the local *curés*. At Nantes the *sans-culotte* municipality was afraid to take the initiative and was constantly seeking the advice of the local representative, Carrier. The wealthy were not afraid to remind their temporary masters that power was economic as well as political. The former supporters of the 'federalist' movement at Evreux, recovering from the fright of the summer, invited the *sans-culottes* to 'choose between Liberty which does not even give you water to drink, and ourselves who provide you with a livelihood'. Not surprisingly, the Minister of the Interior's agent reported that the local Club was 'paralysed by the weakness of the *sans-culottes* and their reluctance to make enemies for themselves by denunciations'. On 31 January 1794, le Bon, in the Pas-de-Calais, enlarged on this problem and explained why he was opposed to the creation of *comités de surveillance* in the country districts. 'Who shall we put on the committees? The rich, the big farmers? That would be putting the wolf in the sheepfold and victimizing the unfortunate. Shall we put in the poor? That would be virtually useless, since they would hardly have the courage to strike at the wealthy on whom their poverty makes them continually dependent.' [1] For le Bon the only solution, until egoism and poverty should dissolve in the revolutionary millennium, was to rely on a few well-chosen agents responsible to the Central Government. Le Bon had put his finger on the dilemma of the *sans-culottes*. Their power was dependent on support from above. When the anarchic autonomy of the representatives on mission was terminated by the growing centralization of power in the hands of the Committee of Public Safety, the *sans-culottes* had no option but to become the agents of the Montagnard dictatorship. Henceforth their fortunes were regulated by the political evolution of the Convention and its committees, and if the Government withdrew its protection from them there was a fearful accumulation of frustrated hatred among the 'people of ability', often the victims of arbitrary arrest and more or less legalized extortion, who were ready to make the *sans-culottes* pay dearly for their brief taste of power.

The Montagnards, whatever their genuine sympathies for their violent partners, intended to retain power in the respectable hands of the Convention and to keep the anarchic force of their allies under close control. It was particularly ominous for the latter that the Convention's concessions of September should have coincided with the final destruction of the *enragés*, the nearest approach to a *sans-culotte* party that the Revolution was to produce. On 5th September the Jacobin Club in Paris quite illegally arrested Jacques Roux, who was to remain in gaol until he committed suicide on 10th February, when ordered before the revolutionary tribunal. His disciple, Leclerc, avoided a similar fate only by abandoning his newspaper and going to the front. When Varlet began to attack the restriction of the meetings of the Sections to two per week (later two per *décade*), he followed Roux into prison. Released in November after Hébert's intervention in his favour, he took care to avoid further trouble. The women's society, the *Républicaines Révolutionnaires*, led by the actress Rose Lacombe, which had supported the *enragés*, was banned on 30th October after an antifeminist diatribe by Amar: 'Women are scarcely capable of

[1] Jacob, *op. cit.*, pp. 315–16.

high speculation and serious meditation. . . . A woman should not leave her family to get involved in affairs of government. . . .' By the end of October the *enragés* had been finally routed, and Hébert, who attracted the support of many of their former followers, was essentially an ambitious politician, intent on using the *sans-culottes* for the furtherance of his own ends.

The veto imposed by the Convention on the daily meetings of the Sections, in spite of the latter's attempt to evade the law by the formation of 'Sectional popular societies' which met on the nights when the Sections themselves were not in session, marked the beginning of their decline as autonomous bodies. The Committee of General Security was beginning to assume control over the forty-eight *comités de surveillance* and to withdraw them from the influence of their parent Sections and of the Paris Commune.[1] The independent power of the *sans-culottes* in Paris was already yielding to the growing strength of the Central Government when it was still at its peak in the provinces. It was only a matter of time before the *sans-culottes* everywhere would find themselves first the agents and then the victims of the middle-class revolutionaries in the Convention.

[1] See Soboul, *op. cit.*, chap. iv and v.

IX

The Failure of Both Principle
and Expediency

Nous sommes placés entre l'anarchie du terrorisme et celle du royalisme.

FLORENT GUIOT, representative on mission in the *Nord*

ALL through the autumn of 1793 the Committee of Public Safety consolidated its authority in the Convention and the country at large. The system of government, based on a sovereign assembly and an executive similar to a war cabinet, evolved, in the British way, both by statutory decision and the accumulation of precedent. The Committee's victory of 24th–25th September, when it was attacked in the Assembly by malcontents of various persuasions, gave it a measure of control over representatives on mission, who were gradually transformed into its own agents. The decree of 10th October, which shelved the application of the new constitution until peace returned, officially entrusted the Committee with the supervision of ministers, generals and local government. The establishment of a national food commission, under the control of Lindet, on 22nd October, greatly extended its control over the economy and partially centralized the system of requisitioning on which towns and armies increasingly depended for their bread. This process of centralization reached its climax with the important decree of 4th December which was intended to substitute a

214

unified national policy for the chaotic local initiative of the autumn.[1] The Central Government now asserted its complete control over representatives on mission, who were forbidden to delegate their powers and to maintain their own revolutionary armies or impose special taxation without approval from Paris. The powerful Departments were replaced as organs of revolutionary local government by the humbler Districts, to each of which was attached an *Agent National*, nominated by the Committee. The latter now assumed the power to dismiss elected local government officials and replace them with its own nominees—a threat to their position on the Paris Commune that was not lost on Hébert and Chaumette. Departments, Districts and their *comités de surveillance*, generals and civil and military courts were each to submit reports to the Central Government every ten days. In this way revolutionary France acquired a bureaucratic organization without parallel in eighteenth-century Europe.[2]

The extent of this centralization was naturally limited by material factors such as primitive equipment and communications no quicker than those of the Romans—although a semaphore was installed to link Paris with the north-eastern frontier in the summer of 1794. The way in which the system of government had evolved also limited the powers of the Committee of Public Safety, for finance was in the hands of an independent committee under Cambon, while the Committee of General Security, in charge of police activities, developed an 'empire' almost equal to that of its more famous partner. But with all its limitations and imperfections the revolutionary government proved powerful enough to overwhelm its foreign and domestic enemies. Lyons fell on 9th October; Toulon was recaptured on 19th December. Three days later the relics of the Vendéan army which had crossed the Loire in October were destroyed at Savenay and the danger of offensive military action from the Vendée was over. By the end of 1793 French territory had been cleared of invaders, with the exception of Condé, Valenciennes and le Quesnoi in the north-east and Port-Vendres and Collioure near the Spanish frontier, and the republican armies had once

[1] See Cobb, *Les Armées Révolutionnaires* II, Book III, chap. i.
[2] See the diagram in Thompson, *The French Revolution*, p. 377; for the text of the decree, see Thompson, *French Revolution Documents*, pp. 262–73.

more penetrated into the Palatinate. The new economic controls succeeded in supplying towns and armies with an adequate supply of cheap bread and in feeding the rapidly-expanding war industries with labour and raw materials. In spite of the enormous war expenditure, prices were relatively stable, and the assignat, which had fallen to 29 per cent of its face-value in September, had actually risen to 51 per cent by the end of the year.

All this was what the *sans-culottes* had demanded in the summer and they had few grounds for complaint. But the revolutionary Government had no intention of sharing its power with any section of the community. Henceforth the *sans-culottes* could exercise local authority only as its obedient agents. When Chaumette, on 1st December, tried to assert the control of the Paris Commune over the *comités révolutionnaires* of the Sections, he was sharply called to order and the Commune was henceforth on the defensive. The political strength of the *sans-culottes* lay precisely in the semi-autonomous authorities— Section, Clubs and well-disposed representatives on mission— whose freedom of action was being continually whittled away by the Central Government. Moreover the Committee of Public Safety, which had shared in the savage anger of the *sans-culottes* in the autumn, now drew back from the anarchic violence that had resulted. On two issues, dechristianization and the more extreme forms of terrorism, the Committee drew away from the militant *sans-culottes*.[1]

In Paris the dechristianization campaign had been exploited by a handful of minor politicians, notably Proli, Desfieux, Pereira, and Dubuisson, in search of popular support. In October the deputy, Fabre d'Eglantine denounced these men to the Committees of Public Safety and General Security as counter-revolutionary agents in foreign pay.[2] Whether or not the committees believed this—probably false—accusation, they had good reason to suspect that the motives of Proli and his associates were primarily political. Moreover the Government and ministerially-minded deputies such as Danton were well aware that dechristianization was creating unnecessary enemies

[1] On the *economic* anarchy of the autumn of 1793, see R. Cobb, *op. cit.*, II, Book II, chap. ii.
[2] See A. Mathiez, *La Conspiration de l'Étranger* (Paris, 1918), chap. i.

in the countryside. Robespierre was sensitive to both these arguments and in addition his religious temperament was probably outraged by the crude blasphemy of the *mascarades* that delighted the *sans-culottes*. Towards the end of November he and Danton took the offensive, had Proli, Desfieux and Pereira expelled from the Jacobins, intimidated Chaumette into repudiating the attack on religion and induced a somewhat reluctant Assembly to reaffirm the principle of freedom of worship. This latter decree was generally disregarded in the provinces, where the dechristianizing campaign had still to reach its peak. Even in Paris the churches remained closed. But the new argument that dechristianization, and extremism in general, formed part of a foreign plot to destroy the Revolution by its own excesses, inaugurated a period of suspicion and confusion in which all the old landmarks disappeared. When an excess of revolutionary zeal was denounced as treason by respected Montagnard leaders, the *sans-culotte militants* began to lose some of their enthusiasm for Sectional politics, which in any case were being deprived of much of their interest as the Government drew more and more power to itself.

Victory in the civil war, at Lyons, Toulon, and round the Loire estuary, brought with it the most furious repression of the whole Revolution. The republicans found themselves confronted with large numbers of prisoners who had taken up arms against the Revolution. Their methods of exterminating opponents, who were all liable to the death penalty on the mere proof of their identity, attained a degree of ferocity almost comparable to those of the twentieth century. At Lyons, Collot and Fouché, finding the guillotine too slow, mowed down over 350 by cannon fire. Eventually almost 2,000 of the *Lyonnais* perished. Carrier at Nantes, with the gaols overflowing with Vendéan prisoners dying of an epidemic which carried off 3,000 in six weeks, tolerated if he did not authorize the drowning of up to 2,000 prisoners in barges scuttled in the Loire, while 3,000 more were shot. Although many of the *Toulonnais* escaped with the British fleet, Fréron and Barras shot 800 in the first three weeks after the recapture of the port.[1]

[1] D. Greer, *The Incidence of the Terror during the French Revolution* (Cambridge, Mass., 1935), chap. ii, p. 196, Table I; for Nantes, see Gaston Martin, *Carrier et sa Mission à Nantes*, pp. 266–96.

To some extent the Committee of Public Safety shared in the responsibility for this slaughter. But towards the end of the year the Government's attitude seemed to be changing.[1] Ronsin, the commander of the revolutionary army at Lyons, was recalled to Paris and arrested, and early in the new year Fréron, Barras, and Carrier were also brought back. Collot felt obliged to hasten back from Lyons in mid-December to defend himself against the changing current of opinion. The terrorists had also been powerful allies of the *sans-culottes*— Carrier was the hero of the Cordeliers Club and Collot the *sans-culottes'* protector on the Committee of Public Safety. Their ruthless punishment of rebels had corresponded to the primitive violence of much *sans-culotte* opinion, and they had tended to combine extreme repression with dechristianization, economic levelling and the promotion of *sans-culottes* to positions of local power. A halt to this policy of extreme Terror, however justified or desirable, was bound to produce a reaction against the terrorists, to confuse the revolutionary rank and file and to prepare the way for the revival of the local bourgeoisie, with bitter wrongs to avenge.

The changing attitude of the Government and the collaboration of Robespierre and Danton inevitably raise the question of whether the Committee of Public Safety was not deliberately trying to moderate the course of the Revolution and return to its conciliatory policy of the previous June. On the whole this appears unlikely, but the obscure political intrigues of the autumn and winter of 1793–4 permit only of the most tentative interpretations. The Montagnards had no sooner won control of the Revolution in the summer of 1793 than they split into warring factions.[2] Hébert and the partisans of violent and extreme measures took the offensive in the Jacobin Club. In November they encountered growing opposition from a number of deputies who, for various reasons, objected to the increasing violence of the Revolution. Among these was Fabre d'Eglantine, implicated in a piece of parliamentary corruption whose exposure would cost him his life.[3] Fabre therefore set out to destroy his

[1] On the Committee of Public Safety, see R. R. Palmer, *The Twelve who Ruled* (Princeton, 1941), *passim*.

[2] R. Levasseur, *Mémoires* (Paris, 1829), II, chap. xi, xx.

[3] L. Jacob, *Fabre d'Églantine, Chef des Fripons* (Paris, 1946), chap. xi; A. Mathiez, *op. cit.*, chap. ii.

accomplices and political enemies and, if possible, to install his friends in positions of power. His associates, commonly known as 'Dantonists', although Danton's own rôle is remarkably obscure, advocated a policy of clemency towards the defeated enemies of the Revolution. Desmoulins' support for this policy was probably disinterested, but for Fabre clemency began at home and could only be guaranteed by a change of government.

At the same time the Committee of Public Safety became convinced, perhaps correctly, that the British Government was employing its agents in France to set the revolutionaries against each other.[1] Robespierre, whose freedom from departmental responsibilities gave him time to concentrate on general policy, had therefore the difficult task of destroying these agents of division while protecting the honest revolutionaries whom they had misled. He apparently regarded the dechristianization movement in Paris and the extremists' liking for the denunciation of their colleagues as confirmation of the foreign plot that Fabre had 'revealed' in October. His alliance with Danton in defence of religious freedom led him to give general support to the 'Indulgents' in December, reading in proof the first two copies of Desmoulins' new journal, the *Vieux Cordelier*. Even when Fabre moved on to attack the structure of revolutionary government itself Robespierre's silence seemed to imply approval.[2] By mid-December it looked as though Robespierre and the Committee of Public Safety were aligning themselves with conservative forces against the advocates of violent terror and their *sans-culotte* supporters.

This situation was transformed by the return of Collot from Lyons on 17th December. Alarmed at the transformation of the political climate in Paris while he himself was still carrying out the old policy of ruthless repression in the south, Collot rallied the 'Hébertist' forces, which returned to the fight in the Jacobin Club. The Committee of Public Safety, threatened with an open breach between Robespierre and Collot, recovered its unity behind a policy of neutrality, Robespierre trying to divert the leaders of the two factions from their war of personalities.

---

[1] For evidence that the British Government was subsidizing some of the speakers at the Jacobin Club, see A. Mathiez, *op. cit.*, chap. vi.

[2] See also Levasseur's conversation with Saint-Just (*Mémoires*, II. 243), and Cobb, *Les Armées Révolutionnaires*, II, Book III.

Fabre's corruption was exposed, and his arrest on 13 January 1794 possibly convinced Robespierre—always inclined to equate corruption with treason—that the foreign agents were as active on the one side as he had previously supposed them to be on the other. Fabre's imprisonment brought a temporary lull, but no reconciliation between the two factions.

In March the Cordeliers Club, perhaps hoping to profit from *sans-culotte* unrest caused by a temporary food shortage, began vague talk of insurrection. Collot tried in vain to induce the Club to resign itself to Jacobin leadership, and on 12th March the leading 'Hébertists' were arrested. Their trial by the revolutionary tribunal was a mere formality, and on the 24th Hébert, Ronsin, Vincent, Momoro, Clootz, Proli, Desfieux, Pereira, Dubuisson and ten others were executed.[1] The Committee of Public Safety had been insisting for months that all its critics, of Left and Right, were the agents of a counter-revolutionary plot. It was therefore not surprising that the trial of the 'Hébertists' should be followed by a blow in the opposite direction—especially since Fabre and his fellow-embezzlers were unlikely to arouse much sympathy. It was presumably not the principle of the *jeu de bascule* that divided the Committee, but the decision to include in the purge eminent deputies with many friends in the Convention, notably Danton and Desmoulins. The origins of this decision are obscure. Robespierre at first opposed the judicial murder of Danton and Lindet refused to sign the order for his arrest on 31st March. Once the Committee had decided to strike, however, it had no alternative but to continue to the bloody end: an acquittal in a political trial is a vote of no confidence in the Government. The Convention was bullied into lifting the parliamentary immunity of nine deputies. The revolutionary tribunal was subjected to heavy pressure until it returned the appropriate verdict. On 5th April Danton, Desmoulins, Delacroix, Philippeaux, Fabre, Chabot, Basire and seven others were executed, together with Hérault-Séchelles, wrongly suspected of betraying the Committee's secrets to the enemy. On the 13th Chaumette and bishop Gobel followed them to the guillotine, with the widows of Desmoulins and Hébert, in one of the most cynical of all Fouquier-Tinville's *amalgames*.

[1] A. Soboul, *Les Sans-culottes Parisiens en l'An II*, pp. 761–823; Cobb, *op. cit.*, II, Book III, chap. ii.

The three trials of *germinal* transformed the whole political situation. The *sans-culottes* were stunned by the execution of the *Père Duchesne*, the commander of the revolutionary army, and Vincent. All their positions of influence fell one after the other: the revolutionary army was disbanded, the inspectors of food-hoarding dismissed, Bouchotte lost the War Office, the Cordeliers Club was reduced to frightened impotence, and Government pressure brought about the closing of 39 popular societies within two months. The *sans-culottes* found their faith in revolutionary men and institutions shaken and the Section of the *Cité*, dutifully congratulating the Assembly, remarked with more truth than tact, 'From now onwards the people will not be so ready to believe those who call themselves its friends.'[1] Henceforth the Sections tended more and more to abandon politics for the collection of saltpetre and the raising of funds to equip *cavaliers jacobins*—a tendency that all of the members of the Committee of Public Safety were sooner or later to regret. The Commune, shorn of Hébert and Chaumette, soon suffered another blow in the arrest of Pache, the mayor. Under his successor, Lescot-Fleuriot, with Payan as *Agent National*, it became entirely subordinate to the Government. The majority of the deputies would have consoled themselves easily enough for the destruction of *sans-culotte* power in Paris, but the execution of the 'Dantonists' had deprived the Convention of nine of its leading members. Robespierre and Saint-Just may conceivably have convinced themselves that Danton was an enemy agent, but they can scarcely have expected the deputies to believe the trumped-up charges against him that they put before the Convention. It had become painfully clear that the 'foreign plot' could be used to secure the conviction of any deputy whom the Government wished to destroy, and such men as Fouché, Tallien and Barras, who had incurred the hostility of Robespierre by their conduct on mission, knew that their lives were now in danger. For the first time the majority of the Assembly went in terror of the Government which it had created, while faithful Montagnards found the criteria of political orthodoxy almost as baffling as did the unschooled *sans-culottes*. All power now rested with the governing committees, isolated but supreme. For the first time since the outbreak of the

[1] A. Soboul, *op. cit.*, p. 778.

Revolution a Government had the power to impose its own policies on both the Assembly and the country at large.

Their speeches suggest that some at least of the members of the Committee of Public Safety had been coming to regard the Revolution more and more as a conflict between moral absolutes. Robespierre had always been inclined to identify his cause with that of virtue and to regard his opponents as *ipso facto* wicked, but this tendency had become more pronounced since his attack on dechristianization. Soon the Republic came to be identified with the reign of virtue; as Saint-Just expressed it: 'Monarchy is not a question of kingship, it is crime; the republic does not lie in a senate, it is virtue.' Naturally such a viewpoint excluded compromise with the unrighteous: 'The republic unites us against all vicious men. . . . One rules the people by reason and its enemies by Terror [an anticipation, in moral terms, of the Marxist 'democratic dictatorship of the proletariat']. The Government of the Republic is the despotism of liberty against tyranny. Whoever does not hate crime is incapable of loving virtue' (Robespierre). Saint-Just, as usual, took the argument a stage further: 'What constitutes a republic is the complete destruction of what is opposed to it. . . . In a republic, which can only be based on virtue, any pity shown towards crime is a flagrant proof of treason.' The ferocity that Robespierre and Saint-Just showed towards the enemies of virtue was the inevitable counterpart to their sincere, if fanatical, vision of a coming utopia in which the repressive State should have 'withered away', leaving a free society of disinterested citizens to live in harmony and peace. For Robespierre the means of ensuring the *civisme* of the well-intentioned but fallible was the conventional one of religion. Belief in an after-life of rewards and punishments was to console the unfortunate and intimidate the unscrupulous. Saint-Just hoped to achieve the same end by essentially secular means, by the formative influence of 're-publican institutions'. 'I imagined that if men were given laws in accordance with nature and their own hearts, they would no longer be unhappy and corrupt.' Hence the duty of the legislator was 'to transform men into what he wants them to be'.

In one sense the ideas of Robespierre and Saint-Just represented the culmination of the eighteenth-century enlightenment, with its belief in the rationality of Man, the identity of public and private interests, the power of environmental influences, and its cult of the civic virtues of ancient Rome, softened by the *sensibilité* of Rousseau. But if they aimed at re-creating the Roman republic, what they produced was a blue-print for twentieth-century totalitarianism, and their ideas have a strangely modern look. The State became all-powerful, the source of moral values and superior to all other loyalties. Robespierre lectured the wives of suspects who appealed against their husbands' imprisonment: 'Is it right that republican women should renounce their status as citizens and remember only that they are wives?' The family became suspect as a centre of loyalty rivalling the State, and Robespierre, Saint-Just, and Barère were unanimous on the need to remove children from its dangerous influence as soon as possible. The individual could claim no rights against the community, which was itself the source of all rights—including those regulating the ownership of private property. The State was also the sole arbiter of taste, and an attempt was made to create a 'republican' style, with the sort of results that one would expect. A logical implication of this moral absolutism was indefinite war until the last 'tyrant' should have been overthrown, since the continuance of 'evil' across the frontiers would offer a permanent danger of the corruption of fallible republicans in France. It was therefore logical for Barère to suggest 'that all our games, all public exercises, should take on a military character', although Robespierre, suspicious of military dictatorship, may not have agreed with him.

These principles, although most elaborately developed by Robespierre and Saint-Just, were not the monopoly of any one group in the Committee of Public Safety. Billaud-Varenne whose economic policies, as expounded in his *Élémens du Républicanisme* published in 1793, were perhaps the most radical of all, made a verbose attempt to define the 'theory of revolutionary government' in terms very similar to Robespierre's, while Barère's 'true humanity consists in exterminating one's enemies' was worthy of Saint-Just.

The policy of the Committee of Public Safety during the spring of 1794 was an attempt to implement these theories. The work of political repression was centralized and accelerated.

The law of 22nd *prairial* (10th June) enormously widened the categories of 'public enemies' until they corresponded more or less to the definition of suspects adopted in September 1793.[1] In trying these people the revolutionary tribunal was henceforth to apply only one penalty: death. The accused were to have no counsel and witnesses were not to be called 'unless this formality appears necessary to discover accomplices or for other important considerations of public interest'. A clause cancelling such previous legislation as might not be in accordance with the new law quietly abolished the deputies' right of parliamentary immunity. The Convention, with the desperate courage of self-preservation, gave the Bill a hostile reception, Bourdon de l'Oise and Tallien in particular indulging in vehement arguments with Robespierre. The latter, who possibly intended to use the new law to dispose of a handful of deputies whom he regarded as particularly 'vicious', appealed to the Centre to agree that 'We cannot have two parties in the Convention, the good and the wicked'. This argument would be more impressive if one of the proofs of Bourdon's treason, in Robespierre's eyes, had not been that he proposed the drainage of marshes during a period of fish shortage! It may be that the hostility of the Convention deterred Robespierre and Couthon from trying to use the *prairial* law against their parliamentary enemies, but its effect outside the Assembly was striking enough. Ever since September 1793 the revolutionary tribunal in Paris had been trying more people each month and condemning a greater proportion of those tried. On the eve of the *prairial* law trials had reached a monthly rate of over 450, two-thirds of the accused receiving death sentences. In June and July the number of executions rose to 1,515—well over half of the total of 2,639 capital sentences during the whole period from the creation of the revolutionary tribunal to the overthrow of Robespierre.[2]

Revolutionary justice was now largely centralized in Paris, which in part accounted for the increase, but the military commission at Nîmes and the tribunals of Arras and Cambrai continued their work, and a new popular commission at Orange,

---

[1] For text, see Thompson, *French Revolution Documents*, pp. 284–7; on the possible significance of the decree, see G. Lefebvre, 'A Propos de la Loi du 22 Prairial', *Annales Historiques de la Révolution Française*, XXIV (1952), p. 253.

[2] D. Greer, *op. cit., passim*.

set up on 10th May, had passed 332 death sentences by the beginning of August.[1] An Orange judge complained significantly of one of his colleagues, 'He has to have proofs, like the ordinary courts of the ancien régime.' Since there was no military crisis and no serious threat to the Government it is difficult not to associate this increasing ferocity with the Robespierrist policy of extending revolutionary justice to the legions of the corrupt and unprincipled.

Significant of the attitude of the Committee, although of little practical consequence, was the decree voted on 26th May that no British or Hanoverian prisoners were to be taken. This seems to have been almost universally ignored, but it did lead to the murder of the crew of a British merchantman, captured in the Mediterranean in July by the frigate *la Boudeuse*.[2]

On the positive side of Government, Robespierre, in a speech on 7th May, declared the need for a moral revolution to complete the work of the scientific revolution of the seventeenth and eighteenth centuries. After attacking dechristianization and the secularism of eighteenth-century intellectuals and stressing the social and political value of religious belief, he introduced a plan for a series of national festivals to inculcate republican principles. The first of these, on 8th June—Whit Sunday—was a festival in honour of the Supreme Being, celebrated with impressive pomp in Paris with Robespierre himself, as president of the Convention, playing the leading rôle. In his mind the new State religion was a general manifestation of belief in God and in the immortality of the soul, which believers in all religions could accept, with a national and patriotic bias calculated to reinforce the *vertu* of the more fallible citizens. By now the provinces had learned to accept without argument the fiat of the Central Government, but Robespierre's intentions were obscure enough to admit of varying interpretations. In some places the new religion was assumed to be a move back towards Catholicism and the Whitsuntide fête was celebrated with incense and prayer. More commonly the Supreme Being was identified with Reason. A journalist at Auch explained to

[1] For a strongly partisan account of the operations of the Orange tribunal see V. de Baumefort, *Episodes de la Terreur. Le tribunal révolutionnaire d'Orange* (Avignon, 1875).

[2] Archives Nationales, BB4 42, fol. 215–18.

his readers, 'We must inscribe on the façade of our temples *To the Supreme Being* instead of *Temple of Reason*. That is to substitute the cause for the effect, but the temple will nevertheless remain dedicated to Reason, since only Reason can render to the Supreme Being the homage which is due to him.'[1] The sacred 'Mountains' which had served for the festivals of Reason were brought out once more and the new celebrations were very much like the old. What was missing was the iconoclasm and the vulgar enthusiasm which had animated the *mascarades*. The new State religion tended to remain an official business, attractive mainly to the Voltairean bourgeois, at home with its abstractions. Once again the Government had lost contact with the ordinary people whom it idealized but never understood.

The social and economic policy of the Committee of Public Safety aimed at creating a viable economy in which all would be guaranteed a livelihood on terms imposed by the Government and not negotiated with sectional economic interests. On 21st February the *maximum* was revised, in accordance with the results of a vast enquiry conducted by the Food Commission. The latter had tried to establish the cost of production of all articles in general use, in their place of origin in 1790. These were increased by one-third, an allowance was made for transport costs, wholesalers were entitled to a profit of 5 per cent on the cost of goods plus transport, and retailers to 10 per cent. The intention was to guarantee the 'virtuous' trader a reasonable livelihood—to 'moralize' commerce—but the effect of passing on the profit margin to the consumer was to raise prices, especially where transport costs were high. In Paris the price of a pound of beef rose from 13 sous 5 deniers to 16 sous; in the District of Crest in the Drôme, sugar, brought from Bordeaux, more than doubled in price. Even if the *maximum* had been honoured the wage-earners would now have been poorer than in 1790, since their wages had been increased by only 50 per cent. In fact, the enforcement of price controls was relaxed after the destruction of the 'Hébertists', with the result that the standard of living of the urban wage-earner tended to fall even more.[2] He was, however, given a measure of security

---

[1] A. Richard, *Le gouvernement révolutionnaire dans les Basses-Pyrénées* (Paris, n.d.), p. 160; see also A. Aulard, *Le culte de la Raison*, chap. xxix–xxxiii.

[2] See D. Guérin, *La lutte des classes sous la première république*, II, chap. xii.

by reason of his daily ration of subsidized bread, and in Paris at least wage rates were often in excess of the *maximum*.

On 26th February and 3rd March Saint-Just introduced his celebrated *ventôse* decrees, somewhat oddly described by Jaurès as *terrorisme nuancé de socialisme*. The principle behind these was simple: traitors had forfeited any claim to property and their goods could therefore be used in an attempt to eliminate pauperism. Six commissions were to try suspects held in prison and the property of those condemned was to be given to the poor. The impact of this legislation would naturally depend on the number and wealth of the suspects, a subject on which no accurate information is available. Estimates vary from the 90,000 of Mathiez to Greer's 500,000.[1] It is not clear whether the intention of Saint-Just and of the Committee was to distribute the confiscated property or to sell it and devote the proceeds to poor relief. At most the measures would have represented a somewhat haphazard and spectacular transfer of wealth and they cannot be considered to have created the theoretical basis for any new social order. They seem, in fact, to have excited historians more than contemporaries. The urban *sans-culotte*, though favourably impressed, was scarcely tempted by the prospect of half an acre in the country and some at least of the rural poor feared that the whole scheme was a cruel plan to transport those who had identified themselves as having no means of livelihood.[2] Since the decrees were never put into operation, discussion of their significance must remain hypothetical.

To cast doubt on the importance of what Mathiez curiously termed 'a vast transfer of property from one political class to another' is in no way to impugn the sincerity of the Committee of Public Safety. On the whole its social policy was both enlightened and benevolent. Barère on 11th May introduced a vast scheme for providing public assistance and free medical attention to a proportion of the elderly and unfit and to nursing mothers and widows, at a total annual cost of nearly 15 million livres. An Education Act, passed on 6th January, provided for

[1] A. Mathiez, 'Quel fut le nombre des suspects', *Annales Historiques de la Révolution Française*, VI (1929), 75; D. Greer, *op. cit.*, pp. 27–28.

[2] See A. Soboul, *op. cit.*, pp. 708–17; R. Schnerb, 'L'application des décrets de ventôse dans le District de Thiers', *Annales Historiques de la Révolution Française*, VI (1929), 24.

three years of free and compulsory primary education. Slavery was abolished on 4th February—it was later to be reintroduced by Napoleon.[1]

The general picture is therefore one of active social reform, but the Government intended to dictate the terms of its own social contract, and its interpretation of the national interest bore hardly on the wage-earner who tried to profit from the labour shortage. On 5th May the Committee requisitioned all agricultural workers for the gathering of the summer's harvest, ordered the payment of the wages fixed by the *maximum*, and threatened with the revolutionary tribunal any who refused to work on these terms. In the naval dockyards and the public arms factories in Paris strict discipline was enforced and any attempts at strike action treated as manoeuvres to paralyse the war effort.[2] On 17th February Jeanbon Saint-André extended to all the minor ports of France the wage rates obtaining in the great State arsenals, perhaps under the mistaken impression that this would lead to the increase that the administrative authorities considered justified. The result was actually to reduce still further wage rates that had already been brought down by the *maximum*. The Minister of Marine seems to have been too frightened of the Committee of Public Safety to point out its mistake and the new rates remained in force.

In view of all these considerations, the enthusiasm of Marxist historians such as Jaurès and Mathiez for the social and economic policy of the Committee is somewhat surprising. The theoretical basis of its policy was the exact opposite to that advocated by Marx. Instead of the moral values of society reflecting its class structure, an attempt was planned to reshape the latter in accordance with moral principles assumed to have universal validity. This was the basis for Saint-Just's notes: 'We must give some land to all . . . we must have neither rich nor poor . . . opulence is infamy.' The egalitarian peasant society that he had in mind had more in common with medieval than with socialist ideas. In practice little was done to modify the social structure of France. The Committee was sincere, but it was not

[1] On the attempt to promote economic levelling by testamentary legislation, see P. Sagnac, *La Législation Civile de la Révolution Française*, pp. 215–33.

[2] For the Paris arms factories see C. Richard, *Le Comité de Salut Public et les fabrications de guerre sous la Terreur* (Paris, 1922); for the naval arsenals, N. Hampson, *La Marine de l'an II*.

concerned to pursue a policy of class legislation. Its vision was of a harmonious society in which all would sacrifice their particular economic interests to the welfare of the community. Consequently it intended to protect the wealthy *patriote* while it tried to relieve the misery of the poor. In agriculture the Montagnards were opposed to an *agrarian law* for the equalization of land-ownership, which was never more than a turnip-ghost with which their opponents frightened themselves. They were probably too ignorant of the infinite complexities of land-tenures to have evolved any concrete policy for the support of the poorer peasants—Collot and Couthon were not even aware, on 20th April, of the existing state of legislation on the sale of the *biens nationaux*.[1] The pursuit of an effective agrarian policy would have demanded far more time than they could divert from the vital business of winning the war. So far as they were concerned, the peasants remained vague symbols of rural innocence and stability rather than tenant-farmers with leases and problems of crop-rotation. In the towns it is difficult to see what the Committee could have done to protect the *sans-culottes* from eventual proletarianization by the industrial revolution. There is no evidence to suggest that the Montagnards were thinking of any radical social transformation, for which the theoretical and material basis was lacking in 1794. Their main concern was victory and their principles centred round the 'moralization' of the *status quo*. *Sans-culottes* and peasants were protected from famine and runaway inflation, but they had probably won a better place for themselves in the free competition of the summer of 1793 than the Committee of Public Safety was prepared to allocate them in the rigorous war economy of the following spring.

So long as it remained united the Committee was virtually invulnerable, but it had scarcely attained the apogee of its power before signs of internal conflict appeared. Attempts have been made to ascribe these divisions to conflicting policies, but the balance of the available evidence suggests that they were due rather to the natural explosion of men of authoritarian temperament, overworked and short of sleep, who had been condemned to each other's continual company for the past ten to

[1] See G. Lefebvre, *Questions agraires au temps de la Terreur*, esp. pp. 57, 115–27.

twelve months. Their success itself had made it safe to quarrel: Spain was invaded and most of the Palatinate occupied in July. The Austrian army in the Netherlands was defeated after heavy fighting at Fleurus on 26th June and the French entered Brussels a fortnight later. By the autumn, with 750,000 men at the front, the threat of invasion had at last disappeared. The naval situation was less reassuring, for the reviving fleet lost six ships of the line captured and one sunk in the western approaches, at the battle of 1st June. But with Toulon recaptured and the Vendée more or less under control, the Republic could not be overthrown by sea-power alone.

Bickering broke out in the Committee of Public Safety, with Carnot describing Robespierre and Saint-Just as 'ridiculous dictators' and Collot making veiled attacks on the Incorruptible. Probably Robespierre, with his peculiar combination of utopianism and suspicion, had become an impossible colleague. From the end of June until 23rd July he appears to have boycotted the meetings of the Committee. After an unsuccessful attempt at reconciliation, the quarrel erupted on 26th July, when Robespierre made a vague denunciation of his enemies on the floor of the Convention. Cambon, Billaud and others who knew or assumed their lives to be in danger spoke up in their own defence and the session closed without any action being taken. The mere fact that members of the Committee of Public Safety were appealing to the arbitration of the Convention implied the end of the Committee's unofficial dictatorship. On the following day, 9th *thermidor* in the revolutionary calendar, Saint-Just came to the support of Robespierre but was howled down by his fellow-deputies. Those whose lives were at stake had devoted the greater part of the night to enlisting the support of the Plain, and Robespierre and his friends appear to have been completely isolated. After a chaotic debate the arrest of Robespierre, Couthon, and Saint-Just was voted, whereupon Robespierre's brother, Augustin, and Saint-Just's friend, Lebas, in a gesture which ennobles themselves and honours their allies, insisted on sharing the fate of the three arrested deputies.

The scene was now complicated by the intervention of the Paris Commune which called for an insurrection to overawe the Convention and reinstate the Robespierrists. The night of 9th–10th *thermidor* was one of great confusion in Paris, as Commune and Assembly competed for the support of the Sections and their troops.[1] How far the behaviour of the 48 sectional assemblies, their *comités civils* and *révolutionnaires*, and the National Guards they controlled reflected the political convictions of the Parisians is very doubtful. It was some time before the public had any idea of what was happening—when the *tocsin* began to ring, many, including the public prosecutor of the revolutionary tribunal himself, thought that the insurrectionary movement was in protest against the attempt, four days before, to enforce wage controls in Paris.[2] The Parisian authorities had been brought very much under the influence of the revolutionary government, which perhaps explains why the Commune itself, dominated by Robespierre's protégés, supported him, while the majority of the *comités révolutionnaires*, accustomed to take their orders from the Committee of General Security, declared for the Assembly. Accidents of geography probably counted for something, much of the support for the Commune coming from Sections relatively near to the *Hôtel de Ville*. Many Sections were deeply divided; in *Mutius Scaevola*, for example, the infantry and the *comité révolutionnaire* supported the Commune, the artillerymen and the *comité civil* the Convention. Although firm conclusions can scarcely be drawn, it does seem that some at least of the Sections that had formerly been distinguished by their radicalism tended to declare against Robespierre and the Commune. Roux's *Gravilliers*, apart from some hesitation in its *comité civil*, upheld the Assembly and Hébert's *Bonne Nouvelle* also opposed those who had replaced the *Père Duchesne* on the Commune. On the whole it seems likely that the memory of dead leaders and the recent attempt to reduce wages discouraged many of the *sans-culottes* from identifying their cause with the Commune and the man who seemed to them responsible for recent policy. The insurrection of 27th July was not a specifically popular revolt directed against a conservative Assembly.

Equally significant was the fact that the Convention entrusted its defence to Barras, whose terrorism at Toulon had earned him the enmity of Robespierre, and to a committee that

---

[1] See P. Saint-Clair Deville, *La Commune de l'an II* (Paris, 1946), pp. 189–315, for an account of events; A. Soboul, *op. cit.*, pp. 996–1025, for an analysis of the behaviour of the Sections.

[2] See G. Rudé and A. Soboul, 'Le maximum des salaires parisiens et le 9 thermidor', *Annales Historiques de la Révolution Française*, XXVI (1954), p. 1.

included both Bourdons, the one 'Hébertist' and the other 'Dantonist'. It was the 'Hébertist', Léonard Bourdon, at the head of the men from the *Gravilliers*, who eventually occupied the *Hôtel de Ville*. On 28th July the guillotine despatched Robespierre and the other three deputies (Lebas had committed suicide), Hanriot, the Commander-in-Chief of the National Guard, Lescot-Fleuriot the mayor, Payan his *Agent National*, and 15 members of the *conseil général* of the Commune. The repression continued on the following day until, of the 140 members of the *conseil général* on 8th *thermidor*, 87 had been guillotined and 40 others arrested.

This is the point that many historians have chosen to conclude their account of the Revolution.[1] Such an implied judgment would have surprised contemporaries and must leave even the least inquisitive reader wondering what happened next. The intention of the Committee of Public Safety was to carry on as before, co-opting new members to replace the three 'traitors'. But the situation had been completely changed by the events of the 9th–10th *thermidor*. The virtual annihilation of the Commune meant that the majority of the Assembly no longer required the protection of a dictatorial Government.

The Centre, with the war going well, could afford to dispense with an authority that it had created with regret and prolonged through fear. The powers of the Committee of Public Safety were immediately curtailed, its authority restricted to war and diplomacy and three of its twelve members ordered to resign each month and not be immediately eligible for re-election. The two absent members, Jeanbon Saint-André and Prieur de la Marne, were ejected and the six new members brought in included the 'Dantonist' Thuriot. Of the remaining members of the old Committee, Billaud, Collot and Barère resigned on 1st September and the three 'specialists', Carnot, Prieur de la Côte d'Or and Lindet, on 10th October, leaving their enemies in command. The revolutionary tribunal also came under attack. A move for its abolition was rejected as premature, but on 1st August the *prairial* law was repealed and henceforth the Court was only to condemn if convinced of the counter-revolutionary

[1] For a good account of the period from the *9 thermidor* to the end of the Convention see G. Lefebvre, *Les thermidoriens*, (Paris, 1937).

motive of the accused—a loophole that transformed the whole character of the tribunal. The arrest of Fouquier-Tinville was itself an indication of the changed attitude of the Assembly and the Government.

The heterogeneous coalition which had been victorious on the 9th–10th *thermidor* had been united merely by its hostility to the Robespierrists and its success created a most confused situation. The relics of the old Committee, supported by some of the Montagnards, hoped to maintain the *status quo*. But the emergence of the Centre as an active political force ensured that the clock would be put back at least as far as the Dantonist past. Individual *thermidoriens*, including some ex-terrorists such as Fréron, Barras and Tallien, went much further. They adopted an aggressively reactionary policy and began attacking their former allies. Under Fréron's patronage there arose the *jeunesse dorée*, recruited mainly from the sons of the bourgeoisie, many of them evading conscription with the connivance of the authorities—a considerably more ⸻ ⸻ilized forerunner of the Storm Troops of a later age. To complicate the situation still further, relics of the *enragés* and the 'Hébertists', often released from gaol in the general relaxation after the 9th *thermidor*, joined in this attack on the Terror, which they blamed for their own misfortunes. Some popular societies were revived, the *maximum des salaires* in Paris was abolished on 31st July and higher rates introduced. In the Meurthe the deputy Michaud reinstated *sans-culottes* who had been arrested as Hébertists, and the Avignon municipality, congratulating the Assembly on its victory of 9th *thermidor*, misread the situation so far as to denounce 'the toad of the *marais* and the reptile of the Plain'.[1] *Sans-culotte* leaders such as Varlet and Babeuf—who for the first time became a public figure as the editor of the *Journal de la Liberté de la Presse* (the title was a programme in itself)—attacked the system of revolutionary government and for a time regarded Fréron and Tallien as their allies against the Montagnards.[2]

Lindet, who had been one of the most moderate members of

[1] P. Vaillandet, 'Les Débuts de la Terreur Blanche en Vaucluse', *Annales Historiques de la Révolution Française*, V (1928), 109.

[2] See J. Zacker, 'Varlet pendant la réaction thermidorienne', *Annales Historiques de la Révolution Française*, XXXIII (1961), 19, and K. D. Tönnesson, *La défaite des sans-culottes* (Oslo/Paris, 1959), pp. 56–62.

the Committee of Public Safety in the year II, tried on 20th September to define the basis of a compromise that would help to bring the revolutionaries together: no return to the law of suspects, the gradual abolition of economic controls, no persecution of nobles and clergy as such, but at the same time no inquisition into past excesses. The Convention voted its unanimous approval, but the passions of the previous two years were not to be so easily exorcised. In October began a reaction against the Montagnards that was to gain momentum all through the winter. The trial of the 94 survivors of the Nantes 'federalists' sent before the revolutionary tribunal by Carrier excited Parisian opinion against one of the most vulnerable Montagnards and discredited those who defended him. The acquittal of the 94 was followed by the arrest and trial of their persecutors, the *comité révolutionnaire* of Nantes. Carrier himself joined the accused on 23rd November and although the verdict of 16th December was surprisingly moderate, involving only three death sentences, the execution of Carrier was a warning to all his fellow-Montagnards.

During the autumn the violence of the *jeunesse dorée* helped the Right to secure control of almost all the Paris Sections. As early as 21st August the payment of 40 sous to the indigent for attendance at meetings of the Sections was abolished and sessions were restricted to one per *décade*. In the following spring the decision to hold meetings in the middle of the day excluded a good many of the *sans-culottes*. The 'regenerated' Sections, unlike the Assembly, shared no responsibility for the Terror and soon began to persecute their old persecutors. At least 37 of the 48 Sections appointed commissions to investigate the conduct of their previous leaders. The extreme violence of the local reaction can be judged from the petition to the Assembly of *Montreuil* on 1 March 1795: 'What are you waiting for in order to purge the land of liberty of these cannibals? . . . Seize them wherever they may be found . . . the sword of the law will despatch them from the atmosphere they have infected for far too long.'[1] Under constant pressure from the Sections, the Convention was pushed rapidly backwards along the road which it had followed in 1793. The violence of the *jeunesse dorée* was turned against the Jacobin Club, whose closure was

[1] Tönnesson, *op. cit.*, p. 107.

ordered by the Government on 12th November, ostensibly in the interest of public order. It was symbolic of the times that on 25th November the 80-gun ship *Jacobin* should have been renamed *9th thermidor*—and perhaps ominous that two months later she sank in a storm!

The governing committees, alarmed by the trend of events, fought a delaying action against demands for vengeance and for a time protected Maignet of the Orange tribunal and his fellow terrorist Le Bon. But on 8th December the Convention voted for the recall of the deputies arrested for protesting against the arrest of the Girondins and the return of these victims of the Terror increased the pressure for reprisals against the terrorists. On 8th March the decision to recall the surviving Girondin outlaws, who included Isnard, Louvet, and Lanjuinais, was accompanied by the abolition of the festival in commemoration of the *journée* of 31st May, and also by the decision to prosecute Collot, Billaud, Barère, and Vadier. The trial of Fouquier-Tinville began on 28th March, soon to lead to his execution, together with that of 15 of his colleagues from the revolutionary tribunal.

The tendency in the provinces was similar to that in Paris in that reaction began in the autumn and steadily gained momentum until the spring. Everywhere the *sans-culottes* were evicted by new representatives on mission from the positions of power in which they had been placed a year earlier. But the intensity of the repression varied enormously in different parts of the country. In the north as a whole, and in parts of the south the movement was surprisingly mild. Rouen contented itself with disarming 37 'terrorists', Bourges 33, and Troyes 74. The District of Sancerre reported that it did not know of any local terrorists.[1] At Melun the new municipality, half of whose members had been arrested as suspects in the year II, arrested six of its predecessors, who were released in the autumn of 1795.[2] At Reims 50 'terrorists' were denounced to the authorities, but only 17 were brought to trial, all of them being acquitted. Chalons similarly put four on trial and subsequently

[1] A. Mathiez, 'La Terreur Blanche de l'an III', *Annales Historiques de la Révolution Française*, V (1928), 401.

[2] F. Courcelle, 'La réaction thermidorienne dans le District de Melun', *Annales Historiques de la Révolution Française*, VII (1930), 113, 252, 329, 443.

released them all.[1] It was no doubt significant that the Terror had claimed only seven victims in the Marne and none in the Seine-et-Marne.

The situation in the south, especially in those Departments which had been 'most involved in the 'federalist' revolt, was very different.[2] Lyons, once the state of siege was lifted on 7th October, rapidly reverted to its former position as the main royalist centre where malcontents, deserters from the army and refractory clergy could find a safe refuge. The local authorities were themselves moderate republicans, but they were not prepared to take effective action against the 'counter-terrorists'. When the National Guard was reorganized in the spring of 1795 one of its three commanders was a man who had taken a leading part in the revolt of May 1793. In the south as a whole, with the exception of Toulon which remained a *sans-culotte* bastion until May, anti-Montagnard representatives on mission had transferred power to the moderates by the autumn of 1794.[3] The new men were often advocates of appeasement, but they had neither the resolution nor the means to protect the ex-terrorists from lynching mobs and organized murder-gangs such as the *Compagnie du Soleil*, which operated with the more or less open approval of the deputies Isnard and Cadroy. During the winter of 1794–5 the murder of individual terrorists became increasingly frequent. Finding that they had nothing to fear from the law—on 15th May assassins were acquitted in Lyons and carried off in triumph—the 'counter-terrorists' began organizing prison massacres as brutal, if not as extensive, as those of September 1792 in Paris. These massacres appear to have started on 19th April at Bourg, where six prisoners were killed. Throughout May and the first three weeks of June they spread to Aix (up to 50 victims), Tarascon (47), Marseilles and Lyons (over 100 each), and there were smaller outbreaks at Lons-le-Saulnier and Nîmes. Toulon revolted in mid-May and tried to come to the support of the Marseilles *sans-culottes*, only to have its forces cut to pieces. The White Terror was mainly confined to the south-east—in the Basses-Pyrénées, for example, repres-

---

[1] S. Blum, 'La mission d'Albert dans la Marne en l'an III', *La Révolution Française*, XLIII (1902), 417; XLV (1903), 193.

[2] On this subject see especially R. Fuoc, *La réaction thermidorienne à Lyon*.

[3] See, for example, Vaillandet, *loc. cit.*, 109.

sion seems to have been as mild as in the north—but in Provence and the regions on its borders the massacres spread panic and left memories as bitter as those of 1793–4.[1]

The Convention found itself helpless to enforce any kind of moderate policy. It attempted to pacify the Vendée and the north-west by conciliation, offering an amnesty to all who submitted, both leaders and rank and file. The result was a number of local armistices, negotiated in the spring of 1795, which amounted almost to the capitulation of the Republic. The rebels were offered an amnesty, the restoration of their property, exemption from military service, freedom of worship, even for the refractory clergy. They were to retain their arms and were entrusted with the policing of their own territory! The consequence was to spread the influence of the Chouans into much of Normandy and virtually to abandon the country districts of the north-west to their influence.

The Assembly also found itself unable to enforce the economic policy of its own choice. On 7th September the *maximum général* was extended for a year, but on 9th November the penalty for farmers who failed to comply with requisition orders was limited to the confiscation of the grain involved. As the reaction gathered pace the *maximum* itself was abolished on 24th December, although requisitioning to feed the towns was prolonged for another two months. The Left made no serious attempt to defend the *maximum*, whose demise it accepted without much immediate regret. On 2nd January foreign trade, with the exception of grain, was freed from all controls, although merchant shipping was not freed from requisitioning by the State until August. The national arms workshops were gradually closed down and a cautious attempt made to return to private war-contracting. But the contractors were unable to fulfil their obligations and the freeing of the grain trade, after the poor harvest of 1794, would have led to the starvation of the towns. Ignoring the central government, local authorities imposed their own controls. The fertile District of Bergues, in the Nord, for the first time resorted to the billeting of troops on recalcitrant peasants—with little success, since some of the

---

[1] S. L. M. Fréron, *Mémoire Historique sur la réaction royale et sur les Massacres du Midi*, (Paris, 1824) *passim*. A. Richard, *Le gouvernement révolutionnaire dans les Basses-Pyrénées*, pp. 211–18.

farmers were glad of this protection against the increasing brigandage in the countryside. The late Professor Lefebvre went so far as to describe the new economic measures as 'much more vexatious and costly, for the majority of the farmers, than the political Terror which had merely intimidated them'.[1] The Convention was eventually driven to reverse its policy and the law of 29 September 1795 introduced the most extensive series of controls on the grain trade that the Revolution had known.

The relaxation of controls during the winter of 1794–5, the continuing high rate of war expenditure, the partial evasion of taxation and the reduction in the sale of *biens nationaux*—for the Church lands had mostly gone and it seemed increasingly unsafe to invest in *émigré* property—all made for inflation. During the first half of 1795 the total of assignats in circulation rose from 10 to 17 milliard livres. Their value had been falling ever since the end of 1793: at 31 per cent in July 1794, they had dropped to 20 per cent by the end of the year and to 8 per cent by late March 1795. Food prices rose even faster than the assignat fell. In Paris they doubled between February and April, while the cost of living in Lyons was much higher than that in the capital, bread selling at 45 sous the pound in March. The household accounts of Madame Hummel at Nantes illustrate a trend that was probably common to much of the country. Her monthly expenditure began to rise in November 1794 and from December onwards never fell below 300 livres. Serious inflation started in March. In May (or more accurately, in *floréal*) she spent 821 livres, and 3,905 in *thermidor* (July–August). Her expenditure fell to 1,331 livres in the following month, perhaps because of shortages rather than reduced prices, but rose suddenly to 25,098 livres in *brumaire* (October–November 1795), bread alone accounting for 17,264 livres. At this point she not surprisingly abandoned the attempt to keep any accounts at all and did not resume until the advent of Napoleon.[2]

The capricious influence of inflation was not exercised in any one specific direction. Madame Hummel's food bill rose by over 50 times, but her rent was unchanged and her landlord had

[1] G. Lefebvre, *Documents relatifs à l'histoire des subsistances dans le District de Bergues*, p. lxxxi.

[2] Gaston Martin, 'La vie bourgeoise à Nantes sous la Convention d'après le livre de comptes de Madame Hummel', *La Révolution Française*, LXXXVI (1933), 236.

presumably his food to buy, too. The wage-earner suffered bitterly from the continuous rise in prices, but the tenant farmer paid a negligible rent and many peasants took advantage of the opportunity to liquidate long-standing debts with almost value-less assignats.[1] It was not until July 1795 that the Convention authorized landowners to obtain half of their rents in kind. The inflation of the year III thus affected all classes, but the wealthy could often recoup themselves by buying *biens nationaux* with their depreciated assignats, and in any case they had reserves of property to tide them over the worst period. When the few possessions of the *sans-culottes* had been sold or pawned they were helpless. Their position was aggravated by a winter of extraordinary severity. Many of the rivers froze and the Seine could be crossed on foot in Paris. Famished wolves appeared even in the streets of the towns. Communications were almost at a standstill and the thaw that followed the great frost turned roads into quagmires and rivers into torrents that burst their bridges. The feeding of the towns became extremely difficult and the poor everywhere were reduced to desperate straits. Cold and hunger left them little time for politics. In the main towns they did at least receive a small ration of subsidized bread, but the increasing evasion of requisitions reduced the Parisian allow-ance to half a pound per head by mid-March, and though rice was issued in addition the poor often lacked the fuel to cook it. In the villages conditions may have been even worse for those who were not self-supporting, and there was rioting in the District of Bergues. Cobb has shown that the death rate at Rouen and le Havre in the years III and IV was abnormally high, and Tönnesson suggests that both the suicide and the death rate increased sharply in Paris in the spring of 1795.[2] If one adds the effects of the White Terror in parts of the south and the more moderate persecution of revolutionaries every-where, with its loss of employment and imprisonment of bread-winners, the full misery of the poor in general and of the former

[1] P. Massé, 'Les Amortissements de Rentes Foncières en l'An III', *Annales Historiques de la Révolution Française*, XXXIII (1961), 349.

[2] R. C. Cobb, 'Disette et mortalité, la crise de l'an III et de l'an IV à Rouen', *Annales de la Normandie*, 1956; K. D. Tönnesson, *op. cit.*, p. 126, n. 29. See also R. C. Cobb, 'Problèmes des subsistances de l'an II et de l'an III, l'exemple d'un petit port normand, Honfleur', *Actes du 81è Congrès des Sociétés Savantes* (Rouen-Caen, 1956).

sans-culotte militants in particular becomes only too grimly apparent.

The contrast between this squalor and the speculative fortunes and sudden wealth of the minority who profited from inflation was made all the more provocative by the changed climate of opinion.[1] Society life re-emerged from the eclipse of 1793. Wealthy bankers and successful speculators and their wives and mistresses embarked on a course of conspicuous expenditure that reflected both their relief and their continuing feeling of insecurity. The salons revived. Fashions, both for men and women, reached strange heights of extravagance with the *incroyables* and the *merveilleuses*, and the winter of 1794–5 was both the gayest and the most terrible of the Revolution. Outstanding, even in the society of the time, were the *bals des victimes*, where the families of the guillotined entertained each other with the napes of their necks shorn as though for the *rasoir national* and a thin band of red silk round their throats. Food was plentiful and luxurious for those who could afford inflated prices, and the contrast between affluence and starvation made the suffering of the poor all the harder to bear.

As usual, the Convention vacillated between approval and alarm. Its growing indifference to the needs of the *sans-culottes* was reflected in its educational policy. The principle of free and compulsory education for all was reaffirmed on 17 November 1794, but on 25 October 1795 education was once more made optional and its cost was to be supported by parental fees. The deputies were more concerned with the provision of adequate secondary education and a Bill of 24th February provided for the creation of one central school in each Department—the forerunner of the *lycée*. The courses provided by these schools were not far short of university level, so they were quite inaccessible to those whose education was limited to what they had picked up in the primary schools. The *écoles centrales* were intended for the privately-educated children of the bourgeoisie. The elaborate provision of post-graduate institutions for the study of medicine, engineering and the fine arts also contrasted forcibly with the neglect of primary education for the population as a whole. A similar class bias probably lay behind the decision on 31st May

[1] For some examples of successful speculation in the renting of *émigré* estates see M. Marion, *La vente des biens nationaux pendant la Révolution*, chap. vi.

to sell *biens nationaux* in large units, without auction, to those who undertook to complete payment within three months. This, however, had to be abandoned when it became obvious that the State was throwing away its assets for a negligible return. However much they might hope to favour the educated and respectable, the deputies were still tied to the Revolution and uneasily aware that the White Terror in the south and the wealthy salons and the *jeunesse dorée* in the streets of Paris were more royalist than republican. Fear of the blind vengeance of a royalist restoration imposed a limit to the concessions they dared to make. Nowhere was this more apparent than in their religious policy.

Once rid of Robespierre and his worship of the Supreme Being, the deputies, most of whom were probably relatively indifferent to the religious question, tried to dispose of this recurrent source of trouble. The official State religion of the Supreme Being was allowed to decline. On 18 September 1794 the constitutional Church was disestablished and a lay State affirmed its religious neutrality. On 21st February the Assembly voted to reserve churches for official State ceremonies, but to allow the constitutional clergy and those refractory priests who had taken the *petit serment* of loyalty to the Republic to hold private worship in such other premises as they were able to buy or hire. What mattered was less the intention of the Assembly than the reaction of public opinion. Although the religious history of provincial France in 1794–5 requires much further investigation, it seems clear that the dechristianization movement had exhausted its momentum—in Beauvais, for example, there were no more marriages of priests after 1794. As usual, there was much local variety: few of those who had abjured the priesthood returned in Lyons, while the majority did so in the Marne and the Aube. There seems, however, to have been a general tendency for the laity to return to church and the Assembly's concessions were frequently made the pretext for the illegal celebration of public services in churches. There may have been a tendency for the educated to retain their Voltairean scepticism when the poor went back to church. One would like to know how typical was the situation in the Marne, where at Reims the reactionary journalist Delloye indulged in Voltairean pleasantries, while at Épernay a man who had just been purged from the *comité révolutionnaire* helped in the celebration of mass.[1] In general the neutrality of the State profited the refractory clergy more than the *constitutionnels*, who had always depended on official support. The non-jurors promptly took the offensive. In the Marne they induced some who had taken the oath to withdraw it; in Lyons, and no doubt elsewhere, they began threatening those who had acquired Church lands. By and large the refractory priests were royalists, and it was this which led the royalist pamphleteer Mallet du Pan to write, with some exaggeration, 'Whoever starts attending mass is an enemy of the Republic.' The Convention dared not allow this source of royalist propaganda to spread throughout the countryside, nor could it ignore the threat to the purchasers of *biens nationaux*, whose interests it had much at heart. Its neutrality therefore rested on an impracticable basis and when the religious revival spread it found itself obliged to resume a persecution that was all the more intolerable for having no religious basis and no positive substitute for the belief that it dared not tolerate.

During the spring of 1795 the desperation of the urban *sans-culottes* reached a point at which violent action became inevitable.[2] In Paris the second half of March was increasingly tense. But the *sans-culotte* agitators, without bourgeois leadership and with no Commune to co-ordinate them, without even control of the Sections, were denied the means of effective insurrectionary action. After a fortnight of petitions and minor riots, on 1st April (12th *germinal*) a large crowd invaded the Convention demanding bread, the application of the constitution of 1793, the release of those arrested since *thermidor*, and the disbanding of the *jeunesse dorée*. The *journée* of *germinal* was no serious danger to the régime for the Sections, their committees and the National Guard all remained loyal to the Government and the demonstrators were ejected from the Tuileries without much difficulty.[3] The main consequence of the insurrection was to accelerate still further the political reaction. The Assembly

[1] S. Blum, *loc. cit.*, XLIII (1902), 417; XLV (1903), 193.
[2] See, for example, R. C. Cobb, *'Une émeute de la faim dans la banlieu rouennaise'*, *Annales de la Normandie* (1956).
[3] For an account of the *journée* see, in addition to Tönnesson, E. Tarlé, *Germinal et prairial* (Fr. trans., Moscow, 1959).

immediately voted the deportation of Collot, Billaud, and Barère to Guiana. Eight prominent Montagnards including Amar and Léonard Bourdon were arrested and Cambon, Levasseur, Maignet, Lecointre, Thuriot and four others went into hiding. The flight of Lecointre and Thuriot, who had been early leaders of the thermidorean reaction, was an indication of the extent to which the Assembly was now bent on undoing the past. The main weight of repression fell on the *sans-culottes*. A state of siege was declared in Paris and many of the *germinal* leaders were arrested. Under pressure from the Sections, the Assembly, on 10th April, ordered the disarming, in Paris and the provinces, of all who had played a leading part in the Terror. The 'disarming' of a *sans-culotte* involved his dismissal from any public employment and the refusal of a passport enabling him to travel in search of work, and could lead to the ostracism of the victim and a general unwillingness to employ him. Tönnesson estimates that in Paris about 1,600 *sans-culottes* were affected by the measure. In the provinces the decree of 10th April was often the signal for the arrest and prosecution of former terrorists. In Lyons and the south-east it probably helped to set off the prison massacres for which it designated the victims.

The continuance of popular agitation in the face of these repressive measures was essentially due to the worsening food situation. In Paris the daily ration of subsidized bread rarely exceeded $\frac{1}{4}$ lb. and was often less. Driven desperate by famine, the *sans-culottes* searched for some political solution to their misery. There were riots in many places, in Amiens and Rouen with the cry of 'Bread and a king', in Paris, 'Bread and the 1793 constitution'. *Sans-culotte* leaders such as Babeuf now preached alliance with the Montagnards, but the latter remained inactive, perhaps as a result of their successful intimidation by the Convention, and the *journées* of *prairial*, like that of *germinal*, were essentially *sans-culotte* affairs. The new movement was organized after a fashion, although very little is known of its planners. On 20th May (1st *prairial*) the Faubourg Saint-Antoine mobilized its forces, and its three battalions of National Guards—whose officers refused to march—provided the main force that once more invaded the Convention, killing the deputy, Féraud, in a scuffle. Again the opportunity was thrown away owing to lack of leadership. The *sans-culottes* appear to have been misled by memories of 31 May, 2 June and 5 September 1793 into imagining that a more or less pacific demonstration would force their will on the Government. They made no attempt to seize the governing committees and were content to occupy the debating hall of the Assembly. When a few Montagnards had come forward and compromised themselves by proposing popular measures the majority of the demonstrators eventually withdrew for the night and the committees were able to clear the hall and arrest 14 deputies, whom they probably suspected of being responsible for the insurrection. The following day saw the crisis of the movement. The Government, which had surrounded the Assembly with troops, brought up the National Guards as well, perhaps with a view to keeping them under the control of their officers. An attempt to organize a new insurrectional Commune collapsed when the Assembly outlawed all who refused to leave the *Hôtel de Ville*. The situation swung in favour of the insurgents when the gunners of Saint-Antoine won over the artillerymen of some of the other Sections who trained their pieces on the Convention. But no one was prepared to take the responsibility for opening fire, and the Government, by fraternizing with the National Guard eventually induced it to disperse. The popular momentum was now broken and on 22nd–23rd May the Faubourg Saint-Antoine found itself isolated. For the first time since 1789 the Government brought up troops for offensive action against Parisian revolutionaries. A first attempt to occupy the faubourg was unsuccessful, but the *sans-culottes* allowed Kilmaine's column to withdraw unharmed. The Committees then threatened to proclaim the faubourg in a state of rebellion if it failed to lay down its arms. No support was forthcoming from the rest of Paris and by the afternoon of 23rd May the insurrection had collapsed.

The repression of the *prairial* rising was severe and effective. A *military* commission—the first to be used against Parisian revolutionaries—tried 149 and condemned to death 36 supposed leaders, including 6 deputies. Romme, Goujon, and Duquesnoy succeeded in committing suicide when the verdict was announced. Duroy, Soubrany, and Bourbotte failed in their attempts and were guillotined. In all, orders were given for the arrest of over 40 deputies and the decision of 19th June to put Le Bon on trial for his excesses at Arras during the Terror justifies his inclusion amongst the victims of *prairial*. Between two and three thousand arrests were made by the Government, while the Sections incarcerated another 1,200. The great majority of these obscure men were eventually amnestied, but their families had often been ruined by their imprisonment, and henceforth they were marked men liable to further arrest whenever subsequent Governments feared trouble in Paris.[1] The reorganization of the National Guard in such a way as virtually to exclude the *sans-culottes* completed their rout. There was no major popular rising in Paris until 1848. But the events of May 1795 left bitter and lasting memories and the historian Buchez, writing in 1838, observed that 'the custodians of the revolutionary tradition were the victims of *prairial* rather than those of *thermidor*'.

The victorious Assembly was not particularly concerned about the revolutionary tradition. For the immediate future the Parisian *sans-culottes* had been reduced to impotence and the Montagnard wing of the Assembly virtually eliminated. The decision of 10th June to offer an amnesty to all who had fled from France after the insurrection of 31 May 1793 confirmed that the predominant opinion was more or less Girondin. But the Girondins in their struggle against revolutionary government had sometimes joined forces with the royalists and the question now was whether it would be possible to prevent the backward movement of the Revolution from culminating in the restoration of the monarchy. There was much to be said for the acceptance of Louis XVII, a boy of nine who might conceivably have provided a symbol for the regrouping of Frenchmen round a moderate constitutional monarchy and offered a way through the labyrinth of hatred in which the country was astray. His death in prison on 8th June put an end to any such hopes. The elder of Louis XVI's brothers, the comte de Provence, now proclaimed himself king. On 24th June he issued a fanatical proclamation of counter-revolution, promising the punishment of regicides, the restoration of the three orders, the parlements and the power of the Church. Any question of compromise between the Convention and the monarchy was now excluded,

[1] See R. C. Cobb, 'Note sur la répression contre le personnel sans-culotte de 1795 à 1801', *Annales Historiques de la Révolution Française*, XXVI (1954), 23.

but there remained the possibility of a forcible royalist restoration, achieved by foreign invasion and domestic rebellion, that would have plunged the country into civil war and further bloodshed. The latest of the innumerable royalist plots provided for the landing of an expeditionary force of *émigrés* in the northwest, to link up with the officially pacified Chouans and Vendéans, an insurrection in the south and an invasion from the east by the forces of Condé, with the connivance of the republican general Pichegru. As usual, the plot was discovered. Vigorous action at Lyons put an end to the massacres, suspended the local authorities and put the city under military rule.[1] The south was intimidated and Pichegru failed to co-operate. All that remained was the forlorn landing at Quiberon on 27th June. Within a month the royalist army had capitulated to Hoche, and 718 of the *émigrés*, including a considerable number of former naval officers, were shot. The expedition was a total failure, but it broke the uneasy armistice in the north-west and revived the civil war with all its cruelty and slaughter. Charette took the field once more and replied to the extermination of the *émigrés* by the execution of hundreds of republican prisoners.

In this atmosphere of hatred, famine and frustration the Convention drew to its end. In the face of the royalist threat the Government swung to the Left. Royalist journalists were arrested and the republican Press subsidized. An attempt was made to catch the young bourgeois evading their military service and it was now the turn of the *jeunesse dorée* to suffer at the hands of soldiers and *sans-culottes*. At the same time the authorities intensified their efforts to exclude the surviving Montagnards from the forthcoming elections. Another ten were arrested on 8th August, including even the experienced trimmer, Fouché. A new constitution was drafted, designed to limit the power of the *sans-culottes* and to preserve a conservative republic from the threat of monarchy or dictatorship.[2] Well aware of their limited support in the country, the *thermidoriens* decreed that two-thirds of the new deputies should be chosen from members of the Convention—probably the only means of securing any kind of workable majority. Both the constitution and

---

[1] See R. Fuoc, *op. cit.*, pp. 165–84.

[2] For an examination of this constitution see A. Aulard, *Histoire politique de la Révolution Française* (Paris, 1921), pp. 543–77.

the two-thirds rule were submitted to a plebiscite. The former was accepted by an enormous majority of 1,057,390 to 49,978, since almost everyone was looking forward to the end of the Convention. The two-thirds rule, obviously aimed against the royalists, passed by a much narrower margin: 205,498 to 108,754. It was rejected by the west, much of the south and by all the Paris Sections except the *Quinze-Vingts*. Suspicions of Governmental fraud in the counting of votes provided the pretext for another insurrection in Paris, on 5th October (13th *vendémiaire*), this time by the royalists. The Assembly turned again to the *sans-culottes* for support, enrolling them for the defence of the Tuileries and repealing the law for the disarming of terrorists. Barras, who had defended the Convention against the Robespierrist Commune, once more took charge of the military preparations. His subsequent report, with its reference to the 'Faubourg Saint-Antoine whose attachment to the cause of liberty is well known', offers a curious commentary on the evolution of official opinion since the *journées* of *prairial*. A crowd of some 20,000 marched on the Tuileries and there was heavy fighting, with some 200–300 killed on each side— Napoleon's leading rôle and the 'whiff of grapeshot' with which he dispersed the royalists are both fabrications. The victory of the Government was followed by the inevitable repressive measures. Although few were arrested and only two executed, the National Guard was disarmed and Paris put under military control. On 26th October the Convention voted a general amnesty for all 'activities arising directly from the Revolution' and at last dissolved itself.

By the autumn of 1795 all the main issues of the Revolution had been decided and the main outlines of future events were becoming visible. The defeat of the *sans-culottes* and of the Montagnards was final and there was to be no further attempt to build a 'social' republic on bourgeois leadership and working-class support. Equally decisive was the breach with royalism, whether domestic or imported. Since these were the only two policies that could arouse much popular support, the conservative regicides found themselves condemned to a fatal instability in every field. Politically they could not create a régime based on free elections and the victory of one extreme or the other in the period from 1795 to 1799 was only averted by a number of more or less violent purges. In the economic field the implementation of the liberal principles in which almost all believed was impossible so long as the war brought continuing inflation. The year III saw striking victories for French arms. Prussia, Spain, and Holland all accepted defeat and made terms with the Republic. But the abandonment of the war economy of the year II ruled out any naval challenge to Britain, the weakened armies were incapable of a decisive blow against Austria and the Government was too confused and uncertain of its own objectives to conclude a negotiated peace. Where religion was concerned the *thermidoriens* could neither enforce a positive policy of their own nor maintain an attitude of neutrality and allow events to take their course. All that was left to them was to maintain an unwanted compromise by alternate blows at the popular forces to Left and Right. This *jeu de bascule* implied an increasing readiness to resort to military force to maintain the uneasy balance. Troops had been used in Paris in *prairial* and the insurgents punished by a military court. It was the army again that saved the régime in *vendémiaire* and the two main cities in France were both under military control. It was merely a matter of time before the army ejected the civilians who were unable to govern without its support and the cynical adventurer who was to seize for himself the heritage of the Revolution was already conspicuous amongst the victors of *vendémiaire*.

X

The Aftermath

Tout le monde est pardonnable quand tout le monde a besoin de pardon.

BAROUD, *Nouvelles observations en faveur des acquéreurs de biens d'émigrés*

F OR many years it has been customary to regard the French Revolution as the decisive turning-point of modern European history, 'the cross-roads of the modern world', to use the expression of R. R. Palmer. Recently, however, there has been a tendency to deny it any such paramount significance. The argument that the Revolution was an essentially bourgeois movement and *ipso facto* an inconclusive one, is developed with much persuasive detail by D. Guérin in his *Lutte des Classes sous la Première République*. More recently, Professor A. Cobban, in his inaugural lecture—significantly entitled *The Myth of the French Revolution*—arrived at somewhat similar conclusions from a very different starting-point. Rejecting the Marxist contention that the Revolution represented the revolt of a rising middle class against a predominantly aristocratic society, he stressed the extent to which 'feudalism' had already disappeared by 1789, the timidity of the anti-feudal policies of the Constituent Assembly and the fact that the initiative was taken not by merchants and capitalists but by lawyers and office-holders in the royal Government. For Cobban, the real motive force behind the movement was the frustration of these royal office-holders, asserting their claim to the high positions from which they were debarred in France by reason of their humble birth.[1] This emphasis on the limited aspirations and achievements of the revolutionaries, with its implication that the Revolution has been to some extent the creation of its historians, requires further examination.

It is immediately clear that the popular conception of the French Revolution as a period of indiscriminate slaughter is grossly exaggerated, for the application of mass-production techniques to the elimination of political opponents is an innovation of the twentieth century. The 'Reign of Terror' up to the execution of Robespierre, probably accounted for less than 30,000 deaths, together with another 10,000 who died in prison.[2] The great majority of these 30,000 were put to death for alleged participation in civil war. The revolutionary tribunal in Paris, the centre of so many grim legends, despatched no more than 2,639 prisoners. It is not to minimize these figures, but merely to set them in perspective, that others are quoted for comparison: 15,000–17,000 *Communards*, almost all Parisians, were shot in May 1871; there were perhaps 40,000 executions after the liberation of France in 1944. Deaths on British roads in 1960 accounted for 13 per 100,000 population; executions for political offences (excluding participation in civil war) in France in 1793–4, for something less than 24 per 100,000.

The popular exaggeration of the scope of the Terror is not entirely to be explained by the argument that,

When beggars die, there are no comets seen;
The heavens themselves blaze forth the death of princes.

The majority of the victims of the Terror were obscure men and women. Of the 14,080 whose social origin is known, only 1,158 came from the nobility and 1,964 from the upper middle class.[3] There were striking cases of the near-extermination of distinguished families, such as Noailles and Montmorin, but the most exalted were not necessarily the hardest hit. The

[1] A. Cobban, *The Myth of the French Revolution* (1955); see also the comments of Lefebvre and Palmer, and Cobban's reply, *Annales Historiques de la Révolution Française*, XXVIII (1956), 337; XXXI, (1959), 154, 387.

[2] D. Greer, *The Incidence of the Terror during the French Revolution*, pp. 25–37, 196.

[3] *Ibid.*, Table VI.

summit of the French aristocracy consisted of the *ducs et pairs*, of whom there were 38 in 1789. Three of these peerages appear to have lapsed owing to death from natural causes. Of the remaining 35 peers I have been unable to trace 7. Two were massacred during the Revolution, 5 executed by the revolutionary tribunal, 16 escaped from France, and 5 suffered no more than a short period of imprisonment. In other words, only one *duc et pair* in four or five lost his life as a result of the Revolution. Taking the nobility as a whole, of whom there had been about 400,000 in 1789, some 1,158 were executed and another 16,431 fled the country.[1] Even if one assumes that each victim or *émigré* belonged to a different family, it is clear that the majority of noble families were not immediately affected, although many, like Ferrières, had a relative amongst the *émigrés*. The Terror was therefore very far from destroying the nobility, even though a considerable proportion went into temporary exile, either to fight the Revolution or to escape from it.

The transfer of property brought about by the Revolution was also far less radical than that effected by the social upheavals of the present century. There was no expropriation of whole social classes, but only of individuals condemned for personal offences. No reliable statistics are ever likely to be available concerning the social consequences of the sale of the property of the Church, the *émigrés* and those convicted of counter-revolutionary offences. Even where evidence survives it often fails to indicate with sufficient precision the social status of the original purchaser. The subsequent history of each holding or building must then be traced, since many who bought *biens nationaux* did so for speculative purposes, and some were relatives or agents of the expropriated *émigrés*, buying on their behalf. On the other hand, some *émigrés*, when they were allowed to return to France, sold part of their surviving estates in order to raise capital. After the Restoration unsold *biens nationaux* were returned to their original owners or their heirs. Political conviction or successful intimidation may also have induced some of the new occupants to sell back property below its market value. The indemnity of almost one milliard francs

[1] D. Greer, *The Incidence of the Emigration during the French Revolution* (Cambridge, Mass., 1951), p. 173, Table I.

voted to the *émigrés* in 1825 was intended to help them to buy back their estates or acquire similar ones. Since conditions varied considerably from one locality to another, and from one family to another in the same place, an exact statement of the effect of the Revolution on land-ownership would require the detailed study of every Commune in France, over a period of 35 years, and even if this were possible the disappearance of many documents and the vagueness of others would allow of no more than approximate conclusions. The following observations, based on detailed studies of the Nord, the Cher, the Gironde and the District of Saint-Pol, in the Pas-de-Calais, are therefore not intended to be more than tentative.[1] Nevertheless, the substantial similarity between these Departments, geographically remote from each other, of different social composition and contrasting revolutionary experience, suggests that the evidence they offer probably applies in a general way to the country as a whole.

At the bottom of the social scale, the attempt to spread land-ownership by the law of 13 September 1793 offering a loan of 500 livres to some of the landless, for the purchase of *biens nationaux*, seems to have been singularly ineffective. Marion found only 40 cases of the use of such loans in the Gironde and only one in the Cher, while Lefebvre discovered very few in the Nord. Sangnier arrived at the same conclusion for the District of Saint-Pol. The Versailles area appears to have been exceptional in that many *bons* of 500 livres were used, but the land thus purchased was frequently resold soon afterwards.[2] On the other hand, the laws of June and July 1793 ordering the division of *émigré* property into small lots were strictly applied. Many lots were sold for less than 500 livres, so that—from 1793 to 1795 at least—the relatively poor were able to acquire some land. In the District of Saint-Pol, lots of five acres and below, which had formed less than one-third of the total number of sales in 1791, amounted to more than nine-tenths in 1793–5.

The purchase of Church property had not been regarded as an act of political commitment—Marie Antoinette had recom-

[1] See G. Lefebvre, *Les Paysans du Nord pendant la Révolution Française*, pp. 11, 495–506; M. Marion, *La Vente des Biens Nationaux pendant la Révolution, passim*; G. Sangnier, *L'Évolution de la Propriété rurale dans le District de Saint-Pol pendant la Révolution, passim*.

[2] Marion, *op. cit.*, p. 212, n. 3.

mended it to Fersen as a good investment—and some had been
bought by nobles who were later to emigrate and by priests
who were to refuse the oath to the Civil Constitution of the
Clergy. But the greater part of these *biens de première origine*,
as they were known, had been acquired by the urban bourgeoisie, whose investment in the Cher amounted to six million
livres, nearly four times that of the peasants. *Émigré* property,
sold in smaller units at a time when the nobility and the wealthy
in general were not anxious to attract attention to themselves,
often went to less affluent bidders. But taking the alienation of
property as a whole, 'those who bought were primarily those
who owned something already', to use Marion's language, and
the bourgeoisie bought more than the peasants, especially in the
vicinity of important towns. The sale of *émigré* property did not
involve the expropriation of the nobility since, as we have seen,
only a minority of the aristocracy emigrated and their families
succeeded in buying back a fraction of their auctioned estates
which Lefebvre puts as high as one-quarter and Sangnier at
rather more than one-tenth. Nevertheless, in the Nord at least,
the nobility seems to have lost much more from emigration than
it acquired from the purchase of Church lands. Lefebvre estimated the proportion of land held by the various classes in the Nord
as follows:

	Nobility %	Church %	Bourgeoisie %	Peasants %
Before 1789 (whole Department)	21–22	19–20	16–17	30–31
About 1804 (one-seventh of Department only)	13	—	28½	42

Relating to different areas, these figures are not strictly comparable and the Nord may not have been typical of France as a
whole. Elsewhere the survival of the *émigrés* as important
landowners can be illustrated from the electoral lists of 1829
in the Gironde and the Cher, where in each case former *emigré*
families provided one-tenth of those subject to the highest level
of taxation. Individual fortunes varied enormously, but over the
country as a whole the landed wealth of the aristocracy had
shrunk but did not suffer anything in the nature of a total eclipse.

The bourgeoisie, in the sense of the urban middle class,

gained most land in proportion to its numbers. If one may generalize from Lefebvre's investigation of a fraction of one Department, this progress was far from evenly spread over the class as a whole. Sixty-two per cent of the bourgeois whose fortunes he examined bought less than five *hectares* (roughly 11 acres) each, while 8 per cent purchased 62 per cent of the land bought by the bourgeoisie as a whole. A very similar tendency prevailed amongst the rural population, where over 60 per cent of the peasants bought less than one *hectare*, while a little over 9 per cent obtained 61 per cent of all the land acquired by the peasantry. In other words, in both town and country, the transfer of land-ownership tended to bring small benefits to many and really substantial acquisitions to a small minority—who had probably been amongst the wealthier members of their classes in 1789.

In general, therefore, it seems reasonable to conclude that the Revolution did not overturn the pattern of land-ownership in France. The transfer of property had important social consequences, but it constituted no more than a modification of the previous distribution and perhaps an acceleration of trends already present under the ancien régime. Important noble estates were fewer but still conspicuous. Some members of the urban middle class became substantial landowners and many more acquired smallholdings. The majority of the peasants still owned insufficient land to support their families throughout the year, but a few emerged from the Revolution as farmers of considerable property. In the matter of cultivation, as distinct from ownership, the consequences of the partial fragmentation of large estates were limited by the fact that these had rarely been farmed as single units before the Revolution, but had been leased as a number of small farms or *métairies*.

Apart from the sale, generally to bourgeois purchasers, of convents, monasteries and private houses owned by the Church, the towns had experienced no corresponding upheaval. The expropriation of the *émigré* nobility was probably less significant here than in the countryside since, if Paris was typical, the aristocracy generally rented their town houses from middle-class owners.[1] Wartime regulations and controls and the severe

[1] G. A. Jaffé, *Le Mouvement Ouvrier à Paris pendant la Révolution Française* (Paris, n.d.), p. 13.

inflation of 1794–5 led to some unemployment and starvation amongst the working class and to some business failures, but did little to affect the basic structure of French commerce and industry.[1] Emergency measures such as the special taxation of the rich and the provision of cheap food and of employment in national arms and munitions factories were essentially temporary. The erratic sword of revolutionary justice and the lottery of inflation destroyed some and elevated others, but left the organization of production and distribution substantially unchanged. It would be virtually impossible to investigate the contribution of inflation to the concentration of industry, but this again is unlikely to have done more than accelerate a previous tendency towards large-scale production. The Convention had at least played with the idea of creating a society of peasant proprietors, but it had no parallel utopia for the towns.

At first sight it might appear that the revolutionary onslaught on the Roman Catholic Church was equally short-lived. The attempt to provide a positive substitute for Christianity never satisfied more than a small minority of the population. The constitutional Church, once deprived of State support proved incapable of maintaining itself. The experiment with a lay State, divorced from any official Church, was too dangerous to survive since it opened the countryside to the counter-revolutionary political influence of the non-juror priests. Eventually, by the Concordat of 1801, Napoleon restored as the 'religion of the majority of Frenchmen' a Roman Catholic Church in communion with the Pope and in partnership with the State, on a basis that was intended to recall the Gallican Church of the 'Most Christian' monarchs of the ancien régime.

In the political field the aspiration to representative government and decentralized administration had already been abandoned at the height of the Revolution itself. The constitution of 1793 was shelved and the Convention dared not confront the electorate in 1795 without the protection of the two-thirds rule. The Departments had been deprived of much of their authority in 1793 and the provinces controlled first by representatives on mission and then by the Committees of Public Safety and

---

[1] For the effect of the Révolution on one enterprise, see the chapter, 'Les mines de Littry', in G. Lefebvre, *Études sur la Révolution Française* (Paris, 1954).

General Security and their agents. Elected councillors were dismissed and their places taken by Government nominees. Napoleon was to carry the process a stage further, by the gradual elimination of representative institutions and the revival of the intendant under the new name of prefect. When Napoleon fell the prefects remained. The Bourbons returned and the brother of Louis XVI at last ascended the throne which he had claimed in 1795 by virtue of the divine right of kings.

There is therefore some apparent justification for regarding the Revolution as a largely ephemeral phenomenon whose relative violence, in an age accustomed to greater stability than our own, led to its being credited with more lasting significance than was actually the case. But to adopt such a perspective is to render subsequent French history largely incomprehensible. It is no coincidence that French historians, whatever their attitude to the Revolution, are virtually unanimous in emphasizing its importance, not merely to France, but to the evolution of Europe as a whole.

The ancien régime had risen with Versailles, and the permanent abondonment of the great palace as the seat of the Court, after the October Days of 1789, signified the end of divine right absolutism. Henceforth, in the nineteenth century, the monarchy was constitutional and the absolutism of the two Bonapartes rested on a precarious basis of violence and demagogy. The hierarchical society fell with the old monarchy. This was not merely a question of opening to the middle classes professions from which they had been previously debarred. What was involved was a whole conception of society, based on the natural and permanent subordination of some families to others. In the countryside change was not merely a matter of landownership. The *fourches patibulaires*, the gibbets which were the outward symbols of seigneurial justice, had disappeared—the physical expression of a transformation of social relationships. The seigneur whose privileges had revolted Arthur Young was now lucky if he retained the influence of the British squire. The Church also lost much of its control over the everyday lives of the people, together with its estates and extensive urban property. Its spiritual authority over the faithful still created strong pressures in the direction of social conformity, but its economic power was shattered and its claim to the automatic support of the secular arm in enforcing its conception of a Catholic society had lapsed. To those who remembered the condemnation of Calas and the chevalier de la Barre this was no small matter. The ordinary Frenchman found the context of his life transformed. Ancient regulations and institutions controlling his employment, his use of his property and freedom to bequeath it after his death, his taxation, relations with his social superiors and with the State had been replaced by a new national uniformity based on the assumption of equality before the law. In many ways the France of 1815 was closer to that of the twentieth century than to the France of 1789.

Even more significant, perhaps, than the magnitude of the social transformation was the manner in which it was achieved. For the violence of the revolutionary movement tore apart the structure of French society, leaving a country so bitterly divided on political, religious, social and economic principles and policies as to be virtually ungovernable. Moreover these tensions and hostilities, arising directly from the Revolution, have perpetuated themselves throughout subsequent French history with frequently catastrophic results that have continued up to the present day.

The most obvious of these divisions concerned the political organization of society. On the surface, this was a quarrel between monarchists and republicans, with the corpse of Louis XVI lying between the regicides and the royalists. But in fact this issue was somewhat unreal, so far as the country as a whole was concerned, for there were less than 400 regicides and the ultra-royalists had never concealed their contempt for the feeble and vacillating policies of the late king. More significant were the divisions within each camp. On the royalist side, legitimists and constitutional monarchists were still as hostile to each other as they had been in 1789. What was at stake was less a type of government than a conception of society. Provence and Artois still hoped in 1795 that when their fundamentally loyal subjects should recover from the madness to which they had been incited by a handful of seditious agitators, it would be possible to restore the ancien régime in all its essentials. Divine-right monarchy would no doubt concede an aristocratic constitution of sorts to the nobles who had supported it in exile, but the royal programme was still essentially that outlined by Louis

XVI at the *Séance Royale* of 23 June 1789: enlightened despotism tempered by such constitutional concessions as the king chose to offer; the alliance of the Most Christian monarch and the Gallican Church; the preservation of an hierarchical society in which status and privilege would be determined by birth. In fact, this combination of royal authority, State religion and aristocratic privilege was never again to be realized in France, but traces of its influence are to be found in much subsequent French history.

The constitutional monarchists realized the futility of any such attempt to restore the ancien régime, but if their programme was more realistic their prospects were no better. Among the *émigrés* they were snubbed and suspected, while in France itself any form of monarchy was associated with treason, civil war and foreign invasion. In purely theoretical terms there was little that divided the liberal monarchist from the conservative republican. Both thought in terms of a rule of law, a constitutional government elected by an educated minority of men of independent means, with an executive strong enough to maintain order but not to defy the will of parliament. Both had in mind a society organized along more or less English lines, where political and economic power would be in some sort of harmony, while liberal policies would allow of social mobility and the gradual enfranchisement of a wider section of the population as it made its way upwards by its own efforts. Moderate constitutionalism along these lines probably offered France the greatest hope of social and political stability, but long years of revolution and bitter civil war had irreparably divided the centre and turned its adherents into the reluctant allies of the extremists on either side.

On the republican side the Revolution had created a new phenomenon: 'Jacobinism'—a Rousseauist conception of the total sovereignty of the State, which was sole arbiter of religious belief and, in the last resort, of the right to own private property. Rousseauist also was the assumption that 'true' democracy lay not so much in the blind acceptance of any majority ruling as in the implementation of an active 'general will' which represented the real interests of the community as a whole.[1] An 'enlightened' minority was therefore justified in providing

[1] See J. L. Talmon, *The Origins of Totalitarian Democracy* (1952), Part II.

the community with policies and institutions which it would eventually come to accept as being in its own interests. These twin expressions of 'Jacobinism'—the right of a revolutionary minority to anticipate public opinion, and the total sovereignty of the State—in contrast to the liberal emphasis on the means rather than on the ends of government, found a permanent home in the hearts of some of the French Left.

In a similar way the religious legacy of the Revolution was not one but several conflicts. The Gallican Church disappeared for ever and its extinction reopened in a more acute form the henceforth insoluble problem of the relationship between a sovereign State and an international Church. Neither Napoleon's Concordat nor its abrogation in 1905 fully satisfied either side or prevented continuous skirmishing along a frontier which each hoped to modify to its own advantage. The religious division did not coincide with the political one and there were constitutional monarchists like Mirabeau who were bitter opponents of the Papacy. While the converse was not strictly true, since allegiance to Rome almost inevitably involved a breach with the Revolution, Montagnards such as Grégoire hoped to reconcile their politics and their religion within a constitutional church that would be theologically orthodox even if not in communion with the Papacy. The situation was subsequently complicated still further when the Pope came to terms with the Revolution in the Napoleonic Concordat. This 'betrayal' was rejected by some of the 'non-juror' clergy and there still exists, in the Vendée, a *petite église* of about 3,000 worshippers which has never resumed communion with Rome, a picturesque confirmation of the tenacity of revolutionary memories in France.

Within France itself the Revolution, by its experiment with the lay State, raised conflicts of equal longevity. The separation of the *état civil* from the Church and the legalization of divorce meant that Church and State applied different standards. More serious was the State's assertion of a claim to control all aspects of the educational system: teachers, textbooks and syllabuses. Here, as in the constitutional conflict, a body of liberal *laissez-faire* opinion, agreeable to the coexistence of secular and religious schools, found itself confronted by the absolutist demands of the two extreme wings. The issue of *laïcité*, born under the Convention, is as vigorous as ever, after five republics, two empires and two forms of monarchy: the Church aims at the education of all the faithful in its own schools while the more extreme anti-clericals advocate a State monopoly of education. Ever since the Revolution the conflicting claims to allegiance of secular and religious authority have been superimposed on political and economic rivalries, multiplying divisions and leading to the fragmentation of French opinion which reduces any majority to a coalition of factions. The religious revival of the nineteenth century aggravated this division of French society since the Church was involved in social and political rivalries instead of transcending them. To some extent friction of this kind is inevitable when the claims of political sovereignty clash with those of an international Church, but in France the Church was also heavily committed in matters of internal politics, and its dislike of republican institutions, as heirs of the Revolution, lasted well into the twentieth century.

A logical consequence of the political commitment of the Church was its alienation of militant revolutionaries. No doubt some of the dechristianizers of 1793–4, like Monestier of the Lozère, received absolution from 'non-juror' priests before they died, but for many the breach with the Church was final. The continuing campaign for the restoration of Church lands, which led some priests, after the return of the Bourbons, to refuse the sacraments to purchasers of *biens nationaux*, probably helped a fraction of the educated middle class to remain true to its Voltairean upbringing. It is difficult to estimate the religious convictions of the *sans-culottes*. But the revolutionary tradition had struck such deep roots and the Church was in such open enmity that it seems highly probable that anti-clericalism, if not avowed disbelief, had become widespread in the towns. No doubt many sceptics still used the Church, as they do today, for the baptism and *première communion* of their children, as a mark of social respectability, but the social reformers grew up in a strongly anti-clerical atmosphere which reinforced their conviction that effective change involved the adoption of revolutionary methods.

Among the population as a whole the interruption of religious practice and the conflict between the rival Catholic churches probably contributed to the growth of religious indifference, whether or not this was masked by an appearance of outward conformity. This was the case in the Loire-et-Cher where, according to the *abbé* Gallerand, the *états de catholicité* of 1797 suggested that the general attitude was one of habit rather than conviction: the majority continued to attend church, but supported Roman or Revolutionary clergy indifferently.[1] If this attitude was widespread, it would suggest another parallel to the political division, with a tolerant centre offset by the existence of powerful militant wings composed of the *dévots* and the anti-clericals.

The social and economic situation presents a somewhat different picture, for in one respect at least the Revolution had appeased more conflicts than it had provoked. The embattled countryside of the ancien régime, with its acute land-hunger and perennial clashes over tithes and feudal dues, became more peaceful after the Revolution. The number of landowners increased appreciably, even though the great majority were still not self-sufficient. Moreover the changes in land-ownership and the division of some estates probably led to a greater amount of land being available to rent. Marion's description of the effect of these changes is perhaps a little too emphatic: 'The sale of the *biens nationaux* therefore made a substantial contribution to the formation and consolidation of that mass of landed proprietors . . . which dominated France in the nineteenth century and exercised a predominant influence over her destiny, which made this country a democracy, but a conservative democracy, revolutionary perhaps in origin . . . but certainly not by interest or temperament.' [2] Though it failed to solve the land-hunger of the overpopulated countryside, the transfer of property was sufficiently general to guarantee the survival of peasant farming into the twentieth century. This development had important effects in various spheres. It probably contributed to delay the agrarian revolution in France and consequently to retard the progress of the industrial revolution. In addition, the old hostility of town and country was perpetuated, in part by the increasing difficulty of feeding the towns, now that the peasants

---

[1] J. Gallerand, *Les Cultes sous la Terreur en Loir-et-Cher*, pp. 136, 742.
[2] Marion, *op. cit.*, p. 419.

were consuming more of their own produce, and in part by the widening gap between a revolutionary urban population and a conservative peasantry that was to become obvious in 1848.

In the towns themselves social conflict was sharpened by the Revolution in the sense that the bourgeoisie had more to fear and the *sans-culottes* had memories of vanished authority. The exceptional circumstances of 1793–4 had accelerated the political education of the working class in French towns as a whole, while the Terror and the reaction of the cruel winter of 1795 provided each side with a bitter distrust of the other. The Revolution had also stimulated the development of social theories that were soon to become socialist. Babeuf, for example, was both a revolutionary figure in his own right and a distant forerunner of Marx. In this way the revolutionary crisis contributed to a dichotomy between theory and experience, the socialist movement first arising not in the evolved industrial society of Britain but in the relatively backward one of France. In consequence the French bourgeoisie found itself, to some extent at least, already on the defensive before the industrial revolution had consolidated its position. The objectives of the nineteenth-century urban proletariat were more ambitious and the fears of the middle class more acute in France than in England, with results that became only too clear in 1848 if one compares the Chartist movement with the June revolution in Paris.

As will already have become apparent, the divisions in French society that sprang from the Revolution were self-perpetuating. This is not merely a question of recollections of the Terror— White or Red—and of family traditions, although these played a part. The events of the Revolution, themselves terrible enough, were soon obscured behind the melodramatic mythology invented by both sides. An illuminating example of this is the account of the Orange tribunal that de Baumefort published in 1875, prefaced by the no doubt sincere invocation of Montaigne: *Cecy est un livre de bonne foy*. In the course of a diatribe against the tribunal and the Revolution in general, de Baumefort repeated the hoary absurdity that Saint-Just had a pair of breeches made from the skin of a young lady who resisted his advances, adding significantly, 'it would be difficult to believe in so many crimes if they were not engraved on the fatal tablets of the Revolution'.[1] In other words, the mention of the Revolution was sufficient to suspend all normal standards of credulity and to induce acceptance of atrocity stories that reinforced the myth from which they originated. The defenders of the Revolution have on the whole shown less taste for macabre invention, but their tendency to justify actions in 1792–4 which they would—one hopes—have violently repudiated in their own times, also helped to reanimate old hatreds. Moreover the perpetuation of revolutionary passions has been a matter of living politics in every generation. The Restoration of 1815 brought a recurrence of the White Terror in the south. In 1848 and again in 1871, there was street-fighting in the streets of Paris. If some of the Free French forces in 1940–4 boasted of their *esprit '89*, there were legitimist influences at Vichy and some of the resistance fighters were not wanting in the *esprit '93*. Specific issues have altered with the generations, royalism has ceased to count as a serious political force and the Right now accepts measures of State intervention, such as a progressive income tax, that would have satisfied an extreme Montagnard of 1793. But the armies do not disband though the battle-fields change. The north-west is still conservative and clerical, as it was in 1793, and the geographical distribution of French party support owes more to tradition and less to economics than is the case in Britain. It is scarcely a coincidence that the Communist bastions in the centre and south-east of France—areas of relatively little large-scale industry—should have been regions where Jacobin Clubs and revolutionary armies were particularly numerous in 1793. The revolutionary divisions, in fact, have never healed; social and political conflicts still tend to be conceived in violent terms, the position of the Church is still a matter of bitter controversy and the political régime an instrument of party rule rather than the symbol of a unified society. Nothing in recent French history suggests that these elements of discord have lost any of their disruptive force.

The impact of the Revolution, both helped and hindered by the progress of the Napoleonic armies, spread far beyond the frontiers of France itself. As Robespierre had foreseen in 1791, its effect was to frighten rulers, nobility and clergy and to

[1] V. de Baumefort, *Episodes de la Terreur: le Tribunal Révolutionnaire d'Orange* (Avignon, 1875), p. 112.

unite them in an unprecedented alliance in defence of the *status quo*.[1] This was the end of enlightened despotism, of the attempt by reforming and often anti-clerical rulers to make political and administrative practice conform to the presumed dictates of 'reason'. Henceforth the appeal was to a 'tradition' that was invented or adjusted to meet the requirements of the age of Metternich. Such tentative reform as was applied, in Prussia, for example, in the hope of tapping some of the latent resources of power which the Revolution had liberated in France, soon withered into insignificance. Hegelian idealism, coloured by the romantic movement, diverted speculation from the reform of practical abuses to more metaphysical objectives—with long-term consequences that were to surpass the wildest excesses of the French Revolution. The new force of romantic, and often racial, nationalism arose at a time when war and revolution had put an end to the traditional restraint that eighteenth-century States observed in their conduct of affairs. While it would be fanciful to attribute the whole of this gloomy picture to the influence of the French Revolution alone, the example of France and the need of aristocratic societies elsewhere for safe weapons with which to combat the French armies no doubt contributed to the spread of the new doctrines. But if the aristocracy feared the middle class, both classes, in England as well as on the Continent, were increasingly on their guard against the working man whose ability, under revolutionary leadership, to challenge the existing social order had been so dramatically demonstrated in France. The new forces of repression and reaction were unable to prevent the onset of the industrial revolution which was to transform the very basis of the society that they sought to preserve, but the fear of 'Jacobinism' probably embittered the inevitable social tensions, made peaceful change more difficult and helped to create the conditions that provided Marx with the material for his theory of class war.

Whether one considers the social changes in France, the way in which subsequent French history has been influenced by the

[1] See E. Wangermann, *From Joseph II to the Jacobin Trials* (1959); W. M. Simon, *The Failure of the Prussian Reform Movement, 1807–1819* (Ithaca, N.Y., 1955); M. Raeff, *Michael Speransky* (The Hague, 1957); for a general survey of the European situation, see the concluding section, by E. Labrousse and M. Bouloiseau, to vol. V of the *Histoire Générale des Civilisations* (ed. Crouzet, Paris, 1953).

divisions and conflicts arising directly from the Revolution, or the contrast between the Europe of Voltaire, Frederick the Great, and Mozart, and that of Hegel, Metternich, and Beethoven, there is no denying the French Revolution its full tragic stature as the profound social convulsion from which modern Europe was born.

Bibliography

A COMPREHENSIVE bibliography of the French Revolution would occupy far more space than the whole of the present volume. Those interested in further information are referred to G. Walter, *Répertoire de l'Histoire de la Révolution Française* (2 v., Paris, 1941, 1951), and to A. Martin and G. Walter, *Catalogue de l'Histoire de la Révolution Française* (5 v., Paris, 1936–43), and to the footnotes to the history of the Revolution by the late Professor G. Lefebvre listed below. The following list of books and articles, roughly grouped according to their subjects, is merely intended to indicate those which I have found particularly useful from the viewpoint of this book. I have emphasized, so far as the material allows, recent works that may not be generally known and books written in English or available in translation. Many of the works listed below contain specialized bibliographies on their own particular subjects. The place of publication is London for books in English and Paris for those in French, unless otherwise stated.

General histories of the Revolution as a whole

P. J. B. BUCHEZ AND P. C. ROUX, *Histoire Parlementaire de la Révolution Française* (40 v., 1834–38).

J. JAURÈS, *Histoire Socialiste* (4 v., 1901).

A. MATHIEZ, *La Révolution Française* (3 v., 1922–27), Eng. trans.

J. M. THOMPSON, *The French Revolution* (Oxford, 1944).

A. GOODWIN, *The French Revolution* (1953).

R. MOUSNIER AND C. A. LABROUSSE, vol. V of the *Histoire Générale des Civilisations* (ed. Crouzet, 1953).

G. LEFEBVRE, *La Révolution Française* (vol. XIII of the collection *Peuples et Civilisations*, ed. Halphen and Sagnac; 3rd ed., 1951), and published lectures, *Les Cours de la Sorbonne: La Révolution Aristocratique; La Fuite du Roi; La Chute du Roi; La Première Terreur; La Convention; Le Gouvernement Révolutionnaire*.

A. COBBAN, *A History of Modern France*, vol. I (1957).

Ancien Régime

A. YOUNG, *Travels in France and Italy* (1st ed., 1792).

P. BOITEAU, *État de la France en 1789* (1861).

C. BLOCH, *Études sur l'Histoire économique de la France* (1900).

H. CARRÉ, *La Noblesse de France et l'Opinion Publique au dix-huitième siècle* (1920).

M. BLOCH, *Caractères originaux de l'Histoire rurale française* (1931).

C. A. LABROUSSE, *Esquisse du Mouvement des Prix et des Revenus en France au dix-huitième siècle* (2 v., 1933).

— *La Crise de l'Économie française à la fin de l'Ancien Régime et au début de la Révolution* (1944).

P. SAGNAC, *La Formation de la Société française moderne* (2 v., 1945–6).

F. L. FORD, *Robe and Sword, the re-grouping of the French aristocracy after Louis XIV* (Cambridge, Mass., 1953).

E. G. BARBER, *The Bourgeoisie in eighteenth-century France* (Princeton, 1955).

J. S. BROMLEY, 'The decline of absolute monarchy', in *France, Government and Society* (ed. J. M. Wallace-Hadrill and J. McManners, 1957).

G. T. MATHEWS, *The Royal General Farms in eighteenth-century France* (New York, 1958).

R. FORSTER, *The Nobility of Toulouse in the Eighteenth Century* (Johns Hopkins University Studies in Historical and Political Science, Series LXXVIII, No. 1, 1960).

P. DE SAINT-JACOB, *Les Paysans de la Bourgogne du Nord au dernier siècle de l'Ancien Régime* (1960).

J. MCMANNERS, *French Ecclesiastical Society under the Ancien Régime. A study of Angers in the Eighteenth Century* (Manchester, 1961).

J. ÉGRET, 'L'Aristocratie parlementaire française à la fin de l'Ancien Régime', *Revue Historique*, CCVIII (1952).

R. FORSTER, 'The Noble wine-producers of the Bordelais in the Eighteenth Century', *Economic History Review*, second series, XIV (1961).

The aristocratic offensive

J. NECKER, *De la Révolution Française* (1797).

B. DE MOLLEVILLE, *Mémoires secrets pour servir à l'Histoire de la dernière année du règne de Louis XVI* (3 v., Eng. trans., London, 1797).

— *Annals of the French Revolution* (4 v., 1800).

CAMPAN, *Mémoires* (2 v., 2nd ed., London, 1823).

CHASTENAY, *Mémoires* (2 v., 3rd ed., 1896).

J. DROZ, *Histoire du Règne de Louis XVI* (Brussels, 1839).

BIBLIOGRAPHY

A. CHÉREST La, Chute de l'Ancien Régime (3 v., 1884).

BRIENNE, Journal de l'Assemblée des Notables de 1787 (ed. Chevallier, 1960).

J. FLAMMERMONT, 'Le second Ministère de Necker', Revue Historique, XLVI (1891).

L. HARTMANN, 'Les Officers de l'Armée royale à la veille de la Révolution', Revue Historique, C, CI (1909).

A. GOODWIN, 'Calonne, the Assembly of French Notables of 1787 and the origins of the "Révolte Nobiliaire",' English Historical Review, LXI (1946).

J. ÉGRET, 'La seconde Assemblée des Notables', Annales Historiques de la Révolution Française, XXI (1949).

— 'La Pré-révolution en Provence (1787–89)', Annales Historiques de la Révolution Française XXVI (1954).

— 'La Révolution aristocratique en Franche-Comté et son Echec', Revue d'Histoire Moderne et Contemporaine, I (1954).

— 'Les Origines de la Révolution en Bretagne', Revue Historique, CCXIII (1955).

— 'La dernière Assemblée du Clergé de France', Revue Historique, CCXIX (1958).

The Constituent Assembly

J. S. BAILLY, Mémoires (3 v., 1821–2).

BESENVAL, Mémoires (2 v., 1821).

FERRIÈRES, Mémoires (3 v., 1821).

— Correspondance inédite (ed. Carré, 1932).

MALOUET, Mémoires (2 v., ed. Malouet, 1868).

A. DUQUESNOY, Journal (2 v., ed. Crèvecoeur, 1894).

A. MATHIEZ, Le Club des Cordeliers pendant la Crise de Varennes et le Massacre du Champ de Mars (1910).

— Rome et le Clergé français sous la Constituante (1911).

G. MICHON, Essai sur l'Histoire du Parti Feuillant: Adrien Duport (1924).

G. LEFEBVRE, La Grande Peur de 1789 (1932).

— Quatre-vingt-neuf (Eng. trans., 1939).

F. BRAESCH, 1789, l'Année Cruciale (1941).

J. A. CREUZET-LATOUCHE, Journal des Etats-Généraux et du Début de l'Assemblée Nationale (ed. Marchand, 1946).

J. ÉGRET, La Révolution des Notables; Mounier et les Monarchiens (1950).

J. GODECHOT, La Contre-Révolution (1961).

A. MATHIEZ, 'Étude critique sur les Journées des 5 et 6 octobre 1789', Revue Historique, LXVII–LXIX (1898–9).

P. CARON, 'La Tentative de Contre-révolution de juin-juillet 1789', *Revue d'Histoire Moderne*, VIII (1906–7).

F. BRAESCH, 'Les Pétitions du Champ de Mars', *Revue Historique*, CXLII–CXLIV (1923).

M. G. HUTT, 'The Rôle of the Curés in the Estates General of 1789', *Journal of Ecclesiastical History*, VI (1955).

V. ALEXEV-POPOV, 'Le Cercle Social, 1790–91', *Recherches Soviétiques* (1956).

M. G. HUTT, 'The Curés and the Third Estate', *Journal of Ecclesiastical History*, VIII (1957).

D. LIGOU, 'A propos de la Révolution municipale', *Revue d'Histoire Economique et Sociale*, XXXVIII (1960).

Institutions; agriculture

P. SAGNAC, *La Législation civile de la Révolution Française* (1898).

M. MARION, *La Vente des Biens nationaux pendant la Révolution* (1908).

A. VIALAY, *La Vente des Biens nationaux pendant la Révolution Française* (1908).

E. SELIGMAN, *La Justice en France pendant la Révolution* (1913).

S. WILKINSON, *The French Army before Napoleon* (Oxford, 1915).

A. AULARD, *La Révolution Française et le Régime féodal* (1919).

G. LEFEBVRE, *Documents relatifs à l'Histoire des Subsistences dans le District de Bergues* (Lille, 1914).

— *Les Paysans du Nord pendant la Révolution Française* (1924).

— *Études sur la Révolution Française* (1954).

— *Questions agraires au temps de la Terreur* (La Roche-sur-Yonne, 1954).

J. GODECHOT, *Histoire des Institutions de la France sous la Révolution et l'Empire* (1951).

G. SANGNIER, *L'Évolution de la Propriété rurale dans le District de Saint-Pol pendant la Révolution* (Blangermont, 1951).

M. GARAUD, *Histoire Générale du Droit privé français*, I. *La Revolution et l'Égalité civile* (1953); II. *La Révolution et la Propriété foncière* (1958).

E. G. LÉONARD, *L'Armée et ses Problèmes au dix-huitième siècle* (1958).

N. HAMPSON, *La Marine de l'An II* (1959).

M. LECLÈRE, 'Les Réformes de Castries', *Revue des Questions Historiques*, CXXVIII (1937).

From the Legislative Assembly to the overthrow of the Girondins

A. SCHMIDT, *Tableaux de la Révolution Française* (3v. Leipzig, 1867).

F. BRAESCH, *La Commune du 10 août* (1911).

A. SÖDERHJELM, ed., *Marie-Antoinette et Barnave: correspondance secrète* (1934).

P. CARON, *Les Massacres de Septembre* (1935).

— *La Première Terreur* (1950).

M. J. SYDENHAM, *The Girondins* (1961).

See also footnotes to chapter vii for local studies on the 'federalist revolt'.

Montagnards and sans-culottes

R. LEVASSEUR, *Mémoires* (4 v., 1829).

A. AULARD, *Recueil des Actes du Comité de Salut Public* (28 v., 1889–1911).

— *Le Culte de la Raison* (1904).

A. MATHIEZ, *La Révolution et l'Eglise* (1910).

— *La Vie Chère et le Mouvement Social sous la Terreur* (1927).

P. CARON, *Paris pendant la Terreur* (5 v., 1910–58).

— *Rapports des Agents du Ministre de l'Intérieur dans les Départements* (2 v., 1913, 1951).

H. CALVET, *L'Accaparement à Paris sous la Terreur* (1933).

D. GREER, *The Incidence of the Terror during the French Revolution* (Cambridge, Mass., 1935).

— *The Incidence of the Emigration during the French Revolution* (Cambridge, Mass., 1951).

G. SANGNIER, *La Terreur dans le District de Saint-Pol* (2 v., Blangermont, 1938).

R. R. PALMER, *The Twelve who ruled* (Princeton, 1941).

D. GUÉRIN, *La Lutte des Classes sous la Première République* (2 v., 1946).

A. SOBOUL, *Les Sans-culottes parisiens en l'An II* (1958).

G. RUDÉ, *The Crowd in the French Revolution* (Oxford, 1959).

R. C. COBB, *Les Armées Révolutionnaires* (2 v., 1961–3).

G. LEFEBVRE, 'A propos de la loi du 22 prairial', *Annales Historiques de la Révolution Française*, XXIV (1952).

G. RUDÉ AND A. SOBOUL, 'Le Maximum des Salaires parisiens et le 9 thermidor', *Annales Historiques de la Révolution Française*, XXVI (1954).

A. SOBOUL, 'Sentiment religieux et Cultes populaires pendant la Révolution', *Annales Historiques de la Révolution Française*, XXIX (1957).

R. C. COBB, 'The revolutionary mentality in France, 1793–94', *History*, XLII (1957).

— 'Quelques aspects de la mentalité révolutionnaire', *Revue d'Histoire Moderne et Contemporaine*, VI (1959).

N. HAMPSON, 'Les Ouvriers des Arsenaux de la Marine au cours de la Révolution Française', *Revue d'Histoire Economique et Sociale*, XXXIX (1961).
See also footnotes to chapter viii for local studies, especially as regards dechristianization.

After 9 thermidor

G. LEFEBVRE, *Les thermidoriens* (1937).

R. FUOC, *La Réaction thermidorienne à Lyon* (Lyons, 1957).

K. D. TÖNNESSON, *La Défaite des Sans-culottes* (1959).

S. BLUM, 'La Mission d'Albert dans la Marne en l'An III', *La Révolution Française*, XLIII–XLV (1902–3).

P. VAILLANDET, 'Les Débuts de la Terreur Blanche en Vaucluse', *Annales Historiques de la Révolution Française*, V (1928).

A. MATHIEZ, 'La Terreur Blanche de l'An III', *Annales Historiques de la Révolution Française*, V (1928).

F. COURCELLE, 'La Réaction thermidorienne dans le District de Melun', *Annales Historiques de la Révolution Française*, VII (1930).

G. MARTIN, 'La Vie bourgeoise à Nantes sous la Convention d'après le livre de comptes de Mme. Hummel', *La Révolution Française*, LXXXVI (1933).

R. C. COBB, 'Note sur la Répression contre le Personnel sans-culotte de 1795 à 1801', *Annales Historiques de la Révolution Française*, XXVI (1924).

— 'Disette et Mortalité, la Crise de l'An III et de l'An IV à Rouen', *Annales de la Normandie* (1956).

— 'Une Émeute de la faim dans le Banlieu rouennaise', *Annales de la Normandie* (1956).

J. ZACKER, 'Varlet pendant la Réaction thermidorienne', *Annales Historiques de la Révolution Française*, XXXIII (1961).

The fullest account of the business of the various Assemblies is to be found in the *Archives Parlementaires* (Paris, 1868–1912, 1962–). The *Annales Historiques de la Révolution Française* is a quarterly devoted exclusively to the history of the Revolution.

Index

Agen, Agenais, 96, 119
AIGUILLON, 53, 65, 82–83, 96
Aix-en-Provence, 41, 236
AIX, (BISHOP OF), 92
ALBITTE, 174
Allier, 201, 204, 211
Alsace, 79, 93, 189
AMAR, 197, 212, 243
Amiens, 243
Angers, 21, 28–31, 95, 188
ANGOSSE, 7
Anzin, 19
Arcis (Paris Section), 152
Ardèche, 144
Arles, 144
Army, 120–24
Arras, 224
ARTOIS, 9, 38, 49–50, 52, 55, 57, 70, 76, 102–3, 108, 123, 257
Assignat, 91, 164–5, 167, 174, 176, 191, 216, 238–9
Aube, 241
Aubusson, 207
Auch, 225
Aude, 158
AUDOUIN, 177
AUGEARD, 38, 49–50
Avignon, 233

BABEUF, 211, 233, 243, 262
BAILLY, 58, 75, 84, 88, 99, 105–6, 197
BANCAL, 166
BARBAROUX, 165, 173, 180
BARÈRE, 157, 165, 178, 180, 182, 190, 202, 223, 227, 232, 235, 243
BARNAVE, 21–22, 66, 68, 78, 86, 97, 99, 104, 107–8, 136, 152, 197
BARRAS, 217–18, 221, 231, 233, 247

BAS, LE, 116, 230, 232
BASIRE, 173, 195, 220
Bas-Rhin, 93
Basses-Pyrénées, 173, 204, 236
Bastia, 98
BAYLE, 173
Bayonne, 208
Béarn, 43
Beaucaire, 79
Beauce, 141, 159, 161
Beaurepaire (Paris Section), 179
Beauvais, 199–200, 203–4, 241
BÉGOUEN, 62
BERGASSE, 87
Bergues, 208, 237, 239
Berri, 96
BERTHIER, 75
Besançon, 77
BESENVAL, 39, 67, 74
BILLAUD-VARENNE, 137, 153–4, 179, 183, 187, 195–6, 223, 230, 232, 235, 243
Blois, 160, 199, 205
BOISSET, 173
BON, LE, 211-12, 235, 245
Bon Conseil, (*Mauconseil:* Paris Section), 139, 147
Bonne Nouvelle, (Paris Section), 231
Bonnet Rouge, (*Croix Rouge:* Paris Section), 146, 199–200
Bordeaux, 7, 18, 26, 42, 77, 115, 149, 172, 175, 207
BORDEAUX, (ARCHBISHOP OF), 65
BOTHEREL, 43
BOUCHOTTE, 209, 221
BOUILLÉ, 97, 104
BOULAINVILLIERS, 5
Bourbonnais, 96
BOURBOTTE, 244

272

INDEX